FREDDY BANNISTER

# THERE MUST BE A BETTER WAY

## The Story of
## The Bath and Knebworth Rock Festivals
## 1969 - 1979

BATH BOOKS

This book published in 2003 by Bath Books
Suite 72, 48 Regent St, Cambridge CB2 1FD

Designed by
Howlett Design, Cambridge, England

Printed and bound in Great Britain by
Antony Rowe Ltd, Chippenham Wilts

ISBN 0 954 5549 0 6

### Acknowledgements

*I should like to thank the following for their help in providing information, photographs, tickets and handbills – Greg Burge, Rufus Hunt, Ove Stridh, Martin Brooks, David Lytton Cobbold, Henry Lytton Cobbold, Chryssie Lytton Cobbold, C.R.Wolfe, Matt Lee, Dave Lang, Dick Appleton, Anthony Booth, Graham Ellwood, Roy Gover, Neil Jackson, C. Johnstone, Peter Still/The Concert Photo Company, The Bath Archives, Brian K Jones, Roger Parkhouse, Simon Phillips, Linda Sawkins, Sandy Prentice, Bill Pritchard, Jackie Ryan, Kelvin Skudamore and Keith Temple.*

www.rockmusicmemorabilia.com

# FREDDY BANNISTER

# THERE MUST BE A BETTER WAY

## CONTENTS

### PART 1   JUST BROKEN EVEN

### PART 2   THERE MUST BE A BETTER WAY

*This book is dedicated to my father-in-law the late Steve Duman, without his encouragement I would never have become a promoter, my daughter Henrietta who badgered me into writing this book and most importantly to everyone who has ever bought a ticket for one of my promotions.*

*Also to David and Chryssie Lytton Cobbold. Without their vision and unfailing enthusiasm, there would not have been any Knebworth Festivals and popular music would have been deprived of what is, in my opinion, 'the best outdoor festival site in the world'.*

# PART 1

just
BROKEN
even

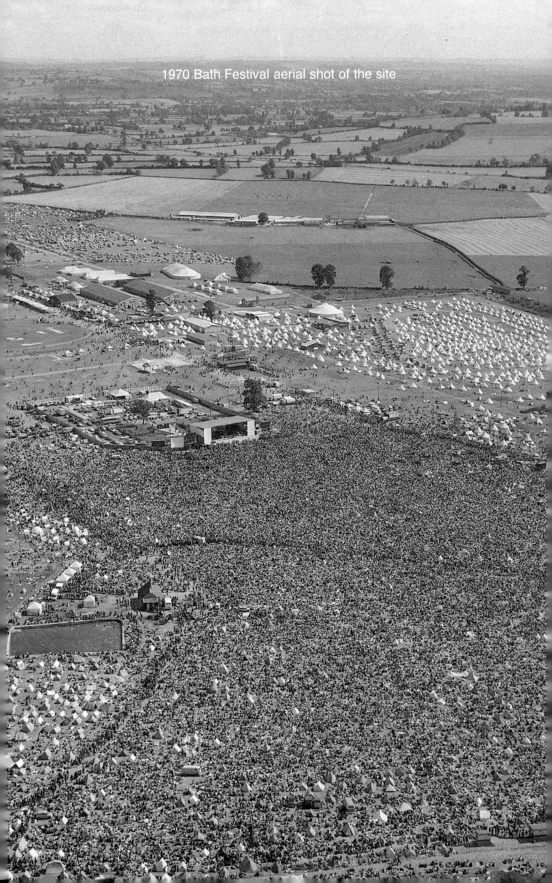

1970 Bath Festival aerial shot of the site

# CHAPTER 1

With a loud bang the door of the admin office burst open revealing an indescribably angry young man waving a large iron bar. How, I thought, could I be all on my own when there were over 130,000 kids outside and a dozen or more staff in the adjoining room? In fact, when it came down to it, what the hell was I doing here anyway?

I had always wanted to be a musician - live a quiet life, have fun. I blamed it all on my father-in-law Steve Duman, at that time the organiser of the London Traditional Jazz Society, who certainly did not want a musician as a son-in-law. In fact, he did not want me as a son-in-law period. However, he only had himself to blame. We lived in the same suburb of London and whenever I played one of his clubs he would offer me a lift home and would occasionally invite me in for a coffee. This was how I met his daughter, Wendy and despite his initial opposition, owing more I think to her tender age than my limited prospects, he reluctantly agreed and we were married at the beginning of 1960.

One day shortly before we were married, after I finished playing a particularly undistinguished gig, Steve observed 'As a trombonist you would undoubtedly make a better businessman' and with these words he brought to a close my less than illustrious career as a jazz musician.

'Why don't you try promoting?' he continued. 'You must be good at something I suppose,' he added somewhat sceptically. 'I'll help you find a venue and show you what to do'.

Our first venture under my (future) father-in-law's guidance was a record hop, or as it would be known these days a discotheque or club night, with myself as disc jockey, Wendy as the cashier and a couple of local bouncers on the door. It was held at a pub called the Woodman in Blackfen, Kent in a small adjoining hall with a capacity of around 150/200. After a slow opening it gradually built up over several months until we had a regular attendance of around 100 -120 or so each week. I thoroughly enjoyed my role as DJ playing the current hits, such as, Jerry Keller's 'Here Comes Summer', Stonewall Jackson's 'Waterloo', Neil Sedaka's 'Oh! Carol' and favourites like 'The Johnny Otis Shows,' 'Ma He's Making Eyes at Me,' until one evening when we arrived to set up we were informed by the landlord that he had decided that he did not like pop music after all and we could bugger off. A simple phone call would have sufficed but I'm not sure he had yet mastered the technique.

By this time we were ready to go it alone and, disillusioned with publicans, but greatly encouraged with our ability to promote, we decided to try a similar event at the Stanley Halls, South Norwood in South East London.

Johnny Kidd on stage at Wallington

It was a substantially bigger venue than The Woodman in Blackfen, but to offset this it was situated in a far larger residential area.

We opened in early 1960 with around 200 enthusiastic teenagers and soon built up to a regular attendance of around 300- 400 every Monday evening. As well as being extremely profitable it was great fun as the kids were generally more aware than at The Woodman and I was kept busy all evening playing requests and dedications, 'This next record is for Norma from Mick.' The girls asking for songs like 'Fall in Love With You' by Cliff Richard, whilst the boys requested Booker T & the MG's and The Bill Black Combo. The dancers, of course, were happy with anything that rocked, particular favourites being Handyman and Good Timin' both by Jimmy Jones.

I was at this time working as a representative for a firm of Hatton Garden jewellers but the directors, with a stroke of deductive genius, decided that my future lay in promoting and promptly sacked me. In fact, it was the push I needed to become a professional promoter.

With this as an incentive we decided it was imperative to open another venue and decided to try the Wallington Public Halls, a relatively smart hall situated on the outskirts of Croydon with an official capacity of 375. We opened with our usual format calling them this time 'Jive Sessions'. Opening night was not an unqualified success with around 80/90 showing up, but it was good enough for us to carry on and try to build things up. It was relatively hard going, my charms as a DJ being somewhat, it seemed, under appreciated (I think it was around this time that I first started loosing my hair) and we soon started using some of the more popular local groups.

Inevitably there were lots of requests for the name bands and armed with an introduction from my father-in-law, Wendy and I visited the George Cooper Agency, one of the largest agents specialising in 'pop artists' to see whom we could book. We were offered a number of acts including Wee Willie Harris, Joe Brown & the Bruvvers and in the end the choice came down to Johnny Kidd & the Pirates for £40 or Billy Fury for £60. In hindsight we should have chosen Billy Fury as he rapidly became too big a star to play the ballroom circuit, but I reasoned that as a ballad singer and heart throb he would appeal mainly to the girls, whereas Johnny Kidd and the Pirates would appeal to both sexes. The fact that Johnny and the Pirates were quite a lot less expensive was a big plus, as we did not want to go too far out on a limb for our first major promotion.

Contracts were soon exchanged and we set about publicising the show. There was, rather encouragingly, an instant buzz at the regular Wallington Tuesday night 'Jive Sessions' but to be on the safe side we placed advertisements in the local papers and fly posted fairly comprehensively. The day of the gig arrived wet and miserable, though this did not seem to bother the excited teenagers who turned up in sufficient numbers to justify our hard work and also, for the first time, gave the hall a really electrifying atmosphere.

It was around 8 o'clock when we started to get worried - no Johnny Kidd, no Pirates and worst of all no equipment. Luckily we had booked a popular local group to play support and these were keeping everyone happy. However, by 9.00 p.m. it was obvious that Johnny Kidd was not going to show up. 'Screwing my courage to the sticking post' I walked out onto the stage and explained that there seemed to be a mix up with the booking and we were going to refund the ticket money. I added that should they doubt my integrity they were welcome to see the contract, which I happened to have with me. Surprisingly, no one bothered to take advantage of this offer - most of the youngsters sympathising with us and wanting to know if a replacement date could be arranged.

The next day, as early as possible, I rang the agency to find that they had in fact double booked the band. They where most apologetic and offered me, as compensation, a replacement date free of charge in three weeks time. When Johnny finally arrived it seemed, to Wendy and me, something of an anticlimax but not to the youngsters who rather surprisingly turned up in even larger numbers than before.

After I eventually got the band on stage I went into the audience to check the sound quality. It was a contractual requirement that the promoter provided a PA for the vocals and I had hired a portable system that in retrospect had less than half the output of a modern domestic Hi Fi unit. I was assured it was state of the art and was just what was required, but even patched into the hall system it was woefully inadequate. I was appalled. You could hear the Pirates very well, but from Johnny Kidd not a word. It didn't seem to matter though, as the girls where screaming so loudly and continuously that no one seemed to notice or care. Amplification, especially of the vocals, was a regular problem in the early 60's it wasn't until the groups, sick of not being heard properly, started to bring their own PA system that things began to improve.

# CHAPTER 2

The Stanley Halls sessions were continuing to thrive. However, after a few months we began to realise that we were attracting a considerable number of Teddy Boys and things began to liven up with rather more fights than we were used to, or indeed wanted. Something had to be done so apart from employing some additional bouncers we decide that an occasional live group would prove diverting.

Once again, as with Wallington, the appearance of live bands led to requests for the better-known groups. This time we chose Screamin' Lord Sutch and the Savages to start what we rather naively called our 'Star Nights'. Sutch was a good choice for South Norwood - loud, unsubtle, entertaining, with a fine rocking band featuring on this occasion pianist Freddie 'fingers' Lee. The high spot of Sutch's act at that time was a number called 'Jack the Ripper' where he emerged from a coffin dressed all in black wearing a top hat and cloak and waving an extremely large and very realistic looking dagger. The crowd loved it and his tumultuous reception earned him a well-deserved return booking.

Initially we booked the band through Tom Littlewood who at that time managed the legendary Two I's Coffee Bar in Soho, but later as I got to know David Sutch better I would call him at home and I would make the booking directly with him. We never had a contract, there were never any problems and he always put on a good show. David was a thoroughly nice guy and is sadly missed.

Although business continued to boom, so did the violence. Even I wasn't immune. I remember one evening looking for Bill Smith, the hall manager, who lived in a house adjoining the hall. I had just knocked on his front door when I realised I was not alone. Two burly youngsters had followed me from the dance and told me in no uncertain terms that they were going to 'give me a going over I wouldn't forget'. It seemed that my stewards had for some reason banned them and they of course blamed me. Just as they were about to get started the door behind me opened and out stepped Bill. Faced with the two of us they decided they didn't like level odds and scarpered.

Apart from the fistfights, which were by now a regular feature of The Stanley Hall dances, one other problem occurred. Whenever it snowed a number of 'Teds' would rush outside and take up a position opposite the hall exit. Armed with a plentiful supply of snowballs they would pelt everyone as they left. Kids have been snowballing almost as long as there has been snow, but not normally with rocks embedded in the centre. It sometimes took over an hour to clear the hall, with our stewards making numerous sorties to seize the 'ammunition'. The police were never interested as no one was ever

Gene Vincent with fan Jackie Ryan

seriously injured and they obviously felt that they had more important things to occupy their time.

At around this time we decided to take another step forward and run our first seated concert. We chose the Davis Theatre in Croydon, soon to be replaced by the Fairfield Halls but at this time Croydon's main venue. Wow!The big time! We managed to secure Gene Vincent already fast becoming a legend as our headline act. Second on the bill were The Viscounts, an excellent vocal duo, with quite a lot of chart success, Paul Raven, who later become rather better known as Gary Glitter, Lance Fortune, Gary Mills and Sounds Inc, one of the best groups around at that time, who apart from their own spot, also backed Gene Vincent. To open the show we had one of the most popular local groups Vern Rogers and the Hi Fi's. Incidentally, Garry Mills whose biggest hit 'Look for a Star' made him into a huge local celebrity lived no more than a couple of miles from us and by one of those strange coincidences his uncle turned out to be our milkman.

Once he found out who we were it was not unusual for him to knock on our door and ask, 'One pint or two and oh have you got a booking for Gary?'.

In the run through before the show one of the Viscounts threw a minor tantrum over the sound mix. It wasn't as though he shouted, but he did pout and sulk quite a lot.

I remember turning to Wendy and saying, 'Ah bless his well permed little head'.

I'm glad he didn't hear me because the singer was Gordon Mills, who founded MAM - soon to be one of the most successful agencies in the country and one with which I subsequently did a lot of business. He also went on to manage both Tom Jones and Englebert Humperdink.

The show was a sell out and as it was our first major concert I was determined that it would run as smoothly and efficiently as possible. We had engaged a professional lighting director from the New Theatre Bromley called Richard Coombs to take care of the settings and lighting and I must say he did a first rate job. The first half ran without problems and on time. It wasn't until midway through the second half and just before he was due on stage that I realised that Gene Vincent was engaged in an in depth interview with one of the national newspapers. Gene was at this time managed by Don Arden. Taking Don to one side I explained rather self importantly that it was imperative that Gene go on stage immediately only to be told, quietly and calmly, that Gene would go on as soon as the interview was finished and not before. When I protested a little too vigorously my cheek was gently tweaked and I was told to be patient. Don must have quite liked me, or at least taken pity on a callow youth because despite his subsequent reputation as a very difficult man I never had anything but pleasant straightforward dealings with him and his company. Gene eventually went on only fifteen minutes late and tore the place apart - it was a fitting climax to our first seated concert.

It was through Gene Vincent that we first met Peter Grant, who in those early days was Gene's tour manager. As we subsequently used Gene quite a lot we came to know Peter quite well. I think he liked us because, unlike a number of promoters, we never talked down to him as a mere 'roadie' but would genuinely enjoy chatting to him. Even in those days it was apparent he had a lot more to him than you would expect and although he was large he was not yet aggressive and always appeared most considerate and charming. It was, therefore, something of a shock when I was woken up one morning, after a very late night, by a phone call from Gene Vincent complaining that Peter had beaten him up. Gene normally spoke with a quiet Southern accent and was often quite difficult to understand, but a slightly hysterical Gene Vincent was virtually impossible. Calming him down I discovered that Gene had had an altercation with his wife, which had ended with him striking her. Peter had arrived in the middle of the row and taking great exception to wife beating had hit Gene, which seemed to me to be fair enough. Gene wanted me to book him into a hotel in central London and, I am sure, pay for it. Instead, rather tactfully, I suggested he talked it over with Don Arden. Luckily I avoided being drawn into this dispute and I never did find out the outcome.

# CHAPTER 3

To add to the complications of our life the traditional jazz revival that had started as far back as 1947 with the George Webb Dixelanders, featuring Humphrey Lyttelton on trumpet had finally made it into the mainstream of popular music giving birth to the 'Trad Boom'. Not wishing to miss out on this opportunity to supplement our income, for various reasons long lost in the mysteries of time, we opened a jazz club in Kidderminster Town Hall. It was an instant success.

The only drawback was the fact that it was around 120 miles from Hayes, Kent where we lived at that time. It wasn't just the distance as I was an extremely enthusiastic driver, but other factors such as the poor road system that existed at that time and of course the weather, especially in the autumn and winter when fog and snow could be a real problem.

Apart from this, running the club was most enjoyable. The audience was slightly older than the one we were used to for pop and were extremely well behaved. Most came to listen but a good percentage came to dance and this helped give the club a great atmosphere, assisted by a number of floodlights which we would take from gig to gig in a little Hillman Husky Estate Car. Crammed with 6 of these enormous one thousand watt floodlights and stands, spare lamps, and an endless supply of red No 6 cinemoid, a gelatine substance which we obtained from a small firm called Theatre Projects, the journey was somewhat cosy. However, it was worth it to give the halls a warm and I hoped extremely sexy red glow.

The only real and regular problem was getting the bands out of the pub, which, fortunately or unfortunately, depending whether you were a promoter or musician, was situated opposite the Town Hall. Come the interval and most bands would leave the stage at high speed and head for the bar. This was fine until it was time for them to resume playing. The more disciplined bands such as The Chris Barber Band, Humphrey Lyttelton, Kenny Ball and Acker Bilk were no trouble, but one band in particular always gave us a problem - The Mick Mulligan Band. The band, helped by the showmanship of their vocalist, George Melly, was extremely popular and appeared regularly for us at the Town Hall.

'An interval looking for somewhere to happen ' was how one of our staff described them and he was not too far wide of the mark.

To overcome this rather annoying habit we developed a technique of sending a steward across to the pub ten minutes before their thirty minute break was due to end and then every five minutes until after thirty five or forty minutes I would personally put in an appearance and remind them of their contractual obligations. This normally did the trick, especially as by then they were beginning to feel no pain and the second half of the gig usually swinging like mad. Nevertheless, despite these minor irritations, the club was a pleasure to run and I even managed to sit in occasionally with old friends such as Dick Charlesworth and the City Gents – bliss…!

The only incident that marred these halcyon days happened one evening, as we were about to count up the night's takings. I was making my way up the stairs that led directly out of the foyer carrying a fairly large case in one hand and supporting our large wooden cash till with the other. I had nearly reached the top when I suddenly experienced a pain so severe that I thought I was having a heart attack I immediately dropped the case and let go of the till, startling the steward who had been supporting the other end. Over a hundred pounds of silver coins cascaded into the foyer - it was a promoters nightmare', a Judgement from God'. However, at that moment I was less concerned with the money than with the thought that I was dying. I couldn't breathe. It felt is if there was an iron band bound around my chest. I sat down and after a few minutes the pain started to subside.

I still wasn't sure what had caused it or in fact what the problem was, but I felt that I would be better of at home where I could contact my own doctor. Unfortunately, at this time Wendy had not yet learned to drive but I found that I could drive quite well if I did not make any sudden movements. All went well until we reached the Old Kent Road, which is exceptionally long and very straight. By this time it was around 2.00 a.m. and, with absolutely no traffic around, I had allowed my speed to creep up a little. The pain, which had pre-viously been sharp and stabbing, had turned into a dull ache and I had prac-tically forgotten about it until I had to make a sharp left hand turn. Braking hard I nearly didn't make it. The pain came stabbing back only this time worse than ever. The more I turned the wheel, the worse the pain. I almost mounted the pavement on the wrong side of the road just missing a parked car. Chastened, I drove slowly home. The next day I could hardly move. Our doctor, when he finally arrived, took one look at me and diagnosed a slipped disc. He advised me to lay on a hard board for about ten days. It was very difficult to spare this much time as we were so busy, but thankfully my father-in-law stepped in to help Wendy with running the clubs. I found it very hard just to lie in bed, especially as after four or five days I felt so much better. However, I stuck it out for the full ten days. In the end it turned out to be good advice, as the problem never reoccurred.

Whilst all this was going on the numbers at the Wallington 'Jive Sessions' were steadily picking up. Instead of a Star Night once a month we had decided to use 'Top Groups' every week and this was proving very popular. We were using artists like Joe Brown and the Bruvvers, even then in those early days a fabulous guitarist and exceedingly popular, as well as

Nero and the Gladiators, Emile Ford and the Checkmates etc.

Situated, as the venue was just 10 miles or so from central London, we began to attract journalists from the major music papers as well as agents and managers and, for the first time, began to feel part of the scene that was fast developing in the early sixties. It was probably a golden age for promoters before they became simply the servants of the groups and I ruled the stage with a rod of iron. Even with the name groups I stipulated that the change over between bands was no longer than one record - around two and a half to three minutes – a tough target but one I often achieved with two records being the norm, unless of course the band had a Hammond organ. I dreaded the appearance of bands like Manfred Mann and The Graham Bond Organisation - they meant good business and good music, but often the delays whilst this temperamental instrument was coaxed into life were interminable.

Whenever I had the time, I really enjoyed standing in the foyer talking to our regulars as they arrived. Amongst these were a young couple around seventeen years old who, most weeks, would come over and talk to me about the groups I had, or in their opinion, should book and about the scene in general. One evening I remember the young boy excitedly telling me he had just joined a group. He was Jeff Beck at the start of his illustrious career. Another young man, a little older than most of our regulars, who came fairly often, was Bill Wyman. He was not yet a Rolling Stone and was still known to his mum as Bill Perks. It was Bill's good friend Stuart Walleans, who was later to assist me both as DJ and stage manager, who told me very early on to book The Rolling Stones.

I remember to this day with ever increasing embarrassment saying 'Good Lord no Stu' we only have a name band policy here!'

One evening, standing in the foyer watching the kids coming in, I was surprised to see coming down the steps of the Ladies' cloakroom one of our regulars, an extremely pretty girl. She was dressed in an ankle length skirt; old brown cardigan buttoned to the neck, granny boots and was wearing her hair in a heavy and rather unbecoming fringe. ' Oh My God!', I thought, she's going to become a nun - but no she'd simply become a Mod. It was then, looking around, that I realised a large number of the girls were wearing similar clothes. Wallington had become a Mod club. I suppose I should have realised this by the large number of motor scooters parked in the lay by outside the hall. The fact that the boys were all similarly dressed in sharp suits and came in wearing Parkas should also have given me a clue, but it was a new phenomenon and at this time only seen in a few isolated spots around London.

# CHAPTER 4

The early sixties saw an absolute explosion of groups being formed and we had enormous number of local bands vying to play support to the main groups. So many in fact, that I would occasionally book the Wallington Public Hall for an evening and hold an open audition. Some of the groups who were just starting out were, as you would expect, pretty dreadful. However, overall, the standard was pretty high. In addition to musical ability it was of course just as important that the band looked good and were properly presented.

We had a pool of bands that I thought were particularly good and would use regularly including Vern Rogers and the Hi Fi's, an excellent band whose singer possessed a really fine voice and who sang in the style of Roy Orbinson and surprisingly pulled it off, Martin Jae and the Hi –Fives, later to be called the Martin Jae Five and who later still recorded under the name Group X and had a hit record catchily titled 'There are Eight Million Cossack Melodies - and this is one of them,' Also very popular were The Strangers - a good straight down the line beat group. Even more popular were Peter Lincoln and the Sundowners led by Peter and Clive, the two younger brothers of Eden Kane, who at that time was most successful with a string of hit records such as ' Well I Ask You, 'Get Lost', and Forget Me not'. Eden, or Rick as his family and friends knew him, was, with his dark good looks undoubtedly everyone's idea of a teenage idol. In fact, all three brothers were successful. Using the family name of Sarstedt, Peter had a hit with a song he wrote himself called 'Where do you go to my lovely', whilst Clive, using his middle name of Robin, had a hit with an old Hoagy Carmichael song 'My Resistance Is Low'. A very talented family.

However, the band that I seemed to become more involved with than any other was one that included drummer Tony Chapman and bass guitarist Keith Temple. Tony was a very bright and likeable young man and was soon helping me as a general 'gopher.' When they brought in a brilliant young guitarist called Steve Carroll I was impressed. Not only were they a very tight little band playing Jimmy Reed influenced rhythm and blues, but they were also all good looking - a fact that didn't hurt their popularity with the girls one bit. I promptly offered to manage them and was accepted, but not before the boys gave me a hard time. We arranged to meet at The George in Hayes and held our meeting sitting out in the garden. I thought it was a formality. However, the boys thought otherwise and quizzed me for nearly an hour before agreeing. The first thing I did was to suggest they dropped their name The Alpha Beats and call themselves The Preachers.

This was a tense time for Tony. Having just been bumped out of The Rolling Stones by Charlie Watts, after doing them the favour of introducing them to Bill Wyman, he was anxious that his new band was successful. I tried to keep them busy playing support at our regular gigs where they often received a better reception than the main group. Although this helped, they needed to reach a far wider audience than our shows could provide. Looking around I found them an excellent agent, a friend of mine called Malcolm Rose. What they really needed though was a record contract so I arranged for them to audition for Pye records. This turned out to be the wrong label because although the boys played well, Pye executives didn't seem to have any real understanding of R & B. I think they were still having trouble coming to terms with pop and with great tact and endless sympathy turned us down.

Whether it was their rejection by Pye Records, or just the constant search for the right sound I don't know, but around this time the trio became a quartet with the addition of Terry Clarke on rhythm guitar. Meanwhile Malcolm was keeping them fairly busy finding them gigs all around the country and the reception they received wherever they played continued to convince me of their potential. Perhaps we were keeping them a little to busy because Keith decided at this point to leave.

'I'm fed up living in a Dormobile and I don't think the band is getting anywhere.' he said.

His replacement was a young guy called Andy Bown. At this stage in his career he wasn't much of a bass player but he did have truly wonderful hair.

I was in Bristol when I heard the news. Tony and Steve had had an accident on their way to one of our gigs in Stourbridge. Steve was dead and Tony was in hospital. The other two were OK. Normally they would have all travelled together in the van but on this occasion they had travelled in separate vehicles. Tony it seems had taken the back street route that I used when I went Stourbridge. On a tricky bend, possibly swerving to avoid an on coming car, they had hit the parapet of a bridge, rolled down the embankment and had been crushed by the equipment they were carrying. Tony was by all reports lucky to be alive. We were all shocked and totally devastated by the news. Steve was one of the nicest of people - tall, good looking, with a slightly shy yet engaging manner. However, it was as a guitarist that he really shone. We were all convinced that Steve was going to be one of the British guitar greats, a view that was shared by many others, including Bill Wyman.

Whilst carrying out research for this book I received a letter from Keith Temple, founder member and original bass player of the Preachers in which his admiration and affection for Steve is evident, as is the respect in which he was held by his fellow musicians.

I quote: ' I was terribly upset when Steve was killed just two weeks after I left the Preachers. Steve was in a class of his own as a guitarist. Despite playing virtually every night with him I never ceased to be amazed

The Preachers circa. 1963  Keith Temple - Tony Chapman - Steve Carroll

Pete Lincoln of The Sundowners
backstage at Wallington

Vern Rogers - A great favourite in
South Norwood and Wallington

at his virtuosity, as were many of the of the top bands we played with. We were on with Manfred Mann at Bromley Court one night and Paul Jones sat on the front of the stage listening, as did the Savages at Redhill and several other bands. If he'd lived he could have been up with the Jeff Becks, Eric Claptons, and Mark Knopflers'.

When he was finally released from hospital, Tony, after much soul searching decided to continue with the band. Realising it would be virtually impossible to replace Steve, he eventually found a guitarist called Gary Taylor who, while not as exciting a player, was still a highly competent guitarist with an excellent image. Slowly things returned to normal and surprisingly the new line up seemed as popular as the old.

Meanwhile I had problems registering the name The Preachers. It seemed that in 1964 anything with religious or biblical references was taboo and our application was rejected. We needed another name. It was Norman Dickens who came up with the new name. At that time, Norman was working for me mainly in the Midlands and had seen the Preachers many times.

'They come on stage like a herd of elephants' he said,' so why not call them The Herd'.

We tried the name out on Tony and he liked it so The Herd it was. Given the amount of promoting we were doing at the time I could never really give The Herd the attention they deserved. So it came as no real surprise when one evening at the Wallington Public Halls I was summoned to one of the dressing rooms and introduced by the band to their new manager, Billy Gaff. I found out much later he and Andy Bown had been partners in a club they ran in Bromley, Kent. Billy Gaff, of course, went on to achieve a degree of fame and quite a lot of fortune as the manager of Rod Stewart.

I suppose I should have been upset but I wasn't. Apart from the fact that that our main interest and income lay with promoting, the band had changed significantly from the early days as the Preachers. They no longer played earthy R & B, but had slowly evolved into a pop group - all pretty hair and posturing. A couple of years later, after The Herd had produced a couple of hit records, we finally received three or four free gigs as compensation for our initial efforts; perhaps in the circumstances I should have held out for more.

# CHAPTER 5

Meanwhile our programme of expansion continued and we opened a new venue in Redhill in partnership with my father-in-law. The dances were held on a Saturday in the Old Market Hall, which was up on the first floor - a little inconvenient for loading in the equipment but a good hall never the less. We stuck to our tried and trusted formula of a name band plus a popular local band. Because of the licensing laws we ran it as a club. Everyone wishing to come in had to first fill out an application form. I shall never forget the look on the face of one young lady.

I was writing out her membership card and, looking at the name on her application form, said, "What a coincidence my mother was an Adcock" and I swear to this day I did not say my mothers 'nickname' was Adcock.

I thought she was going to hit me and she stormed off in high dudgeon. Worse still, when I checked up later, it turned out that my mother's maiden name was Allcock. In the circumstances I didn't think she would appreciate it if I told her of my mistake.

Redhill was the only place in nearly twenty-five years of promoting where we experienced protection of any sort. Because it was a Saturday we attracted a pretty lively crowd determined to make the most of their weekend and our team of six or seven bouncers were hard put keeping on top of the arguments and fights that developed during the course of the evening. On one particularly difficult evening two heavies approached me and gave me a brief but succinct run down on the qualities and abilities of my bouncers.

'They couldn't bounce a fucking ball. If you get rid of them and pay the two of us what you pay all those weedy little fuckers, we'll make sure you won't have any more agro'.

I wasn't exactly overjoyed with their proposition but they made it abundantly clear that if I didn't employ them they would arrange a demonstration of their considerable powers. So, rather reluctantly, I agreed, thinking that if their demands got any worse we would have no alternative but to close down. I must say if this was protection then I was all for it. The fights stopped as if by magic and if there was ever a minor skirmish one look from the terrible two was enough to calm things down. I later discovered that they came from a local estate and as you would expect enjoyed a fearsome reputation in the area. Years later when I was telling Tony Smith, the manager of Genesis, this story he claimed these two gentlemen were his cousins and although Tony grew up in this area and his father, who was himself a highly successful promoter, had his offices in Redhill, I somehow didn't believe him. 'Oh yeah pull the other one, Tony'.

Trad' jazz was undoubtedly in decline. The boom was nearing its end and our club at Kidderminster, along with Jazz clubs all around the country, was experiencing a significant reduction in the number of people attending. In direct contrast, Pop was booming. Kidderminster Town Hall was an excellent venue, so why not, we reasoned, change over? However, before we said goodbye to traditional jazz, one significant event occurred. Don Kingswell, the road manager of one of the better known bands and whom I knew very well as he had previously been the manager of the Cy Laurie Jazz Club (probably one of the most popular of the central London clubs), mentioned that he had recently come across an enormous hall in Bath. He also added that there did not seem to be much going on in the area.

Always the opportunist, I immediately drove down to Bath to look at this venue, which turned out to be The Pavilion. It was large, with an official capacity of 1,000 and, just as Don had said, there did not appear to be a great deal going on. Straight away I sent a letter outlining what I had in mind to the Spa Superintendent, who, amongst many other things, was responsible for the overall administration of The Pavilion and a meeting with him was arranged. Luckily, when we met he approved of my ideas and suggested that we held the dances on a Monday evening when there was a better chance of continuity. We agreed on an opening date of the 21st January 1963 and thus started a relationship with Bath that was to last for more than seven years.

# CHAPTER 6

Just as the future started to look really promising we were about to suffer our first major setback. The dances at the Stanley Halls were still giving us problems. This time what appeared to be an organised gang had laid out my entire team of bouncers. This was it - make or break time. Among my contacts was Paul Lincoln, a professional wrestler and co owner of the 2 I's coffee bar. Once I had explained my problem, Paul gave me the phone number of some one called Bert Assirati, whom he thought would be able to help me. Bert it turned out had been a top-of- the-bill wrestler for many years. Now in his sixties and with failing eyesight, he was still happy to take on the odd security problem and agreed to help me. He explained that he would come himself with four of his boys. When I mentioned that, in my opinion, five of them were not enough to sort out the trouble we were experiencing, Bert assured me they were 'all big lads' and every thing would be 'just fine'.

As soon as I met Bert I was reassured. He was, despite his advancing years, a most imposing figure. He was only around 5' 6' tall but appeared to be the same across the shoulders. He was quite the strongest man I have ever come across. To compensate for his poor eyesight he had one of his young guys at his side at all times acting as his look out. For two or three weeks everything was calm. The local thugs were undoubtedly impressed by Bert and his team and would come over to chat to him. It seemed my strategy was working until one evening, whilst I was up in the balcony checking that all was peaceful in the hall, I happened to look down and there, standing directly under me, was Bert and his young companion. They were totally sur- rounded by a circle of at least twenty of South Norwood's finest. The gauntlet had been thrown down and they were determined that their honour besmirched by these interlopers would be avenged. Looking on in an agony of indecision, I saw the young steward run away to get what I hoped was some help. However, before he could return one of the ringleaders rushed at Bert with an iron bar. This, I thought rather belatedly, is the time I should dial 999 but before I could move Bert had twisted the bar from his attacker's grasp with one hand, while with the other he delivered a short sharp chop to the side of his neck. The boy went down as if pole axed, which I suppose he had been. There was a stunned silence. The attackers to a man fled the building, leaving a very calm Bert to contemplate his victory. In the end it turned out to be a Pyrrhic victory. True we never had another fight, but the local kids stopped coming, and within six weeks the dances had closed.

The transition from jazz to pop at Kidderminster Town Hall went extremely well, attracting even larger crowds. Luckily there was a small hall adjoining the Town hall with large double doors that linked the two together giving a useful increase in capacity. You couldn't actually see the bands but it was great for dancing and other activities. This additional capacity ensured we could afford to use the better-known bands like The Who, The Rolling Stones and The Hollies etc. Rather surprisingly, The Stones did not seem to appeal to the Kidderminster kids. Arriving early the one time we played them at the town hall, we were expecting to see large queues tailing round the block. Instead, all we found was Bill Wyman sitting on a table in the cloakroom chatting to the caretakers. Although the numbers that evening did finally pick up to a respectable level, the hysteria and excitement that we found in other parts of the country was missing. Thinking about it, Wendy and I reached the conclusion that it was probably because Kidderminster at that time was a rather dull and depressing midland town and what the youngsters really wanted in their lives was a little glamour. This was rather born out by the fact that once again Manfred Mann held the attendance record. The screams when Paul Jones came on stage were truly awesome. Then again, it might simply have been the fact that the Rolling Stones phenomena had not yet hit the area. Whatever the reason, there was no doubt that the people were amongst the warmest and friendliest that we came across in our very extensive travels around the country. The two hall keepers were typical examples. In the five or six years that we used the town hall we never had a cross word. Even the Town Clerk, John Evans, whom I suppose was technically our landlord, having as he did the final say on who used the halls, was most affable.

It was at the Kidderminster Town Hall that I first met Robert Plant. I am sure at that time he was playing in Gulliver's People but I could be wrong. It was probably The Band of Joy. Even then he was popular and I remember being extremely impressed by the large number of fans the band brought with them. I also remember thinking what a good voice he had. However, at that time, I don't think he showed any signs of the incredible charisma he went on to possess with Led Zeppelin. In later years he was always reminding me of these early gigs. The one thing that I feel he never got over was the fee I used to pay them. Shaking his head in disbelief, he would recall that it was a tenner for the whole band. Actually, Robert, it was quite a lot more than I paid the other local groups.

Robert obviously remembered these gigs with great affection as I was shown when shortly before Christmas 2002 he phoned me.

'Hello,' said a familiar voice. 'This is Robert Plant. I don't know if you remember me? I used to play for you at Stourbridge Town Hall'.

It seems he had heard about the Bath and Knebworth Commemorative sets my daughter had produced and wanted to buy two of each. I obviously

Nero and The Gladiators - no expense was spared with the costumes !

wasn't going to accept money from him and, ever the nice guy, he insisted on paying. A long argument ensued which was finally ended when I played my trump card.

'For God's sake Robert,' I said. 'There wouldn't have been anything for me to write about if it wasn't for you and Zep'. Not quite the truth but close and it finally convinced him to accept the sets as a gift.

Another of the local musicians to make it was Stan Webb. When I first met him he was leading a band called either the Blue Four or Sounds of Blue. Among others this band included Christine Perfect who, as Christine McVie, went on to achieve fame and fortune with Fleetwood Mac. Stan would regularly call me from the phone box at the end of his street to see if there were any gigs available as support to the more established groups. He eventually changed the name of his group to Chicken Shack, which rapidly became one of the most influential blues bands in the country. We used Chicken Shack a lot in the late sixties including at the 1969 Bath Festival of Blues where Stan, ever the extrovert, using an incredibly long guitar lead, played one of his blistering solos from the middle of the crowd. Stan is one of the great characters of rock and is still upholding the blues tradition playing regularly all over the world.

# CHAPTER 7

Because the Thursday evening shows at Kidderminster were so successful we started to look for another venue in the area, preferably situated a little closer to the well-populated suburbs of Birmingham. After a short search we came up with the Stourbridge Town Hall, an old Victorian redbrick building ideally situated in the very centre of town. If my memory is correct we opened on a Wednesday in November 1962 with the Brook Bros - two young men who, around that time, enjoyed a fair amount of chart success with songs like Warpaint, and Ain't going to Wash for a Week. The main drawback to using Stourbridge Town Hall was the lack of availability and we occasionally lost three consecutive Wednesdays having to move to a Monday or Tuesday in an attempt to maintain continuity. The other was the caretaker, as sullen and un-cooperative, as his opposite number at Kidderminster was helpful and charming. He would sit all evening locked in his little room, glowering at the kids, his only companion a large Alsatian dog which was as anti social as his owner. I think he was just scared of the kids en masse – a bit stupid as they were pretty well behaved and very rarely gave us any trouble.

The lack of continuity was, of course, a real problem as it meant that we had to give more attention to publicity than we would otherwise have done. The cheapest and most effective method of publicising the dances as far as I was concerned was fly posting, which we could carry out ourselves, usually once a month. On these occasions we would book into a local Stourbridge Hotel and start as soon as the show finished, working out from the town centre into the outlying areas. The next day, usually having loads of time to kill before the evening session in Kidderminster, we would drive around checking on our handiwork. I always made sure that I only used existing sites and was particularly careful to cover up only out of date posters as I certainly did not want to spark off a poster war where offending posters were defaced or worse still covered with 'cancelled' notices.

Despite all my care, I still made the occasional howler and on one memorable occasion, what I had presumed was an empty shop the evening before, by day turned out to be a very well cared for grocers whose owners lowered a dark blue security shutter inside the shop window and door as night protection. As we drove by I was horrified to see two staff members slowly and laboriously scraping off the four large posters that I had so lovingly pasted in the dead centre of their large plate glass window. The poster that had led me to the site in the first place, a local production of The Merry Widow, turned out to be sellotaped to the inside of the glass door. Highly embarrassed and wishing to avoid a direct confrontation, we drove to the nearest phone box where Wendy, always the bravest in these sort of situations, phoned apologising profusely for our mistake and offering to have someone call and remove the offending posters. To her surprise, the proprietor was most understanding. Declining her offer he explained that they had nearly finished taking them off and there wasn't much more to do - I could just imagine the reaction if I had done something similar in Surrey.

Like Kidderminster, Stourbridge in the early sixties was not one of the most affluent places in the country and what the kids really wanted it seemed was a little excitement and glamour as portrayed in the various TV shows like Ready Steady Go and Oh Boy, with the emphasis at that time on winkle picker shoes and beehive hairstyles. Mod it was not, which is probably why we continued to do well with Johny Kidd, Marty Wilde and Shane Fenton and the Fentones long after they would have been considered passé in and around London. Like Kidderminster, groups such as the Stones and the Pretty Things took a lot longer to make an impact in this part of the country. I really couldn't image putting on groups like the Graham Bond Organisation or the Downliners Sect in Stourbridge at that time.

The up side, of course, was we did rather better with the pure pop groups such as The Applejacks, Honeycombs etc. and I am indebted to Linda Potter, one of our regulars, for reminding me that on the evening of the Honeycombs appearance, sometime during the changeover, a member of the support band meticulously loosened all the nuts holding the main act's drum kit together, so when the Honeycombs appeared it was only a matter of time before the inevitable happened and the drums exploded every which way across the stage. The female drummer was so upset that she left in a fit of pique bringing their performance to an abrupt and premature end. This of course gave the support band, The Band of Joy, the opportunity they had so deviously sought to save the day and become the heroes of the evening. Even then Robert was already showing the drive, ambition and determination that was to lead him a long way from a rainy, Wednesday evening in Stourbridge.

Although it never managed to hit the heights of some of our other venues and very rarely attracted huge crowds, nevertheless we still managed to run successful nights in the town hall for over four years. Dudley, on the other hand, was a nightmare I would rather forget. When we first discovered the Civic Hall it seemed ideal – large, smart and beautifully maintained. A little discouragingly there was still a large notice at the side of the stage, which had obviously been there since the war that said 'No Jitterbugging' and to which someone, I presume to appear up to date, had added 'Or Stiletto Heels'. However, in its favour, the hall was available for a series of regular Saturday evening sessions.

Opening night started promisingly enough and for the next two weeks just got better. It wasn't until the fourth week that we got our first inkling that there might be a problem. At the end of the evening a young woman came up to me complaining that her coat had been stolen. On questioning her it appeared she had checked it into the council run cloakroom and when she handed in her ticket they were unable to find it. Pointing out politely that it was not my responsibility but the council's, I was met with a torrent of abuse and threats. It wasn't until I looked around that I realised that we had been joined by around a dozen or so of her friends, mainly male and all, without exception, large and very threatening. At this point I waved the white flag and gave her £12, the cost she claimed of her virtually new coat.

I was told later by one of the hall staff that they all came from a local caravan site and were well known in the area and I shouldn't have given her the money as it was a trick they tried to pull all the time. Thinking I would play it safe I arranged for six or seven of our Bristol bouncers to be on hand the next week to augment our local stewards. The following Saturday it seemed as if my fears had been justified, with minor confrontations taking place throughout the evening between the local toughs and our team. As soon as the dance ended we had a council of war and decided that the only course of action was to bar the trouble makers altogether. Our strategy seemed to work. With a local steward strategically placed at the front of house to point them out, our Bristol boys politely but firmly denied them entry. They were helped by the fact that the troublemakers arrived in ones and twos and not en masse.

By 9.30pm the main group was on stage and with one last look around the hall I joined Wendy in a backstage office to cash up the evenings takings. Ten minutes or so later we were interrupted by a knock on the door. It was one of the hall staff who, looking anxious, told me there had been a fight and I was needed urgently. The hall, which a few short minutes earlier had been full of happy, dancing, enthusiastic kids was now virtually empty. Rushing towards the foyer, wondering what the hell had happened, I passed six of my stewards lying unconscious laid out in a neat line. Oh my God! Arriving at the foyer was like entering the front line of a battlefield after the battle was lost. The remainder of my bouncers were standing shocked and bleeding, shirts and jeans torn and ripped. Two of the main plate glass doors were hanging from their hinges, victims of the car that one of the local thugs had driven up a flight of steps and into the foyer in a successful attempt to gain access to the hall for his twenty or thirty friends who were following behind with wooden clubs and iron bars.

The council were most understanding. Perhaps it wasn't the first time this sort of thing had happened and on Monday morning the series was immediately terminated by mutual consent.

# CHAPTER 8

The winter of 1962/63 was a hard one. It snowed – or rather, it didn't just snow - there was a blizzard and the whole of the West Country lay under several feet of the stuff. Driving in and around Bath in the early part of January, with less than three weeks to the opening of our new undertaking, became an adventure. The 'B' roads were barely passable and the minor ones resembled the Cresta Run. Somehow we managed to get out our publicity, greatly encouraged by the excited interest shown by the kids.

We had chosen Jet Harris, late of the Shadows, as our opening act and hoped and prayed for a thaw. We were lucky. By the 23rd of January the roads in and around the city were back to normal and only the minor roads high in the hills surrounding Bath remained affected. The opening night was a great success attracting a large and enthusiastic crowd and this helped to get the series off to a really terrific start. Jet Harris received a rapturous reception with girls screaming and fainting in gratifyingly large numbers. I don't know if this was the sort of reception he was normally afforded but he seemed slightly overwhelmed with the reaction. Jet Harris wasn't the only one who was overwhelmed. A new venue meant that there was no one apart from Wendy and me who had the faintest idea of what was going on. Leaving Wendy to take care of the ticket office, I was busy with the dozens of different jobs that cropped up on an opening night, including talking to the local reporters (most important), supervising the security, stage managing, dis-cussing bookings with the local groups who were keen to play at The Pavilion, sorting out the total mayhem in the car park and generally chatting to our patrons. So busy in fact that I forgot to give Jet Harris a telegram that had arrived earlier that afternoon telling him that he and Tony Meehan were No 1 in the charts with "Diamonds". I remembered it just as he came of stage at the end of his show.

He was less than thrilled, ' What sort of a promoter are you,' he yelled. 'You could have read it out on stage so every one would know'.

Amongst the dozens of people I spoke to that evening was Brian K Jones. Brian it appeared was good friends with The Shadows and had come over from Bristol to see Jet, and to write a piece about him for his column in The Western Daily Press. It also transpired that he managed several of the local groups and knew most of the other groups in the area. This, and the fact that he had some previous experience in stage management, meant that this was a heaven sent opportunity to delegate two of the most important jobs. Brian agreed to help and proved not only to be highly competent, but also a really great guy and although I didn't realise it at the time this was the start of a friendship that has lasted to the present day.

The following Monday was meant to feature Marty Wilde & the Wildcats, but owing to some confusion on the part of his agent, the booking was changed at two days notice to February the 18th. Instead we had Emile Ford and the Checkmates. A hand written notice was placed at the entrance to this effect. However, it did not seem to deter any of the punters, who not having seen Emile Ford before really seemed to enjoy themselves. I, on the other hand, wasn't having such a good time. There were a number of scuffles and incidents and our stewards, whom we had recruited from a local rugby club, were kept very busy. In fact, at one point, they seemed in danger of loosing their grip on things. Oh my God! Not South Norwood all over again, I thought. So it came as something of a relief when I discovered I was being subjected to a little blackmail from a team of young men from Bristol, intent on demonstrating to me that they could do a better job than the stewards I was already employing. Speaking to them afterwards they seemed a decent bunch of lads, most of whom had previous experience of this type of work and as they were happy to work for the same money as the Bath stewards and were even larger. I decided to take a chance and employ them. I need not have worried. They were excellent and stayed with me for the entire seven years we were at Bath. When we opened in Bristol they worked for me there as well.

Wendy and I enjoyed running 'big beat sessions' in Bath. We would arrive early and explore this wonderful city ending up in a Berni's steak bar, at that time very much a West Country phenomenon. The one we frequented was situated just a hundred yards from The Pavilion and from the window we could watch our patrons arriving and judge just when we should leave to open up the box office.

Because of the size of the hall and the fact that there was not a lot going on nationally on a Monday evening, we were in a position to book some of the better-known American acts including Johnny and the Hurricanes, Johnny Tillotson and Jerry Lee Lewis. However, the event that was to put us on the map locally was still some months away. It was while we were up north sometime towards the end of 1961 or beginning of 1962, trying hard to establish a jazz club in Warrington, that I had noticed a poster advertising a 'pop extravaganza' at the Tower Ballroom, Blackpool. Top of the bill was Jerry Lee Lewis, with an exceptionally strong supporting programme of about six or seven well-known groups. Second on the bill was a group I had never heard of called The Beatles. 'Hmm', I thought, they must really have a strong local following to justify that sort of position, so I made a mental note to look out for them and when some time around the end of January 1963 I read that they had just released their first record I was ready to book them. I was amazed when I was quoted a fee of £250 as this was some two or three times the price of a group with a top ten hit, and much more than I had paid any

The Beatles mingling backstage at Bath Pavilion

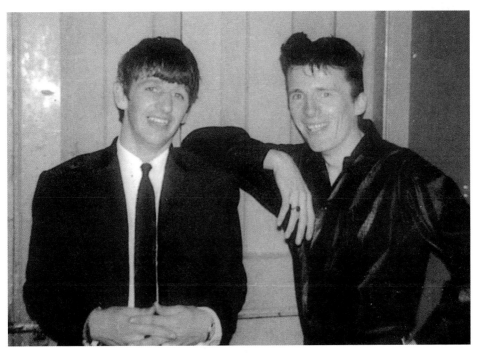

Backstage at Bath Pavilion - Ringo with Chet

group to date. But I had a hunch and agreed to, what I thought of at the time, as their extortionate demands. A date was set for the 10th of June and my hunch obviously turned out to be correct. By the time the 10th of June came around they had had two number one hit singles with Please, Please Me and From Me To You and £250 was looking like a very reasonable figure.

Rather surprisingly, when we gave out our regular monthly flyer, there was very little reaction to the announcement of The Beatles forthcoming appearance, so when the date finally came around we rather naively decided that it was not necessary to set out any earlier than usual. We arrived in Bath around 3.00 p.m. and went straight to The Pavilion to find that there was already a gigantic queue, which was growing by the minute. As a precaution I had already arranged for our staff to be on hand at 6.00 p.m. instead of the usual 7.00 p.m. Nevertheless, it was apparent that unless something was done immediately, the car park in front of the hall would be full to overflowing and the over spill would reach up the steps and onto the main road, creating a potentially dangerous situation. Pausing only to make a swift call to Brian Jones to arrange some urgent assistance, we decided that the only option left to us was to open the hall immediately. Wendy manned the ticket office and I acted as doorman. The hall was jammed full by 5.00 p.m. By this time Brian and some of our staff had arrived and things were slowly restored to a semblance of normality.

It was with a feeling of relief that I saw the band arrive. They were early, thank God - one less worry. While I was up on the stage helping to position the equipment, I was aware of John Lennon and Paul McCartney peering at the audience through a small hole in the curtain. A couple of minutes later they came over and asked me what the kids in Bath were like.

'Wildly enthusiastic' I said which seemed to satisfy them.

It was the support bands I felt sorry for. They not only had to compete with the Beatles for the attention of the fans but because we had opened so early, they had even longer to play. In Chet and the Triumphs and The Colin Anthony Combo we had two of the best bands in the area and somehow they managed, by sheer dint of hard work, to keep the crowd on their side.

It was my normal practice to appear on stage in front of the curtains and give a big plug for next week's attraction, and then introduce the star group. This time when I stepped through the curtains I was virtually lifted off my feet by the sheer, unbelievable volume of sound.

Realising that any announcement was out of the question I simply yelled the magic words, 'It's the Beatles' and as the curtains parted turned and walked back towards these four nodding, shaking, stomping, young men now in full song.

The Beatles at Bath Pavilion 1963

Unforgettable! How anyone in the hall, apart from those in the first two or three rows, could hear anything I don't know but it did not seem to spoil anyone's enjoyment, with this wild barrage of frenzied screaming continuing throughout their performance. Our stewards were fantastic and really rose to the occasion, with some ferrying both the hysterical girls and those who had simply passed out to a quiet backstage recovery area, while others fended off attempts by the more determined girls to get on stage and obtain some little memento of their idols, such as guitars, drums, trousers etc.

After the show came the crunch. I was talking to Wendy in the ticket office when in strode two of the Beatles roadies.

'Our van has been vandalised and we feel that you should pay for some of the damage.'

'What exactly has been damaged?' I asked.

'The wing mirrors have been ripped of, the wiper blades removed and the whole van covered in lipstick graffiti'.

'And where exactly was the van parked when all this happened?' I enquired.

'By the stage door,' one replied.

'What all evening?'

'Yes' came the reply.

'Funny,' I said, 'that several of our kids saw it parked in a side street a mile away and even more unbelievable that you had the time to get every-thing replaced before the show, because I saw it when you arrived and it was certainly in the same state then'.

'Oh" they said and left.

As they did all the hard work and were probably on a fixed salary, I suppose it was a big temptation to raise a little beer money in this fashion. Especially as they could see, what must have seemed to them, so much easy money being made by the band and promoters all around the country.

Next day the Bath Evening Chronicle carried a glowing revue of the show, with most of the papers in the area carrying some sort of report. I am quite convinced this comprehensive publicity helped us establish The Pavilion as one of the most important West Country venues and enabled us to run there as long as we did.

# CHAPTER 9.

The phone rang. Wendy answered it. 'It's George' she called. We had just arrived home from Wallington leaving George, the Hall Manager to see the bands out and lock up. What, I wondered, had happened.

'Its those bloody Pretty Things,' he said. 'When I went to put out some rubbish, one of them long haired gits was fornicating with some groupie by the dustbins, and when I told them to stop he told me to fuck off, and then tipped a bin all over me'.

I commiserated with him. After all, this sort of hazard probably hadn't been mentioned in his job description.

How we managed to get so many great artists to play such a relatively small venue as the Wallington Public Hall I still don't know. I guess I was pretty keen and kept an ear open for what acts were coming in from America. Also, as we opened more venues, we had greater negotiating power. But in the early days I suppose I just played my hunches. I had a pretty good ear for a hit record and used to book a lot of groups on the strength of hearing their latest release just once. I would also listen to our regulars who would come up and request a favourite record or group. This made it possible for us to occasionally have bands appearing for their normal fee the week that they were 'No 1' in the charts. Of course, the agents soon caught on to this, and it wasn't long before contracts contained chart clauses; putting the fees up by specific amounts according to the groups position in the charts on the day of their appearance.

One Tuesday in May 1963 I arrived in Wallington a little earlier than usual as I was expecting a fairly hectic night. The Hall was still and empty. Walking backstage I noticed the lights were on in one of the dressing rooms. 'Christ!', I wondered, did we have burglars? On closer investigation I found Jerry Lee Lewis, just sitting quietly and contemplatively in this empty room. How he came to be there so early and entirely on his own I never discovered. We sat and talked for half an hour or so, an interesting man. Yet while he was happy to chat he never entirely lost his sense of self-importance. However, later that evening I could forgive him any thing. If you haven't experienced a world-class rock 'n' roller at the peak of his considerable powers, performing in a small hall, then you really have missed the point of the music. It was exciting, chaotic, intense, an evening from which neither the piano, nor myself ever really fully recovered.

Another of the pop music giants to appear at Wallington later that year was Roy Orbison. I remember his appearance well because in view of his amazing voice I wanted desperately to improve the sound quality of the P.A. and had hired in some extra equipment. When he came on I was in the

The Brook Brothers backstage at Wallington.
'I'd know those pots and pans anywhere'.

Graham Nash on stage at Wallington

middle of the crowded hall listening anxiously. The sound was certainly better. I could actually hear him. However, what struck me most was that, whilst he was probably a little off the boil at this point in his career, he was still popular enough to sell out far larger venues and yet here he was, standing on a stage barely two feet high, with the audience so close they could have gone through his pockets if they had a mind. He was giving his all for the sheer joy of his music - an attitude that seems to be rather lacking in the vast majority of the current bands.

At last I had rather belatedly followed Stuart's advice and booked The Stones. I should have realised that it was going to be a difficult gig when on arriving at the hall really early I found the area swarming with girls and half a dozen policemen already on duty. I couldn't believe it when I heard an officious inspector tell a group of young girls to get the next fucking bus home. I had a few words with him but it was no good he had a closed mind and wasn't going to be co-operative. He simply told me to get these people inside and off the street as soon as possible. I could feel my respect for the forces of law and order diminishing by the second.

We started to let people in, unusually using two cashiers and were soon full and I do mean full. Trying as hard as possible to appear helpful and get the youngsters off the street, I had rather misjudged the speed with which we were letting people in and we had rather higher numbers than I would usually allow. The officious inspector marched into the hall and all hell broke loose. I thought I was about to be arrested.

'This hall is dangerously over crowded and I am putting an officer on each emergency exit to prevent any one leaving the premises'.

'Very helpful I'm sure luv', I thought.

'In addition I am sending for the Fire Prevention Officer, The Health and Safety Executive, representatives of the Council and my own Senior Officer.'

Bingo, a full house!

What the hell do I do now? The Stones had all ready arrived and were bouncing maniacally around the dressing rooms. In desperation I decided to speak to them.

'How would you feel about going on straight away?' I said, and quickly explained the situation.

'Great,' said Keith. 'We can get back into town earlier.'

While they were getting ready I went on stage and explained that The Stones would be going on a little earlier than usual but would be playing their full set. I was amazed at the speed they got ready. In a matter of minutes, it seemed, they were on stage. Then the mayhem began. Hysterical girls everywhere. One girl in particular had my staff very worried, she was so wound up. We were seriously considering calling for an ambulance, that is until one of her friends turned up, took one look at her and let rip with a back hander so violent that it must have loosened a couple of teeth. If one of my stewards had struck her like this they would have gone to prison for quite some time. It did the trick though!

At last it was all over and the kids, hot and happy, burst open the emergency exits and left – sweeping aside the policemen who were meant to be guarding the doors. Five minutes later the officious inspector returned with his huge posse of officials. Striding into the hall, which was by now comparatively empty, they counted the numbers – 285. They left without saying a word. I understand that the council later wrote to the police telling them not to waste their time. Whatever the reason, we were never bothered by the police again.

# CHAPTER 10

Worthing, despite its image as the geriatric epicentre of the south coast, was probably the liveliest of all the venues we ran mainly due, of course, to its close proximity to Brighton. I shall never forget our opening night at The Assembly Halls in Worthing, if only for the brass neck cheek of the reporter from the local paper.

'I probably won't get here again. I'm very busy you know but do call me if you have any fights.'

'Of course,' I said. 'That's just the sort of publicity we're looking for.'

He gave me a long hard look and left, never to return.

To assure continuity, unusually, we used two halls in Worthing -The Assembly Halls and the Pier Pavilion. Generally, this worked very well but just occasionally we would slip up and forget to include on a contract the correct venue. It wasn't until the group was overdue that I would finally realise what had happened. I would then have to send out a search party for the unfortunate group, who would usually be found sitting outside the wrong venue looking highly bemused and wondering if they were really expected to perform at a Woman's Institute meeting. This confusion continued to dog us when later in the sixties we ran a Sunday evening discotheque we rather fancifully called Albert's Museum, which alternated between the smaller of the two Assembly Halls and a hall at the very end of the Pier. The only drawback to the Pier Pavilion was the fact that it was right on the sea front. Come the summer, huge quantities of seaweed would be washed up on the beach giving off the most appalling stench until council workers would finally arrive and cart it away by the lorry load.

It was at Worthing that we had the dubious distinction of presenting what I was told was the first appearance in the UK by the Walker Brothers and if their amateur behaviour was any indication, it could have been their first appearance anywhere. For a start neither the band nor their roadies could set up their equipment and had to be helped by the local group who were playing support. Even more generously, the support band lent them some of their own equipment to augment what little they had brought with them. It seemed to take forever but finally they were ready to go on and with a great feeling of relief I went on stage to introduce them.

I stood and watched for a few minutes to see if all was well and to satisfy myself that Scott Walker really did have as great a voice live as on record, then went backstage to chat to some friends. Less than fifteen minutes later the band came off stage.

'That's strange,' I thought, 'They must be playing two sets.'

Rushing to their dressing room I found the band changing out of their stage clothes.

'When are you going back on?' I asked to no one in particular.

'We're not' was the reply. 'That's it.'

Focusing my attention on Scott Walker, I tried to explain as rationally and patiently as possible that the contract was for a minimum of 30 minutes and I would like them to perform for at least a further fifteen minutes to avoid disappointing all their fans.

'Too bad' he said. 'That's all we can do.'

I persisted not quite as rationally and certainly not as patiently as before. It was no good he was just not going back on stage. He was arrogant beyond belief and did not seem to care much for either his fans or his reputation. I continued to press him and in the end he said, 'Look you'd better speak to my manager.'

'Thank God,' I thought. 'A professional. The voice of reason!'

'Great,' I said looking around. 'Where is he?'

'In London but you can't speak to him until tomorrow' and with that he walked away.

'I hope you realise,' I said rather lamely to his retreating back, 'if you don't go back on I'm giving the kids their money back and I'll sue you.'

'Too fucking bad,' came the laconic reply.

Giving bad news to 700-800 over excited teenagers was never one of my favourite jobs. Luckily, this time it wasn't so bad, as they had at least caught a glimpse of their heroes and realised that it wasn't our incompetence or dishonesty that had caused the show to be curtailed. Apologising for the brief appearance by the Walker Brothers, which I put down to severe mental exhaustion, I went on to explain that when they left they would receive a ticket allowing them to come to any one of the shows in the next four weeks, completely free of charge. This was a procedure we used at all our shows on the rare occasion that a group failed to arrive, or arrived too late to go on and as a precaution we always kept a set of tickets locked away in the boot of our car. I needn't have worried as my announcement met with an extremely positive response; after all they were getting a free night out. Quickly getting the much put-upon support band back on stage, I made my way to our backstage office. On the way there I passed the open door of the Walker Brothers dressing room and, on hearing lots of noise, I looked in.

'Good grief they're having a bloody party,' I thought.

They were laughing and joking and appeared totally indifferent to the mayhem and disappointment they had caused. I suppose I over reacted but there was only so much of their arrogant indifference I could take. Calling my stewards, I told them to get the little sons of bitches out of the hall and, gently but firmly, they where ejected through the stage door along with their personal possessions. A meaningless gesture, I know, but it certainly made me feel a whole lot better.

Despite these occasional problems, things generally ran pretty smoothly, helped in no small part by the fact that the local police special constables made Thursday evening their regular training night. Stationing themselves near the entrance, they acted as a deterrent to any potential troublemakers without in anyway interfering with the running of the event. However, although the dances were free from fights, they were anything but trouble free. Worthing was primarily a soul venue and, although we put on many different groups, it was the soul bands that normally drew the biggest and most enthusiastic audiences. Artists like Jimmy James and the Vagabonds and Geno Washington and the Ram Jam Band were always popular, as were Herbie Goins and the Nightimers.

Jimmy James was a particular favourite and whenever he appeared it wasn't long before the more enthusiastic fans were up on stage with him stripped to the waist and waving their shirts over their heads in time to the music. Jimmy never seemed to mind. In fact it was probably a scene that was repeated wherever he played. My stewards tried hard to keep the stage clear without being too heavy and spoiling the great atmosphere, but occasionally the stage became one huge seething mass of people and the band was forced to stop playing. I would then take the mic and ask for the stage to be cleared. Amazingly enough the kids were usually most responsive, leaving immediately, inevitably to return after another couple of numbers when the whole process would be repeated once again. Jimmy was a really great guy as well as a brilliant performer and I appeared on stage with him so often that I almost felt part of the band.

Nevertheless, things sometimes did get really out of hand, caused on one particular occasion by an irresponsible agent. We had booked Junior Walker and the All Stars, at that time one of the most popular of the soul acts and we were expecting a large crowd. We were not disappointed. By 8 o'clock the hall was jam-packed. At a quarter past eight, just when I was starting to wonder what had happened to the band, I received a phone call. Junior Walker and the All Stars were not coming - it seemed the drummer had some domestic problem and had flown back to the United States earlier that afternoon and Junior Walker, I was told, was definitely not prepared to play with a dep' drummer. Why the agent had waited for over six hours to let me know I never found out but his thoughtlessness prevented me from making alternative arrangements. If I had known in time I could have probably found a suitable replacement, or at least prepared notices explaining the situation. Alternatively, as a last resort, I could have found an additional local band and given the kids a free dance - anything to avoid the situation that now faced us.

Sounds Incorporated backstage at The Corn Exchange Bristol
Photo by Cliff Bulley

Sounds Incorporated having fun.
The distinguished chap in the middle is me , circa 1964.

Looking at the eager expectant faces of the youngsters cramming the hall I decided that the safest thing, if I wanted to escape being lynched, was to return their money. I delayed making the announcement whilst Wendy and some of the staff made the necessary arrangements. The biggest problem was the lack of change. However, a quick visit to the refreshment bars partially helped matters. My announcement was met with disappointment and anger that rapidly dissipated when they realised that their money was being returned. There was an enormous rush to be first in the queue that very nearly overwhelmed us. We just didn't have the resources to cope, but somehow slowly and surely we managed to get things under control. It was only when things began to calm down a little and I had time to think that, looking at the queue, I realised that I had seen several of these sweet little innocents collecting their refunds earlier in the evening. After a little investigation it appeared that some of the more enterprising little buggers, on collecting their money were being let back into the hall through the emergency exits by their friends and would then rejoin the queue. Some, I learnt later, had managed this little trick three or four times. Whilst all this was going on a couple of even more enterprising punters had forced open one of the kiosks and made off with several thousand cigarettes. A perfect end to a perfect evening. We did ultimately receive an apology and some compensation from the agents for our nightmare, but believe me it wasn't nearly enough.

It was at Worthing that I almost got into a fistfight with one of the artists. Walking around the back of the hall I was nearly hit by a large ball of screwed up newspaper thrown from a dressing room window and which, from the smell, had recently contained fish and chips. Incensed, I picked it up and hurled it back into the room, accidentally hitting the perpetrator smack bang in the face. All hell let loose. It was Ben E King, former lead singer with the Drifters and he was so mad he actually tried to climb through the window to get at me. Thinking quickly, I decided that an apology was probably the only thing that was likely to save me from a good thumping. So with great trepidation I rushed to his dressing room, introduced myself and apologised profusely. Luckily he had a sense of humour and after a short rant at me saw the funny side of things.

# CHAPTER 11

Bristol has always been a great city with an atmosphere all its own, partly I suppose because it is a port and partly because of the merchants the port attracted. Whatever the reason, there is no doubt that it produces people with great character. It is also Britain's sixth largest city and in 1963, apart from regular seated pop shows in the Colston Hall, there was surprisingly little going on. Searching for a suitable venue we came across The Corn Exchange.

'You won't get that for pop,' one of the local promoters said. 'We've all tried and always been turned down.'

Strangely enough we were accepted. Even stranger was the fact that the only other weekly event held there was the "Chinese" Jazz Club run by "Uncle" Bonnie Manzi, an eccentric but very capable promoter from Brighton.

The Corn Exchange was situated in the centre of Bristol just a couple of hundred or so yards from The Colston Hall and drew a rather different crowd than Bath. They always seemed just a little more sophisticated and rather more fashion conscious, although I was somewhat taken aback when I asked one of our stewards where his girl friend was one evening and he replied 'out with Cary Grant.' My immediate reaction was to think it was his way of telling me to mind my own business. But no, it was true. It seemed that Cary Grant's mother lived in the city and whenever he visited her, he had a standing date for dinner with this young lady. Another of our stewards called Steve, not his real name of course, was an Adonis – tall and good looking, with a body builder's physique and a pleasing personality. The girls loved him and he was a great hit with our female artists, especially Marianne Faithful who, I think, given the opportunity, would have had him gift wrapped and delivered to her hotel. If ever we had a situation that called for tact, Steve was the one I would send so you can imagine my horror when one evening, in the middle of the main foyer, he started beating up his girl friend. He was quickly stopped by a couple of our other stewards. When I asked them what the hell was going on, they explained that it was probably just the pressure he was under as he was joining the police the next day - obviously highly qualified I thought.

Normally our stewards were excellent, conscientious, loyal, tactful and tough when required. Nevertheless there were occasions when one or two them could misjudge a situation. On one memorable evening I was standing in the foyer chatting, one of my favourite pastimes if all was running smoothly, when Brian came hurrying up and told me Colin, our largest steward, had just hit one of The Who.

My immediate reaction was 'Oh my God he could have waited until they'd played'; my second was 'Oh shit!'

Hurrying to the back stage area I found Roger Daltrey laying on the floor clutching his stomach and moaning pathetically.

Looking up at me he said dramatically, 'He hit me Fred.'

Well that much was obvious.

'What happened?' I asked a still rather belligerent Colin.

'He tried to bring a girl backstage,' he replied. He then went on to explain that following my long standing instructions, he had told Roger that because of the very limited amount of space he couldn't bring anyone back stage until after the show. Roger continued to insist and things had then got a little out of hand.

But, Colin added in justification, 'I didn't hit him hard.'

That was also obvious because if he had Roger would have been on his way to hospital. Looking down at Roger still lying on the floor, I noticed he was by now neither groaning nor holding his stomach.

'Come on' I said 'Get up. You're going to be late going on' and with that he got to his feet and left. Roger was a great guy and never said another word about this incident, at least not to me.

The Who, in fact, were one of my favourite bands, both musically and as individuals and I got on with them very well, especially Roger who, like me, was a car nut. We were always discussing the relative merits of my E type and the Chevrolet Stingray he owned at that time. Live, they were terrific, generating so much drive and excitement thanks in no small part to their maniacal drummer Keith Moon. Looking back, I must have worked with them more than 40 times over the years and I cannot remember them ever giving a bad performance. Eventually, of course, they become one the biggest groups of the seventies. However, I always felt it was when they first burst on the scene during the mid sixties that they were at their most electrifying and anarchistic best.

We played a lot of groups at the Corn Exchange over nearly five years including the first UK date of Them, the Irish group in which Van Morrison came to prominence. Even at this stage in his career he showed signs of his neurotic personality, asking endless questions about the size and behaviour of the audience. Other legendary artists who played there included Wilson Picket, Gene Vincent, Bruce Channel, The Rolling Stones, The Byrds as well as my particular favourite Bo Didley. We always seemed to draw big crowds and in fact, at one point, the dances became so popular that we were actually turning people away. Now no self-respecting promoter likes to do this and even to this day I start to get the shakes even thinking about it. Giving the matter some serious consideration, I came up with what I hoped would be the solution - a second hall. Checking around I found that the Co-op Society had a suitable venue about 300/400 yards away. It wasn't ideal as it was up on

The Hollies posing backstage at Bristol
Photo by Cliff Bulley

Mike Tobin and The Magnettes.
One of the regular support groups at Bristol and Bath

the first floor. Also it had a very low ceiling, which didn't help the acoustics. However, it was close to the Corn Exchange, which was the most important thing. I decided to try my idea out the next time that we had Manfred Mann. It may seem hard to believe now, but in the sixties this group, with their original vocalist Paul Jones, 'the one in the middle looking sweet', were just as popular as the Stones and the Who. In fact, they hold the record at the Pavilion Bath for the largest attendance at one of our dances. They readily agreed to my harebrained scheme for a small additional fee, as I think they were just interested as I was to see if we could make things work. When the evening finally arrived we were ready. Well, perhaps not entirely ready because nowadays we would have rented extra equipment and had it all set up. But in those days the economics did not allow for such luxuries. So, instead, after the band finished playing their set at the Corn Exchange, there was the extraordinary sight of the roadies, bouncers, stage manager, musicians and even the promoter loading equipment into a van and, in some instances, carrying it along the street, then lugging it up several flights of steps to the first floor of the Co-Op. As Manfred Mann's equipment, besides the normal compliment of amplifiers and instruments, included the dreaded Hammond Organ, plus a drum kit and endless amounts of cable you can imagine the complexity of the operation. Somehow I couldn't imagine Blur or Pulp mucking in in the same way. My idea wasn't a great success. We tried it another couple of times with other groups but the logistical problems, coupled with the unsuitable hall, prevented it from being a practical proposition. It was an interesting experiment and something I felt I had to try.

We had been married around four years when Wendy decided we should have a dog. Whether or not it was her thwarted maternal instincts I wasn't sure but I thought it was a good idea. We were both keen on Basset Hounds, having met several belonging to friends and admired both their good nature and idiosyncratic personalities. The first thing I did was to buy a couple of books on the subject the second was to phone the Kennel Club for a list of reputable breeders. We were in luck. Not only was there a kennel in West Meon specialising in Basset Hounds, conveniently placed for us mid way between Bristol and Worthing, but also they had a number of puppies for sale. We stayed over in Bristol after the gig and set out the next morning full of eager anticipation. When we arrived at the kennels it turned out be a small bungalow in the middle of nowhere. Knocking on the door we where greeted by an elderly man, unshaven and wearing a shabby overcoat that reached down to his ankles. He appeared a little confused as he explained that his wife, who actually ran the kennels, was out. However, he eventually agreed to show us some puppies. We explained that we wanted a male hound. As he walked back inside, we were both more than a little surprised to see that the floor of the hall was totally covered in straw. A couple of minutes later he was back with this little furry bundle, which he gently placed on the ground. It was a delightful little creature - black white and tan with its feet stained a bright yellow from the straw that was obviously laid throughout most of the bungalow. Following the advice I had gleaned from the books I asked to see the sire. Leaving Wendy with the puppy, I was led around the back of the building to a wire enclosure and shown the largest Basset I had ever seen.

'Fine' I said. 'Now can I have a look at the puppies pedigree?'

Name: Burgundy Cameo, sex: male - excellent we'll take him. On our way to Worthing we decided to call him Claud, a fine name with an appropriately Gaelic ring. Arriving at Midhurst we decided to stop to allow the puppy to pee. Walking a little way from the car it squatted down to wet - squatted down? 'Dogs don't do that', I thought. Gently turning the little animal on to its back, I peered apprehensively at its genitals. Just as I thought - a female. We'd been sold a pup! I was all for going back but by then Wendy, of course, was totally smitten with the creature and we decided to keep her. I'm glad we did because for nearly fourteen years she was our constant companion, travelling to practically every gig and, in return for her keep, providing great devotion and loyalty.

# CHAPTER 12

Without doubt The Pavilion Bath was our flagship. Its large capacity allowed us to present some fabulous groups and over the years, as well as the very best British bands, we were lucky enough to book some exceptional American acts. There were, of course, notable exceptions and one that I remember all to well were The Byrds. In 1965 they were riding high with their version of Bob Dylan's 'Hey Mr Tambourine Man' - a great song with Jim McGuinn's twelve-string guitar playing particularly impressive. We were lucky enough to book two dates on their short U.K. tour and because of the spectacular hype surrounding the visit, we were all looking forward to seeing them live. On the evening of the gig, as I heard Brian introduce them, I walked into the hall with eager anticipation. They looked fabulous - the absolute personification of the sixties, all capes and granny glasses. However, when they started to play it was a different matter. They were simply dreadful - nowhere as proficient as any of our local support bands. Their rendition of Hey Mr Tambourine Man raised a small cheer. Other than this their performance was a sad disappointment. Ironically, later on in the seventies, we used The Byrds a great deal and by then they had turned into one of the tightest and musically proficient bands in the business. Jim had by then become Roger, because I believe a fortune-teller had once told him that Roger was more charismatic. David Crosby, Chris Hillman, Gram Parsons etc had given way to Clarence White, Gene Parsons and Skip Batten and it was this later line up that helped to re-establish The Byrds as one of the greatest live groups ever.

I would like to say that the Jimi Hendrix date at The Pavilion stands out from all the other great acts we played there, but unfortunately I can't. Possibly because we used him quite regularly at this time in our other venues and possibly because I was too unaware to recognise his unique talents immediately.

Ike and Tina Turner on the other hand will always remain in my memory. It's hard to choose a favourite performance out of around 350 shows in nearly seven years, but theirs definitely made my personal top ten. They arrived early, as they were doubling up that evening between Bath and a venue in Bristol. I must say I was a little surprised when Ike introduced me to Tina as his sister. Possibly he meant it in the ethnic sense, or there again, perhaps he was really into incest and was desperately short of female relatives to fantasise about. Whatever the case he was in a good humour.

I had heard that he could be difficult, but when I asked him if he would mind if I filmed one of their numbers he just said, 'Sure if it's for your own use.'

The Who on stage at Bath

Bo Didley and The Duchess
backstage at The Pavilion Bath

Keith Moon and Pete Townshend
on stage at The Pavilion Bath

I had recently bought a 16mm Bolex cine camera with a Synchroflex sound recording attachment and I was really keen to try it out. This was, of course, long before today's home video cameras and amateur sound films were still something of a novelty. By present day professional standards, sound was not very good. O.K. for speech but, with only one microphone, pretty inadequate when it came to recording a group, especially one as big as The Ike and Tina Turner Revue. Nevertheless, when it was time for the show, I was ready. I had set up on the right hand side of the stage and most fortuitously this was the side where Tina was performing. No prizes for guessing what number I chose to film. 'River Deep' had always been a favourite of mine and I was interested to see how their live performance compared to the record, which was so brilliantly produced by Phil Spector. I soon got my answer. Live they were even better - a little less polished perhaps but with even more raw blasting energy. The band, led by Ike, really cooked and Tina, along with the Ikettes in their shimmering micro skirts, were just too much. The Ikettes were three great looking girls who sang as well as they looked. One of these was the young P.P.Arnold who went on to have a fair amount of success in her own right. Nevertheless, as you would expect it was Tina who stole the show. Only 25 years old, she was dynamite. Seeing her thrusting and twirling only four or five feet away was a moving experience and I was glad the camera was securely mounted on a tripod. The film, in glorious black and white came, out rather better than I thought it would. Even the sound was just about passable. It was and still is a great reminder of that fantastic evening.

As I have previously mentioned, we rarely had any trouble at the Pavilion. However, the fight on this particular evening had been a doozy. Two boys, no doubt for all the usual good and profound reasons, i.e. booze, girls, territorial invasion, or just plain stupidity, had knocked seven kinds of hell out of each other, with both inflicting quite a lot of damage in the short time and it took the stewards to pull them apart. After the show, I was standing in the now empty hall, mop in hand, gently dabbing at the rather worryingly large pool of congealed blood, philosophising on the futility of young men, when I was woken from my reverie by a loud and cheery voice.

"Hello". It was the Mayor of Bath. He lived near by and would occasionally pop in on his way home.

Hurriedly and as surreptitiously as possible, I pushed a large bucket full of warm soapy water across the floor in an attempt to hide the blood. Luckily, he didn't notice or at least if he did he was to well mannered to mention it.

"Was it a good evening? " he enquired.

" Very" I said "Very lively", I added, thanking my lucky stars that he had arrived just to late to see just how lively it had really been.

The Animals backstage at The Bath Pavilion after
hearing they had reached No. 1 in the charts

We had an excellent relationship with the all the staff of the Bath City Council with whom we came into contact, especially the youth officer, who would look in from time to time to chat and to his credit, never attempted to interfere with the way we organised things. I should have learnt from him and stuck to what I knew best - promoting. However, it's very easy to be wise in hindsight and one evening, when I received a phone call from the Bath police regarding one of our regulars, I decided that the very least I could do was to offer this poor unfortunate some assistance. It seemed this young man had borrowed a car forgetting, of course, to ask the owner's permission and wanted me to post bail of £25. I should have realised then that I was going to be the patsy. If I was the only person that he could think of to help him then obviously he had exhausted all other contacts and he probably wasn't the little innocent that I had so naively imagined. At the police station I duly completed the formalities, which, amongst other things, involved making myself responsible for him appearing in court at a later date. I then drove him back to The Pavilion, where with a perfunctory 'thanks' he disappeared into the hall not even bothering to go through the pretence of offering to pay. What I wondered had I let myself in for? At the end of, what was for him, a most enjoyable evening he left never to be seen again either by the police, or more importantly the local magistrates and I never saw my £25 again.

I suppose you could call it artistic temperament but we normally had more trouble with the groups than we ever did with the audience. The Kinks and Small Faces were the worst offenders, normally turning up late, if at all and on one memorable occasion the stewards had to break up a fight on stage, when Mick Avory, the Kinks drummer hit Dave Davies over the head with a cymbal. Amazingly enough, this was not the end of their set, although the atmosphere whilst they remained on stage was tense to say the least. I suppose we persevered with both groups because they were popular and drew large crowds – also, because, on a good night, they played some of the very best pop music of the sixties.

The Four Pennies, who had a No 1 hit with Juliet in May '64, on the other hand were usually a model of reliability, so you can imagine my surprise and alarm when on one of their regular appearances at the Pavilion they were late. So late in fact that I was just preparing to make an announcement apologising for their absence when I was told they had arrived. Without any apology or a word of explanation they disappeared into the dressing rooms and seemed in no hurry to change into their stage clothes. I decided to see what was going on and shot back stage to speak to the leader Lionel Morton. Rather surprisingly, he seemed unprepared to talk to me and in fact, with two rather terse words, indicated that I should leave. Not wanting to delay their appearance even further, I decided to have it out with him after the show. His rudeness was totally unnecessary and I was seething. Rather fortuitously the first person I bumped into on leaving the dressing room was Colin, our super heavyweight steward. I quickly explained the situation and told him that as soon as the gig was over I expected an apology from Mr Morton. It was with a great feeling of relief that I finally heard Brian announce the band, but my relief quickly turned to something approaching horror when a couple of minutes later I saw Colin stride onto the stage, walk up to Lionel Morton, by now in full song and, placing a hand under each arm, pick him up and carry him off, leaving the rest of the band totally dumbfounded. Much to my surprise they did not stop but like the true professionals they were continued playing. My horror increased when I realised that Colin was heading towards me.

'My governor wants an apology,' he said quietly, lowering a petrified Lionel to the ground.

There was no argument. At that moment I think he would have given me his entire fortune and thrown in his wife, the actress Julia Foster, for good measure. It was not what I wanted and was certainly not the way I normally ran my gigs. But before I could say anything, and I swear this is true, Colin picked him up again and took him back on stage, placed him gently back on his feet and with only the slightest of pauses to dust him down, left. When they finally finished their performance, which, as usual, was very well received, I decided that this time it was me that owed them an apology. It was very graciously received. In fact, I couldn't believe it was the same belliger-ent guys I had been speaking to just a couple of hours earlier. It was only when I turned to leave and saw three of my stewards standing in the doorway grinning like idiots that I realised they had followed me in to the dressing room to keep an eye on me. Talk about gunboat diplomacy.

Although there were some very good hotels in Bath they were relatively expensive so it made more economic sense to return home to London after the show. On one occasion Freddie Garrity, leader of Freddie and the Dreamers, who were very big at the time with hits such as, 'I understand' and 'If you gotta make a Fool of Somebody', arranged a lift with us back to London. Freddie, who was more of a comedian than a pop star, seemed in those days to be permanently on television and with his bright and breezy personality eventually went on to be a very successful TV presenter. He was excellent company but after half an hour or so sitting contentedly in the rear seat of our car, fell asleep. Just before we reached Newbury, the police flagged us down. Now this was most unusual. However, it was the time of the Great Train Robbery and a nationwide search was being undertaken for both the robbers and the missing money.

"Where exactly are you going at this time of night sir?" said a studiedly polite policeman. You must remember it was 1963 and most respectable members of the public were expected to be home and in bed by midnight.

Before I could reply a voice from the back of the car said, 'they did it officer. They are the ones you're looking for. They've got a suitcase full of money in the boot'.

Pandemonium. One policeman immediately became three, a torch was produced and shone into the back of the car. Instant recognition.

'Oh it's you,' said a rather exasperated voice.

Exasperated they may have been. However, it didn't stop them from asking for Freddie's autograph. On the other hand, it did stop them from looking in the boot. I often wonder what they would have said if they had bothered to look and found our case which contained a suitcase full of money from a number of shows.

Looking back on the sixties, I often think what a godsend a mobile phone would have been. With seven or eight regular gigs to book each week it was a continuous problem and not the sort of thing you could delegate. I was the only person who knew the preferences of each venue and what I could afford to pay, so each journey was normally planned around telephone boxes, either at the M1 Motorway service stations on our way to Kidderminster and Stourbridge, or along the A4 to Bath & Bristol. Our other venues were not such a problem as the journeys were all relatively short and I had time to call people before leaving home. Most of the calls made on the road were to see if my various offers and counter offers had been accepted. If they had been, fine - if not, utter panic whilst I either raised the amount I was prepared to pay, or came up with a totally new group to try. Altogether it wasn't an ideal arrangement as booking the programmes for each venue was the most important part of our business and of course too many misjudged bookings could result in heavy losses. But even worse was the loss of atmosphere a poor attendance caused and too many evenings like this could cause a venue to close. Even in the halcyon days of pop you had to be careful who you booked as not every chart-topping group drew large crowds.

To try and improve matters and make life a little easier, we decided to open an office and quickly found premises in Basil St, just a short distance from where we lived. We recruited a young man called Chris Brown to run things and employed Sue Young, an extremely pretty young lady, as our secretary. It made no difference. I was still running round the country from phone box to phone box, only this time I had the added responsibility and expense of an office. I am without doubt the worst person ever when it comes to delegating responsibility, preferring to take care of everything myself wherever possible. So I suppose it was no surprise that our circumstances did not improve. Apart from arranging the printing of our regular monthly handbills and the occasional poster, there wasn't a lot for them to do except pass on messages. If I'd had more time to spare I am sure that I could have found a way to make this new arrangement work. As it was, things drifted along for several months until one day Sue inadvertently sent a letter to The Town Clerk of Leamington Spa whose Town Hall I was trying to rent for a regular series of dances that ended with the words 'and I will gladly come to Tunbridge Wells to discuss this matter with you'. The Town Clerk was most understanding but I am afraid to say I was not, giving Sue a real ticking off - something she has never held against me, as far as I am aware, as she is still one of our very closest friends nearly forty years later. Within a few weeks Chris left to commence a very successful career in advertising and with a great sigh of relief I closed the office. It wasn't a total loss though, as one of the tenants in the next office was expanding his business and was prepared to pay us a premium to move out. So after some fairly intense negations I was finally persuaded to leave!

# CHAPTER 13

Standing in the middle of Malvern, an hour or so before the doors of the Winter Gardens opened for another of our 'Big Beat Sessions', I wondered what, apart from the beauty of the area, had led me to open a club in such a remote place? True, Worcester, a reasonable size city, was just five or six mile away, but at 6.00 p.m. on a Tuesday evening in the mid to late sixties, apart from a few cars, there were often no more than half a dozen people to be seen on the main street. By eight o'clock it was normally a different matter. Kids just seemed to materialise out of thin air and to this day I am not sure where everyone came from. On a busy night, I was told people travelled in from Birmingham, which was over thirty miles away, as well as from other exotic locations such as Cheltenham and Gloucester. Whatever the explanation we generally did very well, born out by the fact that we ran at this venue for nearly three enjoyable years.

One other phenomenon that I found difficult to explain was why Malvern slowly turned into the hippest club we ever ran. True, by the late sixties the emphasis had changed from pure pop to more R & B based music - witness the success of bands like John Mayall's Blues Breakers and Fleetwood Mac and the thriving blues and soul scene. The pop charts were still hugely influential, but it was the album charts that dictated more and more the bands that we would use especially in venues like Malvern. Where else in the country on a Tuesday night, I wonder, could you count on an attendance of at least five or six hundred for Zoot Money's Big Roll Band?

As you would expect the Spencer Davis Group from Birmingham always pulled them in, as did The Who, Cream and Manfred Mann. However, it was the lesser known bands like Creation, Herbie Goins and the Night Timers and the Alan Bown Set, all of whom also drew very respectable crowds, that I think really showed how aware were the kids in the area.

For the relatively short time they were in existence we used Cream a lot, usually without any problems. They were enormously popular and always drew a large crowd. This particular evening in Malvern was no exception. The place was packed. Cream was due on stage around 8.45.p.m. By 9.15.p.m.they still hadn't arrived. I was pretty pissed off. These were professional musicians being paid an extremely large fee and the least they could do, I thought, was to arrive on time, after all they had the whole bloody day to get there. I was, I must admit, in a pretty foul mood and finally decided I had no option but to give the kids their money back and sue the band. Informing my stage manager that I would make an announcement at 9.30.p.m. I stormed back to the box office. Two minutes later the door opened and in marched Eric Clapton, Jack Bruce and Ginger Baker and without a single word of apology for their late arrival demanded to know why the stage manager had refused to allow them to play.

'Because your too bloody late,' I said bluntly.

That did it. Instant mayhem - all three of them shouting at me at the top of their voices and all at the same time.

'We got lost,' one of them explained when they had calmed a little down, as if this feeble excuse made everything all right.

'Too bad' I said. 'You should have given yourselves more time. Anyhow I'm giving the kids their money back so you might as well bugger off.'

With that they left the office and I prepared to go on stage and make my announcement. Before I had time to leave the office, one of my stewards came rushing up and told me that Ginger Baker was on stage explaining to the crowd that this arsehole of a promoter was preventing them from playing and it wasn't their fault, as they didn't want to disappoint the audience. Running like hell, I arrived towards the end of his tirade and, grabbing the mic', pointed out that it was the bands fault for arriving so late, and to compensate for this I was prepared to give every one a full refund. However, to be fair to everyone who had turned up that evening, I was offering to put it to the vote to see whether they wanted to see Cream perform or have their money returned. It was a landslide victory for the band. I don't think there was a single vote for a refund. I had lost in the biggest possible way. However, I consoled myself with the thought that at least I didn't have to return the evenings profits. Pausing only to check with me that they would definitely be paid, Cream at last started to play. A large percentage of the audience relied on public transport, which finished running at some ridiculously early hour, so after the show there were long queues for the telephones to call taxis or poor long suffering parents. This didn't concern the band of course as by then they were long gone - I bet they didn't get lost on the way home.

The audiences at Malvern were generally very well behaved - nice kids who had come to see the bands and enjoy themselves and like most teenagers in the sixties were pretty broadminded and not too easily shocked. So I was a little taken aback when two young men approached me and complained about the language used by the illustrious Arthur Brown during his show. They were about seventeen years old and from their general appearance and manner probably came from Malvern College, the distinguished boys' school, near the town centre. They must have been destined for the church because they seemed deeply and sincerely shocked by what they had witnessed, explaining to me that the gratuitous use of obscenities was a really bad influence on young people in the audience, many of whom were still in their formative years. Not knowing what to say exactly I decided I would let them tell Arthur of their concerns face to face. Leading them round to his

The Searchers backstage at Wallington.

The Kinks on stage at Wallington

dressing room I asked them to wait outside while I explained the situation to him and I was relieved when he agreed to see them. Arthur sat impassively while they expounded at some length on why they found his language offensive and what his responsibilities to his audience were.

When they had finished Arthur without any change of expression leant forward and slowly and earnestly said just two words - 'Fuck off '.

Geno Washington, I was reminded a short while ago, still holds the all time attendance record at the Winter Gardens but the Who couldn't have been far behind, consistently packing the hall every time they appeared. Every Who gig, while usually fun, was more often than not a somewhat traumatic experience. This time to make matters worse they were bringing with them a CBS film unit - any excuse I thought to play up to the cameras. I could already picture the performance - smashed guitars, amps destroyed and the drum kit kicked to the four corners of the stage. Ironically enough, when the band started to play they were moderately subdued, well at least by their own manic standards. Not so the audience who were surprisingly high-spirited, bouncing around in front of the stage like loons and generally having a great time. It was halfway through the set when one of the handheld cameras disappeared. It wasn't stolen you understand. It was just borrowed from the cameraman who had positioned himself in the crowd to take audience reaction shots and who happened to be using it at the time. There was a short pause while I went on stage and appealed for its return. Miraculously it turned up safely at the back of the hall where some one had left it on a chair. By this time every one connected with the show was in the hall lending a hand including Wendy and Chris Stamp, the co -manager of the Who. Ten minutes later it happened again. You would have thought by now the cameraman would have learnt his lesson or at least asked for a minder. Once again I went up on stage and asked for the camera to be returned. This time, however, I was interrupted in mid flow by one of my stewards urgently whispering in my ear.

Turning back to the audience and only just managing to keep a straight face I added 'Oh, by the way, it would be really great if we could also have our camera man back!'

# CHAPTER 14

Besides being a golden age for promoting, the early sixties were also, for me at least, a golden age of motoring. Cheap cars, cheap petrol and no speed limit helped me indulge in my passion for cars - that and the fact that we covered over 50,000 miles a year running the gigs. It was also a period that coincided with our increasing affluence. My first sports car was a Jaguar XK 150 3.4 drop head in BRG, with a sage green interior - very tasteful, if not incredibly quick. I part exchanged this for a real sports car - a 1962 3.8 E Type Jaguar Fixed Head Coupe. I bought it from Col. Ronnie Hoare, who at that time owned F. English Ltd; the Ford distributors in Bournemouth and from a small corner of this enormous garage also ran Maranello Concessionaire, the Ferrari importers. The E Type was his own car and had been taken apart and carefully re-assembled by his Ferrari mechanics when they had a quiet moment, which in those days was quite often as Ferraris had yet to be imported in significant numbers.

The E Type Jaguar was the embodiment of the sixties. Introduced in the autumn of '61, it was an instant sensation. With most of the production earmarked for export, even in 1963 it was still a fairly uncommon sight so that on the rare occasions that I took it to Wallington it created quite a lot of interest amongst the musicians and I was kept fairly busy giving demonstration runs. I had a favourite route that I would use that took in various types of roads from country lanes to dual carriageway and I usually ended the demonstration with a three-figure blast along a suitable stretch of road. Much as I loved the E Type, I had fallen for a Ferrari 250 GT 2+2 so it had to go. The dark blue Ferrari with its Pininfarina designed body was a beautiful car. However, it was the superb V12 engine that really excited me. Developed from a long line of racing engines it was extremely responsive and made the most wonderful spine tingling noise at high revs. Unfortunately, both the handling and road holding were initially disappointing especially in the wet as I soon discovered when I nearly spun it into a river just outside of Salisbury. I was advised to fit a set of Dunlop SP tyres, which had recently been introduced and these totally transformed the car. Incidentally, this was the car in which I nearly cut short the career of Sounds Incorporated. I had taken three of them for a short demonstration run around the roads near Bath, when for some reason I took a wrong turning and found myself in an area I barley knew. Entering the outskirts of a village at some considerable speed, I lined the car up for what appeared to be a fast right hand bend when I suddenly realised to my horror that it was a complete right-angled bend. Bracing myself for what seemed to me to be an unavoidable and rather serious accident, I braked as hard and as late as I dared and the car just went round as if on rails. Shaken and most decidedly stirred I looked at my passengers calmly sitting there, obviously thinking it was just another example of Bannister's brilliant driving technique. I realised after this occurrence that the harder you drove the car the more responsive it became, helped of course by those superb Dunlop SP tyres.

Ferraris in those early days sometimes lacked the reliability of the cars of the larger manufacturers, due in part, I suppose, to limited development funds and my period of ownership of this great car was by no means trouble free. It was the brakes on this particular example that gave the most trouble. On one occasion, I just managed to get home by driving slowly and pumping the brake pedal whenever I had to use the brakes. It was obvious that there was a leak in the system so it was trailered down from London to Bournemouth for the attention of Maranello Concessionaires. It was, as you would expect, an expensive exercise but at least I reasoned it would be worth it as reliable brakes were a prerequisite in such a fast car. When it was ready, Wendy and I caught the train down to Bournemouth intending, once we had collected it, to drive over to Bristol for our Wednesday gig. It was about 10 miles into our journey that I decided to see just how good the brakes now were. Accelerating up to about 80 mph I hit the brakes hard and the car started to slow in a thoroughly satisfactory manner. Suddenly there was a loud bang and the brake pedal hit the floor. This time there was no possibility of pumping up some pressure, as there was absolutely nothing there. We were still doing around sixty but luckily, although narrow, the road ahead was straight for about a quarter of a mile. Letting it roll to a stop I discovered quite providently that we had come to rest right outside a phone box. Still shaking, I called Maranello's service department and gave them hell for about 10 minutes. There is nothing that is guaranteed to bring out the garrulous worst in me than self-righteous indignation and I must say I made the most of every one of those minutes.

Despite this experience I still loved Ferraris and it was while I was waiting to pick up the 2+2 that I first noticed the white GTO sports racing car standing in the corner of the workshop. To say it was love at first sight is to understate the obvious. It was simply stunning. It had been owned by John Coombs, an extremely affluent Guildford garages owner who also ran his own racing team. The car had been pretty successful over the two previous seasons driven by such people as Graham Hill, Innes Ireland and Mike Parkes who later went on to be a Ferrari works driver. It was now rather uncompetitive and was subsequently up for sale for the princely sum of £6,250, even then more than the price of a new Rolls Royce. It would, I thought, with just a few modifications to make it road legal, make the most amazing road car. I could think of little else over the next three or four weeks and finally rang the garage to see if it was still for sale. It was and I immediately arranged a test drive. Arriving in Bournemouth, I found the car untouched since my last visit. It was still virtually as it had left the racetrack. Deciding to chance a short and highly illegal drive around the outskirts of the town we set out with Donald McLeod, a director of Maranello Concessionaires, at the wheel. Things were fine until it was my turn to drive. Up to that point we hadn't exceeded 3,000 RPM. Without thinking of the consequences, I pulled away using around 5000 RPM in each of the lower gears. All hell let loose. The noise was enough to break glass in the windows of the nearby houses. People were diving for cover. I had forgotten the car was running on short pipes without any silencers. Backing off immediately I drove slowly and circumspectly back to the garage. I was sold. I offered £5,750 for the car providing they fitted long pipes with silencers and lowered the rear axle ratio. They said they would think about it and let me know. They must have been quite keen to get rid of it as they had in fact rung and left a message before I arrived in Bristol - the car was mine. It would be two weeks they said before I could collect it. Two weeks that seemed more like two months but at last the day I had been so impatiently waiting for arrived. Setting out for Bournemouth in the 2+2, which I had part exchanged for the GTO, it started to rain and by the time we got to Ringwood it, was really pouring. Sitting at some temporary traffic lights just outside of the town I happened to glance in my mirror and to my horror I saw this old fifties Rover bearing down on me obviously out of control. Frantically putting my car in gear I tried desperately to move out of the way but without success. Wallop! My seat collapsed and I found myself lying flat on my back looking at the roof lining. Scrambling out I went to look at the damage. It wasn't too bad but the boot lid had taken on a distinctly concertina-ed look.

By this time, I had been joined by the driver of the Rover who explained to me that his brakes had failed. However, when I looked at his car I couldn't help notice that the tyres were balder than I was. Whilst we were swapping insurance details, Wendy rang Maranello Concessionaires to tell them of the accident.

'Don't worry' they said, 'the insurance will take care of all that'.

After this experience I was relived when we finally arrived at our destination. In view of the damage to the 2 + 2, I was expecting a long delay. However, the formalities did not take as long as expected and within the hour we were on our way. The GTO was unbelievable - still rather noisy despite the two silencers but incredibly quick, as you would expect from around 300 hp in such a lightweight car. The lower gearing limited the top speed to a mere 142-MPH but of course improved the acceleration, which was now in the order of 0 -100 in around 11 or 12 seconds. Pretty impressive in 1964 when most family cars barley reached 80 MPH and had 0-60 times around 20 seconds or more. I was by now pretty familiar with the roads between Bournemouth and Bristol with their many twists and turns and I couldn't wait to explore my new car's road holding. Coming up to one of my favourite bends, I went in fast and deep and promptly scared myself stiff. The car just wouldn't slow down quickly enough. Using the steering wheel for leverage and rising out of my seat I managed to exert enough pressure on the brake pedal to slow down sufficiently. It was then that I realised that no one had bothered to change the hard brake pads that had been used for racing.

I used the GTO, as often as I could but there were drawbacks. It was sometimes difficult to start and as we had just moved into Trevor Place in Central London there was no garage where I could tinker with it. The fact that there was no speedometer and that luggage room was non-existent also did not help matters. In spite of this, we still had some terrific runs commuting between the clubs. My favourite road at this time was the A4 between Bath and London. This was long before the M4 linked these two cities. I knew the road well as I used it regularly a couple of times a week and although there was no dual carriage way, except for the 30 or so miles of the M4 that started at Maidenhead and ran past Heathrow Airport into central London, it was still a fairly fast road, especially late at night when the traffic was light. It was while coming back from Bath on one invigoratingly sunny day, full of the joys of spring, and I must emphasise, full of absolutely nothing else, that I let the GTO run to its maximum revs in each gear. These days 142 MPH may not sound fast but on a main road in 1964 with on coming traffic it had its moments. All perfectly legal in those days I hasten to add. However, seeing the look on the faces of the drivers of the oncoming cars when we passed with a closing speed of nearly 200 MPH caused me to moderate my driving habits. Now motorways, that was a different matter.

Eventually after a year or so the GTO became just too much of an expensive liability and I decided to sell it. This was not as easy as I had thought. Nobody it seemed wanted an old retired sports racing car. Eventually I sold it for £4,250 to a man named Pearce who paid for it with used notes he kept in a large biscuit tin. Altogether my indulgence had cost me around £2,000, almost double a mans average salary for a year. Nevertheless I did learn something from this experience. In future I just con-centrated on the earlier Ferraris and great English sports cars like Frazer Nash and Bentley and never again lost money on my hobby. The irony was, if I had put the GTO away for 24 years, it would have made a fantastic pension fund. In 1989 a Japanese collector paid ten million dollars for a similar car.

The Ferrari GTO

# CHAPTER 15

Business that night at the Pavilion had been a little slow, so it came as a welcome diversion when we received a visit from Naomi Page, the administrator of the Bath Festival Society and her young assistant Luke Ritner. They explained that the society had been receiving quite a lot of criticism from local people for being too elitist and they wondered if we might be interested in running an outdoor event, in conjunction with The Bath Festival Society, for the young people in the area. Naomi explained that the Bath Rugby Club had recently organised a barbecue on the Recreation Ground, which had been most successful and she thought we would do very well if we used the same place. Now the Rec' Ground was less than 75 feet from where we were standing talking and I passed it every time I came to the Pavilion. For some reason, probably to do with my blinkered vision, I had never ever seen its potential as a festival venue. Suddenly I saw the light. It was a brilliant site about 20 acres in size, give or take the odd tennis court. Absolutely ideal as it was bang slap in the centre of Bath with all the attendant facilities like car parks, restaurants, hotels and loos, in addition to tier upon tier of Georgian terraces providing a simply superb backdrop. Like all converts, I was suddenly, wildly, enthusiastically sold.

'It's a great idea' I told Naomi and Luke. 'We would love to do it.'

As soon as we got back home I shot of a letter to the Parks Department outlining our idea and mentioning, of course, our tie up with the Bath Festival Society. We then crossed our fingers whilst we eagerly waited for the reply. When it finally came we were delighted. Not only could we use the Rec' Ground, but it was available on June 28th - the day we had requested. The rental charge was £40, which I remember thinking at the time was not totally unreasonable!

My first job was to draw up a list of groups I would like to use. However, before I even had time to start enquiring about their availability, I received a phone call from Richard Cowley, a senior booker and director at the Chrysalis Agency. Richard was a good friend and we had recently been carrying out a lot of business together, mainly due to the fact that the agency had an extremely large roster of top groups.

'Before you book anyone' Richard said, 'I'll send you a list of our acts that are available on the 28th and also their prices'.

When it eventually arrived I was most impressed and in fact, after the normal haggling over prices, booked nearly 80% of the programme through Chrysalis, including Led Zeppelin for £125. Even by 1969 standards it wasn't a great deal of money for an outdoor show. However, this was a group that had only drawn around 200 to the Pavilion less than a couple of months earlier. By June, Zeppelin was just starting to break in America and Peter Grant, shrewd and conscientious as ever, called me and re- negotiated the fee, pushing me up to £200. Still a bargain as it turned out!

The rest of the programme was made up groups that I felt we required to make a well-balanced programme and three local bands that, in my opinion, deserved a wider audience. The final programme was Pete Green's Fleetwood Mac, John Mayall, Ten Years After, Led Zeppelin, Nice, Chicken Shack, John Hiseman's Colosseum,Blodwyn Pig, Keef Hartley, Group Therapy, Liverpool Scene, Taste, Champion Jack Dupre, Savoy Brown, Clouds, Principal Edwards' Magic Theatre,Babylon, Deep Blues Band and Just Before Dawn. I also added John Peel as compere. John, with his huge knowledge of the scene, then as now, stamped his quiet authority on the event in a way no one else at the time could have done.

With the programming out of the way, it was a relatively simple matter to cost the festival and set a ticket price. We always tried to offer the best value possible whatever the event and I must say, looking back, our first festival really was pretty good value at 18/6 (92.5p) for an all day ticket.

Our regular poster suppliers at this time were a company called Impact, who not only designed but also printed the posters themselves. We asked them to produce a design we could send to our numerous ticket agencies and social secretaries at the principal Universities. I must say that both Wendy and I were extremely pleased with the final result, which was very much in keeping with the period and featured a drawing of a young girl, almost wearing a flowing gown. It was totally innocuous. So much so that we were somewhat taken aback when we started to receive complaints about our 'obscene' poster from one or two of our ticket agents. The worst area was, not surprisingly, Bournemouth, where our agents Austin Reed were instruct-ed to remove the offending posters from their windows. On closer inspection, the girl's 'flowing gown' was quite revealing – showing perhaps more anatomy than was acceptable to an easily offended public. To overcome this problem we had Impact produce another design, this time featuring the head and shoulders of a typical sixties hippie girl complete with headband and this was eventually sent out with the original poster as an alternative choice.

It must have been around seven or eight weeks before the festival that the handbills were finally ready. Eager to obtain a reaction we chose, logically I suppose, The Pavilion to see how the programme was received. We were rather disappointed and not a little worried as we had a lot of money riding on this one. There were pockets of unbridled enthusiasm but the general mood was one of rather blasé indifference. Maybe our clientele at The Pavilion were too spoilt because later that week we were down on the south coast for one of our regular gigs when Wendy, unable to stand the suspense any longer, decided to call some of our key ticket agents to see if they had started to sell tickets. I remember it was a warm sunny day and she was standing barefoot in a telephone kiosk in Hove. Suddenly she let out an almighty yell, at the same time leaping in the air.

'Good news'? I enquired hopefully. 'Or have you just trod in something?'

'What do think?' she said scornfully.

'We've sold a ticket?' I said.

'Better than that' she replied. 'Every single bloody agent that I've rung has sold out.'

Wow! It looked like we were off the hook.

After the euphoria came the hard work. Well, to be honest, apart from the publicity and ticket distribution, there wasn't a lot to do, certainly not compared to some of our later events. My main concern was the sound. Amplification for outdoor festivals was still pretty hit and miss and I wanted the best sound we could obtain. Asking around the general consensus seemed to be that Charlie Watkins of WEM was the man for the job and so it turned out. Charlie was fantastic, totally involved and very professional and did a truly great job.

We had arranged with a local scaffolding firm to build two stages. My reasoning was that this way, with nineteen groups playing on one day, we could keep the time between changeovers as short as possible. By today's standards they were very modest structures, each measuring approximately 40 feet wide x 20 feet deep, with the stage placed 4 feet above the ground. Small they may have been. However, they did have rather expensive roofs just in case we were in for a wet day and because of their compact size we were able to place them so we did not have any problems with sight lines. In fact, almost unbelievable now, it wasn't until the day before the event that we drove to Bath to supervise the set up. Even this wasn't especially arduous consisting mainly of citing the stages, portaloos, and a catering marquee. We also had the none too taxing job of indicating in which areas we wished canvas screens to be erected to stop the public from obtaining a free view. Finally, we placed four tables borrowed from The Pavilion at the appropriate entrances and we were finished. If I remember correctly, Charlie Watkins did not arrive until early on the morning of the show to set up and test the PA system.

After supper on the Friday evening, Wendy and I went for a walk around town. Bath that evening was an unforgettable sight - blue denim everywhere. There was even an impromptu concert being given in the Abbey precincts by some very earnest, young folk singers, watched attentively by a crowd of several hundred, probably the largest audience they would ever perform to. Youngsters were settling down for the night everywhere and anywhere they could find space - in shop doorways, on public benches, along the banks of the River Avon (such a feature of the city) and probably in many other places I didn't care to think about. However, most cheekily of all, several had actually pitched their tents on the large grassy traffic island in the middle of the main road opposite the Abbey. By the time we got back to our hotel, although everyone we saw was wonderfully well behaved, we were already a little worried about what would be the City Authorities reaction to this peaceful invasion.

# CHAPTER 16

Early on Saturday morning my deep and untroubled sleep was disturbed by a strange noise. I looked at my watch. 7.00 a.m. The noise was still there - a steady rumble. Pulling the curtains, I looked out of the window. The noise translated itself into a steady stream of youngsters heading towards the Rec' Ground. Good grief! The festival! In my sleep induced stupor I had actually forgotten it was the big day. Hurriedly getting ready, we made our way over to The Pavilion, which was to be our headquarters. Although it was still only 7.45 a.m., there was already a huge crowd milling around in the car park and, as far as I could tell, there was a similar scene at each of the other entrances. Displaying our total lack of experience of this sort of event, we had arranged for our staff to be on duty at 9.00 a.m., assuming that as the first band wasn't due on stage until mid-day, this would have give us plenty of time to get everyone in. Fighting down an increasing urge to panic, I was extremely relieved when the first of our stewards, using their own judgement, started to arrive just after eight. By half past eight we had sufficient staff to open the doors. I was extremely impressed by the patience and good nature of the youngsters, some of whom had been waiting for several hours for the gates to open. There was no rushing and pushing. In fact, this laid back attitude was typical of everyone who attended the festival.

Once we were up and running I was free to turn my attention to other problems, such as the lack of a sound system. Well, technically that wasn't correct. The PA was on site but having arrived late, it was still being set up and tested. As it happened, after a lot of frantic activity, it only delayed the start of the festival by twenty-five minutes. However, with so many bands scheduled, it was still enough to affect the running times. Quite providential-ly, as it turned out, and I still don't know why, Group Therapy failed to turn up which kept the status quo.

Wendy was finding the size of the Recreation Ground difficult to cope with. The four entrances were spread out over a comparatively large area and she was finding it quite exhausting walking around collecting the cash, making sure the cashiers had sufficient float and that everything was running smoothly.

Some one had a brainwave, 'What she needs is a bike.'

One was duly provided, although I have no idea where from. It solved the problem though and she was able to whiz from gate to gate quickly and easily. That is up to the time the ground started to fill up. Now Wendy has never been one of the world's great cyclists and in the general excitement and with satchels bulging with cash, she managed, on several occasions, to ride over the legs of kids. Whether it was the warm sunny weather, the fact that dope was just beginning to be more widely used or possibly because they were all amazingly well mannered, I don't know. However, whatever it was, every time it happened, the kids apologised most profusely to Wendy for getting in her way.

Nevertheless, even the best mannered people have the odd grouse and the main complaint seemed to about the lack of pass outs. Now to be honest, we really did not want to give them out as it immediately gave rise to all sorts of security problems. However, around 3.00 pm, we relented and started to issue them. It just happened that some time later I was standing close to the stage on which The Edgar Broughton Band were performing when Edgar launched into one of his famous tirades. He started telling the audience in great and forceful detail that, without pass-outs, they were virtual prisoners of these evil promoters. I tried to get his attention but it was no good. He saw himself as the leader of his people and he wasn't going to stop for anyone. Angry and upset I reached up and grabbed the nearest part of him, which happened to be his ankle. He still wouldn't stop his diatribe so I pulled harder. This time his foot came off the stage leaving him hopping on one leg. Success. I finally had his attention.

'What,' I yelled pointing at the nearest exit, 'do you think they are - Scotch fucking mist?'

He at least had the good grace to look slightly embarrassed and mumbled a few words of explanation to the crowd before continuing with his set.

Meanwhile' back stage' in The Pavilion all was surprisingly well ordered and calm. With only four actual dressing rooms available I expected some problems, but Brian seemed to have everything under control. The rather surreal sight of a number of roadies playing darts and table tennis, which we had so thoughtfully provided, further enhanced the calm and peaceful atmosphere. Well they had to have some outlet for their pent up hostility I suppose. The only place that was really crowded, of course, was the bar. It was packed with the agents and managers of the groups who were performing, augmented by a considerable number of music industry people, who, chancing a day out in the provinces, had come to see what the festival was all about. Not all of them were delighted that the festival was a financial success. Amongst these were Terry Ellis and Chris Wright, the founders of the Chrysalis Group, who had provided most of the groups performing that day. I was told later by one of their staff that they were really disappointed that we hadn't fallen flat on our faces. I must say I found this difficult to believe because apart from the fact that they had acted as our main agents and had earned from our event, both of them were already hugely successful and had absolutely no reason to be jealous. There was no doubting the sincerity of

Tony Stratton Smith, founder of Charisma Records, who the following year was to become the manager of Genesis. Seeing me later that evening he was full of enthusiasm, greeting me with a big bear hug that practically lifted me off my feet.

'Congratulations! It's a truly great show. I'm really pleased for you,' he said, before praising the location of the Rec Ground, how ideal it was, and what a great city Bath was. It seemed he had never visited the place before. Tony's early death was a great tragedy and an enormous loss to the record industry.

Like true love, nothing ever runs totally smoothly and we finally had a problem big enough to stop me becoming too bored and complacent. The right hand stage started to collapse. Nice, not satisfied with bringing along an enormously heavy Hammond organ, had added four big, burly Scottish Bagpipers to their line up and it was all proving too much for our temporary structure. There was not a great deal we could do about the problem, short of stopping the show, which was just about unthinkable. So, I put two of the biggest stewards I could find under the stage to hold up the weakened area, whilst Nice completed their set. It must have been quite literally back breaking work and it saved the day but not before we sent in a further four stewards. Luckily the scaffolding company had left a couple of their men on

A great shot of the audience with Bath in the background taken at the 1969 Festival

site just in case of such an eventuality and an effective repair was made whilst the other stage was in use. I often wonder if Nice were aware of the drama that was taking place under their feet.

One other problem we had was with the caterers. Our initial agreement was that all drinks were to be sold in plastic containers and nothing was to be served in a glass. Unfortunately, not believing my pre-event estimates of the numbers we were anticipating, they under-ordered and not surprisingly, started to run out of drinks fairly early on. It seemed they were unable to find a supplier with a large stock of soft drinks in plastic bottles so they settled for glass bottles. This would not have been so bad if they had just delivered the stock at one central point and distributed it to their sales outlets by hand or even if they had used a trolley. The trouble was that they used a large lorry to take the cases of drinks around the site. Whilst this was not initially a problem, as the day wore on, the lorry started to run over the bottles it had previously delivered, not only breaking them but also grinding them deep into the ground. I eventually noticed what was going on and actually chased the lorry around the ground yelling hysterically for him to stop. However, by then it was too late. The damage had been done.

While these minor dramas were taking place, the audience had been

enjoying some great music with Ten Years After, featuring the amazing Alvin Lee, blowing everyone's minds. There was also a nice set from the idiosyncratic blues veteran Champion Jack Dupre, who in my opinion showed everyone how the blues should really be played. However, it was left to Led Zeppelin to steal the show. Peter Grant, already showing his managerial flair, made sure the band was on stage at just the right moment for them to make the maximum impact. Wendy and I were in the office with some friends when we heard this tremendous commotion. I immediately shot out to see what the hell was happening only to bump into Brian doing the same thing.

'I think there's a riot going on,' he said.

When we reached the stage area we both relaxed as we realised it was nothing more sinister than the audience reaction to Zeppelin's set.

Later that evening Peter Grant called into our office for a chat.

'Good crowd wasn't it? Done all right today - just broken even?' He enquired politely. He went on, 'see Freddy, I told you the boys wouldn't let you down. They were worth the extra money weren't they?'

He was obviously delighted with the way they had been received and he was right. Zeppelin was already worth a great deal more than we had agreed to pay them. It was obvious, even then, that they were going to be really huge. Listening to the departing kids all I could hear was Led Zeppelin this, Zeppelin that. It was the biggest buzz since we saw the Beatles break some six years or seven earlier.

The day finally drew to a close. The parks department who were responsible for the Recreation Ground surprised us all by allowing people to stay on site overnight. Tired but euphorically happy, Wendy and I drove the hundred yards or so to Pratt's Hotel. You may think this was sheer laziness on our part but we had a rather large case with us, packed with the cash we had taken that day, including a large amount of pre-decimal silver coins. The case was so unbelievably heavy I could hardly carry it. Staggering with it into the foyer of the hotel I needed all my strength to keep from dropping it. We were greeted by the elderly night porter whom we knew well from our regular visits to the hotel and who would always, with great courtesy, carry our luggage to our room. Before I could stop him, he rushed over to the case and started to lift it. The case stayed obstinately glued to the floor. However, not so his feet, both of which were lifted into the air. I just managed to catch him before he fell backwards. Getting his breath back, he looked at me rather accusingly.

'What have you got there? Been robbing a bank?'

'Something like that', I replied.

He then very graciously allowed me to risk a hernia and struggle up to our room, while he confined himself to bringing us our gourmet supper of stale ham sandwiches.

# CHAPTER 17

The next morning we walked over to the Recreation Ground. In the bright sunlight it looked a little sorry for itself with loads of litter everywhere. However, apart from a little damage to one or two fences, it seemed to have survived its ordeal pretty well. There were still a large number of young people around and we quickly engaged fifty of them to help with the clearing up. They were surprisingly conscientious and soon The Rec' Ground was looking its old self – well, superficially, at least. The problem that they just could not solve was removing the broken glass. Although they tried as hard as possible, our inexperienced temporary helpers were simply unable to cope. On Monday morning Mr Daw, the head of the Parks Department, took over. He and his staff had obviously experienced this problem before as they quickly roped off individual areas and made sure that they were totally clear of glass, before moving on to the next section. This thorough attention to detail was necessary, of course, as the ground was normally used for both Cricket and Rugby. The thought of diving onto the ground after a ball and jamming your hand into a shard of glass just didn't bear thinking about. We eventually received a bill for around £300 for all of this additional work, along with an apology from Mr Daw for the high cost involved. Personally, I thought it was excellent value and I was very grateful to him and his department for all their hard work.

After the event came the post mortem. Most reviews of the event, whether in the local papers or in the national music papers, were sympathetic. Not so the spinsters and retired colonels of Bath. Letters started appearing in the local paper, 'The Bath & Wilts Evening Chronicle' which, whilst trying hard not to seem too prejudiced against the young, contained complaints ranging from 'I was unable to hear the commentaries from the test match' to 'If we must have this deplorable type of event, may I suggest we ask the noble Marquis to accommodate it at Longleat? No doubt the lions would clean up some of the leftovers.' This letter caused such a furore that the writer was compelled to send another clarifying his point 'I did not say the lions (at Longleat) would welcome the campers. Indeed, I doubt if they would: I asked if Lord Bath would consider it.' The writer then overdid it a little, I thought, by finishing, 'Yes, I like the neat neckties and polished shoes. In 1945 my generation wore them whilst defending our country. We sometimes wonder why, when we see mobs like those of last weekend'. However, by and large, most of the correspondents confined themselves to simple prejudices regarding the appearance of the youngsters' sometime outlandish clothes and the boys' long hair. 'Simply couldn't tell the gels from the chaps'.

To be fair, we received almost as many letters of support as we did of complaint. The one thing that came over clearly though, was that the local people, both young and old, felt that The Blues Festival had brought a proper sense of festivity to the town - something that the actual Bath Festival had up until then failed to do. However, the most important commendation as far as I was concerned was that the Bath Festival Society had intimated that they would be happy to work with us again. Wendy and I had a long discussion with Naomi Page and various members of the organising committee. We were delighted to find that, much as they needed additional funds, there was a strong desire within the society to make the Bath Festival more attractive and accessible to young people. This was especially true of Lord Strathcona, the Chairman, whom we discovered was particularly keen to see our sort of event actually held in the city.

The upshot of our various meetings was that Wendy and I would once again apply to the Parks Department for the use of the Recreation Ground. This time we didn't think it would be quite as easy to hire and we, of course, expected to pay a considerably higher rent. We also expected to have to comply with a number of special conditions regarding the use of glass, extra entrances, stewards etc. So we were more than a little surprised and rather concerned when we were informed that our application would have to go before the Parks Committee for their approval. When the long awaited letter from Mr Daw finally arrived, we were dismayed to find our request had been categorically refused.

We were not the only ones to be surprised as the event had the support of quite a few influential people in the city, including a number of local councillors. Nigel Dando, at that time the youngest member of the council, included in his maiden speech an impassioned plea to save the Blues Festival and Councillor Clem Fox was quoted as saying,

'It would be grossly unfair to the organiser of the festival if it was banned from the Recreation Ground. If it was banned because of the danger of broken glass, then the annual festivities of Bath Rugby Club and Somerset County Cricket Club ought to be banned as well. It looks like a small minority dictating to the city.'

To which Coun Walter Huggett Chairman of the Parks Committee replied, 'Don't let it go out from this council that we are against the young people or the blues festival.'

Others suggested alternative venues such as the Norwood playing fields, that later became the main campus of Bath University and Victoria Park.

The outcome of all this kerfuffle was that the Bath City Council asked the Parks Committee to reconsider its decision to ban the festival from the Recreation Ground. They also asked them to meet me to discuss alternative sites. Before a formal meeting with the Parks Committee was arranged, I had several informal chats with Councillor Huggett, a very pleasant man whom, it seemed, was very much in favour of the festival returning to the Rec' Ground. In the Chairman, it appeared, we had a very significant ally. When the evening of the meeting arrived I was fairly optimistic that I could persuade the committee to change its collective mind. An optimism that was further reinforced when I met the rest of the committee members. They seemed such nice, reasonable people. I was invited by the Chairman to address the meeting and explain why I thought the Recreation Ground was such an ideal place to hold the Festival and what ideas and suggestions I had to prevent a repeat of the various problems. After I had finished speaking, I was then asked a large number of relevant questions, most of which I found easy to answer. I felt overall I had made a good impression and was feeling even more confident that we would succeed. The motion was finally put to a vote and to add to the drama it was split fifty/fifty. I was delighted with the result. With the Chairman on our side, his casting vote would ensure that we would carry the day. It was then that I learnt my first lesson in local politics - he voted against us. 'The hypocritical son of a bitch', I thought. However, I said nothing. It wouldn't help our cause if I lost my temper.

We were on our own it seemed. There was nowhere in Bath that was suitable so there was no alternative than to look at the surrounding area. I wasn't entirely upset by the decision, as I had been rather concerned that with the proliferation of events like the Isle of Wight Dylan concert, we would have to book an even stronger programme and probably add an extra day to stay competitive. We certainly could not have expanded the event if we had stayed on the original site in the centre of Bath. But where to go? The first place we decided to check out was Corsham Court, a stately home standing in an enormous park about ten miles from Bath. The owner, it seemed, was a great patron of the arts and Naomi Page offered to make overtures on our behalf. Unfortunately, it didn't seem as if popular music qualified as an art form in his eyes and we were turned down. Naomi then suggested that we meet Farmer Sparrow, a local character who, apparently, knew all the farms and estates in the area. He turned out to be a first rate contact and a real character. Asking around, he found out that there were quite a lot of farmers who, for a sufficiently high rent, were prepared to allow us to use their land. The trouble was that not many owned land that met our requirements of situation i.e. away from neighbours, reasonable size, good access. Eventually, after a great deal of searching, we found a large farm on the Lansdowne, just three or four miles from the city centre. It seemed ideal and we asked Farmer Sparrow to arrange a meeting with the owner. Trying hard to be as ingratiating as possible, we suggested meeting for lunch in one of the better hotels in Bath. However, it seemed that the farmer hardly ever ventured into Bath and in fact it had been some years since his last visit and anything as sophisticated as a hotel was something he avoided at all cost. We finally arranged to meet at his farmhouse and an agreement was reached, subject to the necessary planning consents being obtained. Our initial enquiries with the local authorities seemed to show that there wouldn't be any major objections but we were advised to speak to the local Water Company as the area in which we proposed to run our event was situated in a catchment area. This proved to be a major problem. It appeared the water table all along the Landsdown was extremely high. In fact, it was just a couple of feet below the surface. This being the case, they certainly didn't want tens of thousands of youngsters urinating into the water supply. I must say I thought it would give an added piquancy to the local tap water. However, this was, of course, just my personal opinion and one that I didn't think the Water Company really wanted to hear. Nevertheless the loss of the farmland was a major set back.

# CHAPTER 18

While our search for a festival site continued, it was business as usual. We were still travelling around the country a great deal. However, instead of our regular weekly shows, we were now promoting a larger number of seated concerts. I had also been thinking about expanding into management so it seemed a good time to take on an assistant. We quickly found a young guy named Ian Tilbury, who had previously worked for Blackhill Entertainments run by Pete Jenner and Andrew King. Two influential figures, they had managed the Pink Floyd in the band's early days and also organised the Rolling Stones concert in Hyde Park. Ian's main claim to fame was that he kept thousands of butterflies in a comatose state in his refrigerator the night before they were released from the stage, in a symbolic gesture by the Stones. He came highly recommended and was an excellent and meticulous organiser, qualities that we really needed at this time.

Over the years I had booked quite a lot of acts through Barry Dickens and Tony Burfield, two great guys who worked for the Harold Davison Agency, one of biggest agencies in the country. After the 1969 event, Tony and I had discussed the possibility of them becoming the sole bookers for the 1970 festival. To make the event successful, we both felt that what was needed were exclusive appearances by American bands that were seldom if ever seen in the UK. Shortly after our chat, I used Tony to book us a Canned Heat gig at the Dome in Brighton. It sold out as soon as the tickets were put on sale and it was clear from the way the band was received on the night that they were hot. Tony, who had come along to see that all was well, suggested that we talked with their manager Skip Taylor to see if we could persuade Canned Heat to appear at the 1970 Festival. Skip was enthusiastic and a deal was done. We now had our first band - a venue would have been nice!

To say we were anxious was something of an understatement. We were now into the New Year and we were still without a suitable site. Talking to Naomi Page, I had the first indication that the Bath Festival Society had been carrying out a little 'behind the scenes' activity.

'Why don't you give the secretary of the Bath and West Agricultural Society a call? They have a massive show ground near Shepton Mallet and they just might be interested,' she said.

The Secretary turned out to be The Lord Darling.

'Come and see us,' he said and a meeting was arranged.

Before keeping the appointment, we drove out to the show ground to check it out. It was, as Naomi had said, massive with good access from a main road. It was also far enough away from any built up areas to avoid problems of noise. There was one area of about thirty to forty acres that immediately caught my eye - it sloped gently away up hill and was the perfect location for the concert arena. The showground's one drawback was the fact that it contained a comparatively large number of permanent buildings. However, a definite plus was that some of these buildings housed properly plumbed loos - luxury indeed.

Lord Darling turned out to be a very correct and courteous English gentleman. But however polite he was, I could never quite overcome the feeling that he thought promoters came some way below rat-catchers on the social scale. At least rat-catchers, I could imagine him reasoning, did something useful. Nevertheless our initial meeting went fairly well, after we adjusted to both his interrogation technique and the fact that his society was thinking of a rent of £10,000. Rather more than the £40 we paid last year, I thought ruefully, though to be fair we were now planning a far larger event. At the end of our discussions he told us that he would report back to his committee and let us know their views as quickly as possible. He was commendably efficient and we received a letter within the week. The committee it seemed, subject to certain safeguards, was prepared to let us use the Showground - at last we had a site.

After the normal and expensive negotiations between our respective solicitors, the contract was ready to be signed. The day chosen for this momentous event was the Saturday of the Bath and West Societies annual show. When we arrived, we were shown into the Secretary's office where we were introduced to a number of the Society's committee members. There was, it seemed, one last problem that they had omitted to mention at any of our previous meetings and this was that they required Wendy and me to personally guarantee the conditions of the contract. There wasn't a lot we could do. We had already committed ourselves to a number of groups and we desperately needed a site, so we signed. Afterwards, six or seven extremely charming members of the committee took us for a tour of the show. Thirty years on it is difficult to recall their names. However, I do remember that there was a Colonel, a couple of Lords, an Admiral and a one armed Viscount. The one thing I am really certain about though is that we had a great time, which finally ended with all of us piling into an enormous vintage steam driven swing boat.

After all of the problems finding a suitable site, it was a great feeling to be able to start work on the festival in earnest. While we had been rushing around looking for a site, Tony Burfield and Barry Dickens had been checking on the availability of the groups in which I had expressed an interest. They had done their job well and we had a choice of some of the very best of the American West Coast bands. Our first priority was to confirm the pencilled bookings. When we had finished we were confident we had put together a fairly strong programme. Nevertheless, knowing the Faulk Brothers were planning an even more ambitious event on the Isle of Wight than the one they had organised in 1969 featuring Bob Dylan, I felt we had to go for overkill to be sure of not being eclipsed. I was desperate to book Led Zeppelin but Peter, as usual, was exercising his managerial skills and not committing himself. The other act I was really keen to book was Frank Zappa and the Mothers of Invention. Tony had spoken to Herb Cohen, their manager, who had expressed some interest. However, since the initial enquiry we hadn't heard from him. That was soon to change. I heard from Tony that Herb was flying into London and would like to meet me to discuss matters. It seemed he was going to stay at a hotel just a few hundred yards from where we lived and it was decided that I would collect him from his hotel and bring him back to our house. I took an immediately liking to him. He was nearly as wide as he was tall and looked rather intimidating, but he had great charm and a laid back manner which tended to disguise a very shrewd mind. The meeting initially went well. That is until, in the middle of a question, he went to sleep. I was not sure if this was some American negotiating ploy designed to put me at a disadvantage, or just the result of jet lag. After an hour or so of embarrassed indecision, I decided to wake him up and take him back to his hotel. As he got out of the car, he promised to give me an answer regarding the festival as soon as possible. As I got to know Herb better, I found he would often cat nap. If he wasn't jet lagged, after ten or twenty minutes, he was fine and raring to go again.

Eventually, after several telephone conversations, I finally discovered exactly what it was that Peter Grant wanted for the band - lots of money and clear top billing. The money, surprisingly, wasn't a huge problem but the billing was. I had already promised Bill Thompson, the manager of Jefferson Airplane, that they would receive equal top billing. Also, there was a lot of talk among the American bands about invoking the Favoured Nation clause. This in effect ensured that all of the groups would be paid the same amount. Of course, when it came down to it, although all groups were equal, some were undoubtedly more equal than others and this idea died a natural death. It was a very difficult decision, as I really didn't want to break my word to Bill. On the other hand, Zeppelin was potentially the hottest band in the world and would be a real coup. In the end I simply could not afford to loose them so I agreed to Peter's terms.

We now had our complete line up and I started to order the publicity material. A week later Herb Cohen rang.

Zappa will do it,' he said.

That was it, the icing on the cake. Of course, we had to reprint the posters and flyers but that was a small price to pay for what I like to think was

**TRANS WORLD AIRLINES, Inc.**
(INCORPORATED IN THE U.S.A.)

214 OXFORD STREET
LONDON, W.I.
01-636 5411

S T A T E M E N T

Bannister Promotions,
22 Trevor Place,
London SW7.

AMERICAN FEDERATION OF MUSICIANS
New York /London: June 22, 1970

| | | |
|---|---|---|
| Fare basis:  Group Affinity New York/London return 43 Economy seats at £104.4s.0d. | £4480. | 4.  0. |
| 25% cancellation fee for 6 group members (in accordance with the conditions contained within 'Application for International Group Travel Fares') | £ 156. | 6.  0. |
| 2 First Class returns New York/London | £ 625. | 0.  0. |
| 1 First Class return  New York/London (infant) | £  29. | 9.  0. |
| TOTAL        ..    ..    ..      .. | £5290. | 19.  0. |

| | | |
|---|---|---|
| less 10% deposit | £ 572. 19.  0. |
| less payment received from Coca Cola Ltd. | £1612.  2.  0. |
| less payment received from Bannister Promotions | £3105. 18.  0. |
| TOTAL | £5290. 19.  0. |

The original invoice for the Bath Festival 1970 charter flight.
Note the contribution by Coca Cola

a rather good programme, consisting of on Saturday: Maynard Ferguson, Joe Jammer, Keef Hartley Band, Fairport Convention, Colosseum, Johnny Winter, It's a Beautiful Day, Steppenwolf, John Mayall, Canned Heat, Pink Floyd and on Sunday: Hot Tuna, Flock, Santana, Country Joe, Doctor John, The Byrds, Moody Blues, Frank Zappa and the Mothers of Invention, Led Zeppelin and Jefferson Airplane, with John Peel and Mike Raven providing continuity.

I was also able at last to get the journalist from the local Bath paper off my back. For over a month he had called me repeatedly to find out the full line up.

When I finally told him his only reaction was 'Led who? How the hell do you spell that?' Even after I told him he still managed to print it as 'ledzeppelin'.

Luckily that wasn't the reaction of the journalists on the music papers who were pretty enthusiastic; otherwise I would have been really depressed. Perhaps, once again, this lack of enthusiasm was just confined to Bath because when we tested the reaction to our programme at the Pavilion, the response was again most blasé, with the comments.

'Seen them, don't like them, who the hell are they?'

Fortunately, the rest of the country didn't feel the same way and once the tickets went on sale, Wendy found it very hard to keep all of our ticket agents supplied, so great was the demand.

As well as the local Bath journalist, another persistent caller was Angie Bowie, David's wife who was really keen for me to add her old man to the bill. Space Oddity had just charted and I had already made a mental note to watch out for this obviously highly talented young man. So although I was sympathetic, I had to explain that I thought his musical style was incompatible with the type of event we were presenting - I often wonder how he would have been received if he had actually appeared.

After the initial euphoria came the reality of to what we had committed ourselves. The fees for the dozen or so American bands had been easy to calculate. Not so easy to determine, we found, were the costs of the airfares and freight, which were our responsibility. Working out the expenses, based on each band travelling independently, was really frightening. It came to a truly enormous amount of money and was distinctly uneconomic.

'Perhaps it would be better to charter an aircraft', some one suggested.

We obtained quotes from a number of companies and surprisingly the American company, TWA, one of the largest of the airlines at that time, was the most competitive. Economically, the charter made sense and, providing we could get the bands to agree, we had solved the problem. The fact that it was an American airline helped to persuade them that it was a practical and safe alternative to scheduled flights and they all finally agreed, but not before the normal obligatory hassles, of course. These included a total disagreement over the departure dates and to make matters worse, as the plane was already pretty full, some of the bands renegotiated the number of tickets they required, to include seats for parents, friends, second cousins, ex-wives, accountants etc.

# CHAPTER 19

As the date of the event grew ever closer, so our visits to the Bath and West Showground increased. As it was a round trip of over three hundred miles it was something of a nuisance as it cut down on the time I could spend in the office. However, it was a necessary chore, as we needed to tie up important details with the Society's Secretary and also meet with our local contractors. Why we arranged a meeting with Peter Grant for the same day as one of our trips to Somerset I simply can't remember. Perhaps we had a long-standing appointment with Lord Darling and Peter was unable to meet us any other time. Whatever the reason, it led to a mad cross-country dash. If the roads had been traffic free we could have made good time on our journey back to London but, mid-afternoon in 1970, the A303 was heavily congested. I tried very hard to make up time. However, after a succession of near misses as I tried to leapfrog convoys of lorries, I gave up and phoned home to explain we were going to be a little late. Peter was having afternoon tea with Wendy's mother and was quite happy to wait for us. Unfortunately, as we got nearer to London, the traffic became even heavier and we arrived tired, irritable and extremely frustrated, just ten minutes after Peter had left. I rang him later that evening to apologise.

'Don't worry,' he said, 'these things happen.'

This was typical of the easy going Peter we knew in those days. Very different from the power tripped bully he became over the next decade.

Somewhat to our surprise several of the more conscientious mangers flew in from the States to check out the site including Bill Uttley, who looked after Steppenwolf and Bill Thompson, manager of The Jefferson Airplane. This added still further to the time we were out of the office but it helped iron out problems that could have arisen over the weekend of the festival. It was on our visit to the showground with Bill Thompson that Claudie, our basset hound, really let us down. On our arrival, we had stopped at the Secretary's office to chat. Afterwards we set off with Lord Darling to show him exactly where we wished to position the stage. Driving slowly to avoid the many sheep that were grazing in the area, we finally arrived at the chosen spot. As I stepped out of the car, Claudie, who had been sitting quietly dozing in the back of the car, seized her opportunity to escape. She had never shown the slightest interest in chasing sheep before, or in anything else for that matter, but now she excelled herself. Ears flying and baying with excitement, she started to have the time of her life, causing sheep to scatter in every direction. I was distraught. Just when I wanted to make a good impression, this had to happen and to make matters worse, I suddenly remembered that the penalty in the farming community for sheep worrying was death. Hoping fervently that this applied to the dog and not the owner, I realised that something had to be done quickly.

I had already shouted myself hoarse to no avail so the next time she came reasonably close I ran as hard as I could and launched myself into a spectacular and successful flying tackle - luckily, without coming into contact with any of the cow pats and sheep droppings which generously covered the ground. I probably over reacted because later that afternoon, sitting in the Secretary's office, a tiny rabbit ran in and was promptly and, it seemed to me callously, thrown out to the waiting Labradors.

On the way back to London, I discovered that while I had been making a total prat of myself, Bill had been watching my antics. He had, it seemed, been most impressed with my style and agility and thought that I had a great future in American football. He also, thank God, liked the site and was happy for his band to appear. Dropping him at his hotel we asked him what he was doing that evening, rather expecting him to explain that the Harold Davison Agency had something planned for him.

'Nothing,' he replied, so we arranged to meet him later.

Bill was something of an anomaly. His philosophy was pure hippie, as you would expect from some one who was part of the Jefferson Airplane family and who, because of his position as manager of a band that was considered by the American authorities to be subversive and his colourful appearance, was automatically subject to a search for drugs every time he passed through JFK Airport. Yet his interests ranged far and wide. Extremely well read, he was just as happy discussing the beliefs of Sartre and Jung as the rather more contentious convictions of Leary and Ginsberg. He was also a keen and very knowledgeable connoisseur of fine wines. Showing our own prejudices, or at least our preconceived ideas, we expected that he would want to go to a club like the Revolution or the Speakeasy. Instead, he chose to see a film based on the life of Anne Boleyn called 'Anne of a Thousand Days', followed by a nice leisurely supper. We saw a lot of Bill over the next three or four days and became good friends, which was why I was so anxious not to break my word regarding Jefferson Airplane's billing. When he finally discovered my perfidy, he was initially rather annoyed with me. However, being a realist, he soon got over it and as our friendship grew we went on to become The Airplane's European representatives.

As the Festival approached, we had many requests from companies eager to film the event. Most of them wanted us to do the most difficult, if not impossible job, of obtaining clearance from the groups involved and were then prepared to offer us something like 2.5% of any net profits. A company called Gentle Ghost eventually came up with the best offer. Although there was no up-front money, they were prepared to give us a reasonable percentage of any profits and, best of all, they were prepared to negotiate the film rights with the groups themselves.

Another decision we made which showed our inexperience at that time was to allow a young man named Tony Elliot, who had just recently started a magazine called Time Out, to have a free hand with the editorial content of our festival programme. As usual, we were frantically busy when we received a call from him suggesting that he produced the programme for us. We thought it was a great idea- anything to reduce the workload. If we had been a little less involved with other things, we would certainly have insisted on vetting the content. It wasn't until the middle of the festival that I actually had a chance to see a copy. Although I thought that the layout and general production was excellent, I nearly had a fit when I read the unpleasant and politically loaded things Elliot and his colleagues had to say. It must be the only time a promoter has paid for the privilege of being so thoroughly castigated.

As soon as we realised we were going to be running a two-day event, I decided that it was important to provide additional entertainment for the periods when the groups were not on stage. Film seemed to be a good idea and we planned two independent cinemas, housed in large marquees. For those who did not want to give up their position in front of the stage, we would erect a giant screen some forty feet wide in the concert arena. Finding films to show in the two marquees was not a problem. However, it was difficult to think of something suitable to show on the big screen. In the end we settled on Walt Disney's masterpiece 'Fantasia' – a film that had become increasingly popular since the advent of psychedelic drugs in the early sixties. Ian was truly excellent at tracking down difficult to find items and, once he had found them, even better at convincing people to rent them to us. However, even he found it difficult to persuade the Walt Disney Corporation to let us borrow a copy of this film. In the end we had to agree to pay for one of Disney's own projectionists, complete with a full size 35mm cinema projector to come to the festival to ensure that the film was presented in an appropriate fashion. The irony was that due to the playing schedules becoming so disrupted, the bands were forced to play throughout the night and there was no opportunity for the film to be shown. Among the other things we initially planned were lectures by such people as Allen Ginsberg and Timothy Leary. However, whether through lack of interest by these luminaries or because of the expense involved (I can't remember), this idea was rapidly dropped.

One wet and windy day towards the middle of May, a deputation of half a dozen or so students visited us from Reading University. It seemed they had heard about the festival and wanted to help. One of these was David Campbell, better known for some obscure reason as Thump. David, a very engaging young man, had elected himself the spokesman for the group and volunteered to liase between the students and us. As the size of the event was growing all the time, it was obvious that we would require a large pool of casual labour and we were very happy to employ him and his friends to help with the preparation and build up of the event. However, our biggest difficulty was finding a person with experience of all aspects of the construction industry, to act as our site manager. The problem was solved when Ian contacted a specialist employment agency and found Mike Good. Mike was just what we needed. He supervised the jobs we had agreed to undertake ourselves, such as erecting the perimeter fences, manufacturing extra loos and urinals. He also liaised with our subcontractors and generally made sure that every thing was carried out to the satisfaction of the Bath and West Society.

Wendy and I always felt, wrongly as it turned out, that if we gave the people a good deal, they would reciprocate. We therefore decided not to turn the concert area into a virtual prison by erecting hundreds of yards of eight-foot high corrugated iron sheets, as they had at the previous Isle of Wight Festival. We resolved, instead, to erect a six and a half foot high chain link fence running parallel, some fifteen or twenty feet inside the fairly secure existing fence that ran all the way around the show ground. We reasoned that this would give us a suitable 'no go' area, that, if policed with a sufficient number of stewards, would keep out most gatecrashers. What we initially failed to do was accurately measure the distances involved. When we finally did, the existing perimeter fence turned out to be well over a mile and a half in length. If we had thought things through properly we would have perhaps been a degree less idealistic and opted for the cheaper and more practical way of securing the arena. However, in retrospect, had we done this, I think we would have spoilt the very special atmosphere the festival created.

In addition to using the permanent buildings available on site for sleeping accommodation, we decided we would also provide individual tents. Rock festivals were still something of an unknown quantity to most companies and, quite understandably, they were concerned that their property could get damaged, lost or even destroyed. So it was something of a surprise when Ian discovered a firm in Liverpool that would supply us with as many small tents as we required. Taking them at their word, we ordered a thousand made up from a selection of ridge and bell tents. Initially we had intended to make a small charge for the use of a tent over the weekend, but shortage of staff and general administration difficulties meant that these small tents, along with virtually every other facility, were provided free of charge.

As the expenses continued to mount, so our thoughts turned more and more towards sponsorship. Encouraged by the fact that both the Milk and Cheese Marketing Boards had approached us to book stands at the events, we fired off letters to a number of multi national companies. Of these, only Coca Cola replied and although they were not interested in becoming the event's main sponsor, they did give us a large number of cans free of charge and also agreed to supply us with further stock at a heavily discounted price, for which we were extremely grateful. More importantly, though, they contributed to the cost of our charter flight to the tune, if you will forgive the pun, of close on £2,000. The various record companies representing the groups playing at the festival were another thing altogether. They were delighted with the extra exposure for their artists, especially as so many of them were rarely seen in this country. However, when it came to digging into their more than ample coffers to provide some support for our event, it was a very different matter. We had asked them to sponsor individual items that directly benefited the audience such as polythene sheets - in case it rained, the cinemas, some silly games and some extra loos. We also asked them to help with the cost of the trailers we used backstage to house their groups. We figured this would give them some good publicity, something at that time they desperately needed. We should have known better. Not one came across. Selling 'product' was one thing, but giving money to some upstart promoter was unthinkable.

Negative co-operation seemed to be the only answer, so when the time came for them to request tickets and passes for their support staff, we ignored them. I was, I believe, accused of power tripping. However, this was just so much bluster from brain washed record company executives who did not understand the public's poor perception of the part they played at that time in the music business. In the end some sort of compromise was reached. The details are hard to recall. However, it was just the start of an ongoing dispute that I had with the record industry that was to continue of and on for the next ten years.

# CHAPTER 20

Ten days or so before the festival was due to start; we moved our office to the showground. Lord Darling had found us a smart building of our own, with a reception area and two or three separate rooms. It was ideal and we immediately started to get ourselves organised. To save running up colossal hotel bills, some weeks earlier we had agreed to rent a rather fine six bedroom house from Colonel Bullivant, a member of the Bath and West Society Committee. When he first mentioned the property to us he had rather modestly described it as his daughter's cottage. 'Some cottage', I thought. It was absolutely enormous. Nevertheless, it was ideal for us as it was situated only two or three miles from the festival site and comfortably accommodated Wendy and me, Ian and his wife and other members of our administrative staff.

My first job was to position the stage. It was not a task that I enjoyed, as it was such a responsibility. Get it wrong and all sorts of problems could arise as only a certain percentage of the audience would have a clear view and some poor unfortunates would be peering into the wings. Anticipating a much bigger crowd than at the Rec' Ground the previous year, we decided to build one large stage with the floor at a much higher level. As it was almost impossible to visualise anything at all from ground level, I asked the stage construction company if I could use one of their flatbed lorries as a makeshift stage. After much manoeuvring, I finally found a satisfactory position, which took full advantage of the gently slopping ground and still left enough room for a decent size backstage area.

We soon got into a routine of starting at around eight in the morning and working through to seven or eight in the evening. After such a long and exceedingly hard day, there wasn't a great deal for our team to do with their evenings. Actually, there was only one thing that they could do unless they had their own transport and that was to visit the local pub that was virtually a part of the Bath and West Showground. The big draw back to this arrangement, as far as I was concerned as the promoter, was the fact that the 'speciality of the house' was rough scrumpy. This potent cider was available, I was unreliably informed, for about a £1 a gallon, or was it a £1 for ten gallons? Anyway, no one seemed to neither know nor care when I asked, as they were either too inebriated to remember accurately or too hung over the next morning to give a damn. The upshot of all this was that most evenings around 11 p.m., I would drive around the site looking along the verges and in the ditches for members of my valiant workforce and if I found anyone too far-gone to stagger home, I would push or haul them into the car and drive them back to their accommodation. Recently, looking through old copies of the local paper, I was amused to find a report of a meeting of the local licensed victuallers association where their chairman recommended that all the pubs in the area should close over the weekend of the festival. I think he must have been drunk because if they had followed his advice they would have missed out on what must have been the best weekend of their careers.

Construction on the site was now well under way and although we had our students from Reading University, we were still short handed. Our problem was soon solved as word had obviously gone out that there was work to be had and we soon had a steady stream of callers offering their services. Most of these were local people. However, a small number had travelled from Europe and even the USA specifically to help with the event. One of these was a young Texan called Tree. I never did find out his real name but everyone called him by his nickname for obvious reasons. He was at least 6ft 7ins tall and weighed around seventeen stones and always insisted that he was the baby of his family, with two even larger older brothers, which I must say I found just a little difficult to believe. He was an utterly tireless worker and really did do the work of at least three men. He stayed with us for nearly two weeks and when the time came to leave he refused to take a penny of the money he was entitled to. If only I could have found another couple of dozen just like him!

Jonathan Smeeton, our electrician, was another great find and was at that time working as the lighting director with Hawkwind. He had many responsibilities on site, which he always attacked with great enthusiasm. Probably his single most important job was to provide the security lighting for the perimeter fence. This consisted of assembling something like a mile and a half of cable and inserting a bulb holder every ten or so feet, a gigantic undertaking that appeared to leave him totally unfazed. Whenever I wanted a word, I would pop into his workshop where he and his two assistants were usually to be found busy manufacturing this simply enormous string of lights.

'Hi' I would say to him in greeting.

'Sure am,' would be the inevitable reply.

Nevertheless, he still managed to complete this mammoth task with plenty of time to spare. Unfortunately, it turned out to be something of a waste of time and money. At around 2.00 a.m. on the eve of the festival, some clever little bugger, obviously looking for a way to bypass our ticket office, removed a bulb, inserted a thrupney bit and instantly plunged the entire length of the security fence into total darkness. He probably did us a great favour as we suddenly realised that the lights were showing the kids, intent on crashing the festival, exactly where the fences ran in the more remote areas away from the main road.

One of the conditions imposed on us by the Bath and West Agricultural

Society was that we provided a Fire Engine and trained crew throughout the duration of the festival. They were also keen that we generally liased with the local Fire Brigade. I couldn't exactly blame them as they did have rather a lot of wooden buildings. The Society actually owned an old rather decrepit fire engine of their own, which we could use. However, as we were not sure where to find experienced fire fighters, we decided to arrange a meeting with the local Brigade to obtain their views. Wendy and I found them to be most helpful and although they were unable to commit an engine specifically to our event, they were pleased that we had made them aware of the festival. They also helped us with suggestions as to how we could find suitable people to man the Society's fire engine and where we could find emergency water supplies. They were so affable and helpful that the meeting ran on rather longer than we had expected. We were by this time rather anxious to get back to the site to see what nasty little surprises were waiting for us. We shot off down the road for the short journey back to the showground and it was only as we were turning into the main entrance that we both remembered, virtually simultaneously, that we had stood up the Bishop of Bath and Wells, whom we had arranged to meet later that afternoon. Hurrying to the telephone, Wendy apologised most profusely. We were supposed to have met to discuss how we proposed to look after the moral welfare of the assembled multitude and how exactly we intended to keep the sexes apart in the tents! In the end we compromised by allowing the Bishop to conduct a short service from the stage on Sunday morning.

We must have been crazy to have even contemplated such a thing. However, whilst we were rushing around organising the Bath Blues Festival, we were also arranging a folk festival for later in the summer. Although there were already a number of pop festivals held each year, we felt that folk music, which was at that time enjoying a large mainstream following, had been rather neglected. We had already found a superb site near Reading called Swallowfield Park and had even gone as far as booking the programe which included such luminaries as Tom Paxton, Incredible String Band, Tim Hardin, Tom Rush, Julie Felix, Fairport Convention, Matthew's Southern Comfort, John Fahey, Ralph McTell, Shirley & Dolly Collins and Home Brew, Mike Chapman, Al Stewart, Famous Jug Band, Fotheringay, Pigsty Light Orchestra, Ian Anderson and Storyteller.

Unfortunately, when negotiating for the park, I had made the mistake of presuming the man I was dealing with was the owner and not just the tenant. Whilst we were preparing for The Bath Festival, he rang me at the show-ground to tell me that the owners had heard about the folk concert and had expressly forbidden him from renting the park to us. Any other time and I would have tried to get them to change their minds. As it was, I was up to my

The Bath crowd and stage 1970

ears in problems and I just could not spare the time to bypass the tenant, track down the landowners and arrange a meeting, especially as there was still no guarantee that I would be successful. In the end I had no option but to cancel the event. I was really disappointed as I always felt that because folk music was far more low key, plus the superb setting and great programme, this could have been one of the very best festivals we ever promoted.

In the week before the event, time just seemed to disappear and we were all beginning to wonder if we would get every thing ready in time. To make matters worse, I suddenly realised the charter flight bringing the bands and their managers was due in shortly, making even more demands on my time. Tony Burfield and Barry Dickens had, thank goodness, taken care of all the work permits and M.U. exchanges and other logistical problems and were planning to be on hand at the airport to make sure all went smoothly. However, they thought that as I was the promoter, it was a good idea if I met the plane as well. Leaving Cannards Grave (the name of the village where The Bath & West showground is situated) really early, we arrived at Heathrow with plenty of time to spare as the charter flight was just a little behind schedule. Leaving Wendy in the main concourse, Tony, who had had plenty of experience of this sort of thing and I contacted a senior Immigration Control officer who allowed us to stand beside the staff working at passport control. They were all terrifically helpful. ' Just point your people out to us as they arrive and we will deal with them as quickly as possible'. We didn't like to tell them that it would be abundantly clear whom we were waiting for as soon as they appeared. They only had to look for the hair.

It soon became clear that we had lost Dr John. Tony was frantically busy sorting out the various groups, so I was handed his work permit and told to go and look for him. Setting off down a corridor in the general direction of the arriving aircraft, I soon spotted a lone figure standing in the middle of the passageway staring at the wall in rapt attention. He appeared to be totally oblivious to the other passengers trying to pass round him and to add to the totally surreal nature of the scene, he was wearing full Gris Gris man regalia and holding in one hand something that looked suspiciously like a spear.

Making my way up to him I drew myself up to my full height, and in my best colonial explorer's manner said 'Dr John I presume. Welcome to England.'

En masse, such a large number of musicians appeared a little overwhelming. However, at least they all seemed to be pleased to be in England at last. It was good to see people that we had worked with previously such as Bob Hite. Even I couldn't miss seeing him. Bill Thompson took the opportunity to introduce me briefly to the members of Jefferson Airplane. I wasn't sure what to expect, certainly not six such charismatic people. I had, of course, heard their records and seen their photographs and yes, Grace was even more striking in person, but I was still somewhat surprised by their charm and intelligence. I learnt later that two of them came from families in the diplomatic service - I wasn't at all surprised.

Leaving Tony with the unenviable job of making sure that every one was transported to the correct hotel, Wendy and I headed back to Somerset. On our arrival, as we feared, people were beginning to arrive early in significant numbers and we were not completely ready for them. We had only erected about half of our small tents and we still had something like five hundred to go, plus numerous other jobs that needed finishing. We decided our only option was to recruit some of the new arrivals and work flat out. To everyone's eternal credit, we managed to get most things finished and put up a further two hundred and fifty tents before we were forced to call it a day.

The entire admin team, all eight of us, moved onto the site early Friday morning, the day before the festival was officially due to start - ready as we'd ever be for the weekend ahead. We were already tired after the intense pressure of the previous week. A bigger and better financed company could have afforded the luxury of a larger executive team. This would have enabled key persons to share responsibilities and work in shifts, spreading the workload and ensuring that every one enjoyed sufficient sleep. However, these were early days for us all and we were learning the hard way.

Through contacts, word of mouth and adverts in local newspapers, we had managed to assemble a formidable army of stewards. A few of them had worked for us before at our gigs in Bristol and Bath including some who had even travelled from as far as Worthing. However an army is only as good as its leaders and its command structure and for once we seemed to have too many Indians and no chiefs. Well a few, as I was using some of my old stewards as section leaders. Communication was almost impossible, as this was long before walkie-talkie radios were widely available and we had neither the time nor the wit to install temporary landlines. Nevertheless, with a great deal of thought and a little careful briefing, we eventually came up with a system that worked quite well. If only we had worked things out before the event instead of during it, life would have been considerably easier for everyone concerned, especially me.

We had situated the campsite just outside the boundary of the show-ground and close to the main entrances. No mention had been made in our pre-event publicity that the campsite would be open on the Friday but this did not seem to deter anyone. By midday we realised we had underestimated the numbers arriving early as they were simply pouring in, in a never-ending stream. We immediately set about increasing the number of loos, adding extra water bowsers, and most importantly firewood. What they did with the stuff besides burn it I'll never know, but by the end of the festival we had paid for and transported close on fifty tons of good quality firewood. Each lorry load becoming ever more expensive as we searched the area for supplies. This, of course, was in addition to a large number of wooden fences and horse jumps on adjoining land that were also burnt - expensive campfires.

Unlike the atmosphere of the festival itself, which turned out to be utterly fantastic, the mood on the campsite was initially rather threatening. Continuous chants of 'out devils out' reverberated across the fields. In our efforts to keep everyone entertained, we had arranged for a number of artists to play on the small stage we had set up in the middle of the campsite. These included solo singers, several comedians and an excellent American group called Formerly Fat Harry who was to play an important and unscheduled role in opening the festival the next day.

Friday night was a long one. Cars just kept coming and coming and suddenly we were running out of places to put them. Around 1 a.m. I got a message from Lord Darling to meet him in his temporary office, a large caravan strategically placed to give him the best view of what was happening. He was armed with a list of local farmers whose land adjoined the Bath and West Showground and who, for an unspecified sum, were prepared to let us use their fields as overflow car parks. Handing me a phone, he invited me to get on with it. It wasn't my finest hour. In fact, it was something of a blood bath. The farmers, knowing full well I had no alternative but to rent their fields, or face even greater chaos, charged a figure that in normal cir-cumstances would have been sufficient to buy their fields outright. By 3 a.m. I had hopefully, at some considerable cost, secured enough fields to contain all the vehicles we were expecting.

# CHAPTER 21

As it started to get light on Saturday morning, I was stunned by the sheer size of the crowd that was revealed. There must have been some thing approaching thirty to forty thousand people spread out over the campsite and various car parks waiting to be let in. How many, I wondered, had actually bought tickets?

At the beginning of the week leading up to the event, Wendy had phoned our ticket agents in an attempt to obtain an accurate idea of the numbers we could expect. Much to her surprise, she found that despite having been given large allocations, everyone of them had sold out over the previous weekend. We immediately set about remedying the situation. However, by then it was far too late. By the time the tickets finally arrived with the agents, the vast majority of people who had been unable to buy a ticket had already left to start their journey to Evercreech, intending, we hoped, to purchase one on their arrival. Nowadays any promoter would make advance ticket sales an absolute priority but in 1970 we put the welfare of the audience first and concentrated instead on providing the best facilities possible to the exclusion of all else. It was a costly mistake as we left ourselves vulnerable to gate crashers and dishonest stewards and very nearly jeopardised our future.

To say the first couple of hours after the gates opened were chaotic is to redefine the meaning of the word. Even with a fairly substantial army of stewards we learnt the hard way that our idealistic approach to security couldn't work. The boundary fences were too long and the entrances too far apart. The real problem, of course, was there were just to many people. They seemed to be growing like crops in the fields and this was just the start. Whether by accident, caused by so many people trying to crowd through to few entrances or by intent, I don't know. However, soon large gaps started to appear in the fences and our security was breached. To make matters worse, whilst all this was taking place, several of the stewards we had recruited from the Bristol area, not our regular stewards, well not directly anyway, took advantage of the situation. The opportunity to acquire what they saw as easy money proved too strong a temptation. They wangled it so they could work at one of the more distant entrances well away from Wendy's direct supervision. In the general confusion around the gates (and any one who attended a festival in the late sixties or early seventies will know exactly what I mean), they managed to set up in competition with our own ticket sellers and discretely started to let people in, at what I am sure was a generously discounted rate. Wendy had her suspicions about what was happening but without proof it was hard to take any action. As a precaution I had all the stewards on the entrance in question transferred to other jobs inside the showground, as far away from the perimeter fences as possible. If I hadn't been so totally engaged in other matters I would have realised that they wouldn't give up as easily as all that and checked up on them. As it was, it wasn't until some months later that I learnt from a friend that the worst offender had been heard boasting that he had stolen nearly £1,500, a sizeable amount in 1970, which probably equates to something like £15,000 to £20,000 today. The thing that really hurt was the fact that he turned out to be the brother of one of the stewards who had worked for me from the time we first started to promote at The Pavilion in Bath. I was so upset that I wanted to report the matter to the police. However, as my informant refused to make a statement, and I had no other proof, I had no alternative but to forget the whole affair. It did leave me wondering just how much we had lost in this way.

The festival was scheduled to start at noon. By 11.30 a.m. not one of the bands scheduled to play had arrived. The roads around the site were totally jammed. According to the Somerset Standard, 'There were solid jams of stationary traffic up to 10 miles long around Shepton Mallet.' The paper then went on to quote one of their reporters who was stuck at the tiny hamlet of Cannards Grave just a few hundred yards from the Bath & west Showground who wrote in all seriousness, 'People on their way to Cornwall from the north are finding Cannards Grave a dead end. They are stuck. Traffic is moving 20 yards every half-an-hour.'

Matters weren't helped when some of the festivalgoers added to the chaos by abandoning their cars at the side of the road and walking the last mile or so. If things were difficult for the punters, it was doubly frustrating for the artists sitting in all this traffic wondering if they would ever get to the gig. This was just another example of our inexperience. We should have anticipated these problem and made alternative arrangements. Probably the answer would have been to use helicopters to bring them in. However, this additional expense was just not within our budget. This sort of situation really was a promoter's nightmare and it was probably the only time in the entire weekend that I was close to panic. All those paying customers and nobody around to entertain them. If only, I thought, I had remembered to bring my trombone! Luckily on Saturday we still had formerly Fat Harry on site as well as Brian Jones and Tony Burfield, who had bravely, if rather foolhardily, volunteered to assist with the stage management and they managed to wing it until some of the scheduled performers finally arrived. Despite our best efforts, Sunday morning was initially just as chaotic until Donovan who, unbeknown to anyone, had come along to the festival and had been sitting in the audience waiting like everyone else for the music to start, very generously offered to fill in. He played for several hours whilst Brian and Tony struggled to bring some semblance of normality to a nightmare scenario. Donovan really saved the day and I don't think I ever thanked him, so Don if you read this - thanks -thanks a lot!

By mid morning on Saturday we were also facing our first staff casualties. The first to keel over was Ian Tilbury. Ian, always a highly-strung, nervous individual was overcome with a fit of the shakes and had to lie down - he just could not handle the continual pressure. He became progressively worse and, in fact, eventually left the site altogether. This, of course, left me in something of a spot as he was responsible for making many of the arrangements and I was counting on him to take care of the more routine tasks. In normal circumstances, Wendy would have filled in. However, she was in charge of finances including collecting cash from the gates and arranging payments to staff, groups and contractors, an enormous responsibility. In the end I delegated whatever jobs I could and just had to work a 24-hour day to compensate. Other casualties followed thick and fast. Our Worthing stewards, who had been truly excellent over a four-hour stint on a Thursday evening at The Assembly Hall, could not cope with the total chaos of such a large event and wanted to go home. Worse still, I found Mick lying down in one of the caravans sobbing like a baby. I was flabbergasted. He had been one of the toughest and most reliable bouncers at the Pavilion and had worked with me for nearly six years. Like most of us he had been up all Friday night and, like the Worthing stewards, he had obviously found the sheer pressure of the event impossible to deal with and wanted to leave. This was a more serious blow as he was to have been my general gopher and minder.

One other minor casualty was Dr Sam Hutt, better known these days as Hank Wangford, the singing gynaecologist who had been given the job of organising our medical team. By lunchtime Saturday, Sam, who I think had probably been analysing various substances in a quest to better his scientific knowledge, was a little overcome by the results of all his research and had to rest. This, of course, was not a real problem as he had brought along three other doctors in addition to a number of nurses and they could cover for him until he was fully recovered. In fact, he and all our medical team did a tremendous job and along with Release coped with a lot of drug-induced problems, as well as with the more routine sprains, headaches and the consequences of exposure to the inclement weather.

Gradually things started to settle down, or perhaps to be more accurate we started to become a little more organised and began to get on top of things. I even had time to check on the sound quality, which, thanks again to Charlie Watkins of WEM, was pretty good despite the somewhat blustery conditions.

While I was in the arena I was rather surprised to see that quite a number of tents had been erected amongst the crowd, cutting of the view of the stage for those unfortunate enough to be sitting behind them. I would have liked to have done something about removing them, but I felt that it could have been rather inflammatory, so I left them. No one seemed to mind, which says a great deal about the patience and good nature of the audience.

The position on stage also started to improve as the bands finally began to arrive. This was an enormous relief and removed some of the pressure from our stage managers. Unfortunately, it was to be rather short lived as, along with one of the bands, came the Hell's Angels. It was only recently that I found out, from an article written just after the event by an American journalist, that Fairport Convention was involved in bringing them onto the site and I quote:

'It happened that Fairport Convention were late arriving because of traffic and eyeing the bikers on the road, scrounged lifts straight to the stage. It just seemed natural then to invite the scruffs in for ringside seats in the press enclosure. While the Fairport jig band zapped through their fast electric blue grass and amplified polkas, the Angels did their Aztec two step, staged mock fights and played grab ass and French kissed for anyone with a camera'.

If this was true, and I had known at the time I don't think I would have used Fairport ever again. The Hell's Angels were an absolute pain in the arse and a problem that I could have done without. Although they were nothing like as tough and violent as their American counterparts, their presence was inflammatory and as the day wore on they became ever more outrageous. For a start, they stopped John Peel from reaching the stage. If he had only walked the short distance over to my office and told me, I would have got him on even if it meant using a tank. As it was, tied up in the admin office dealing with the thousand and one problems that always seem to occur at rock festivals, I knew little about these events until Brian sent me a message outlining the situation. He didn't make it sound too serious - just an irritant, so I sent a message back telling him to offer them some money to leave. They obviously declined his offer, as some time later Brian himself came over to the office and explained that things were getting a little out of hand and the Angels were starting to attack members of the audience. He thought it would be a good idea if I had a word with them, as it seemed the only person they were prepared to talk to was the promoter. I have never been a hero. In fact yellow is my favourite colour and I have streak of it a mile wide running down my back. But a man has to do what a man has to do etc and it was with some trepidation that I made my way backstage. In later years I wouldn't have dreamt of such a confrontation without taking with me a small army of heavies, but this time I went alone. After all their bluster, I was relieved when the Angels turned out to be more West Country than West Coast. It seemed they really didn't want to become involved in a pitched battle, particularly after I explained that my stewards outnumbered them by at least ten to one and, if necessary, I was prepared to use rather a lot of force to remove them. To soften the threat and as an added inducement, I increased the amount of money Brian had previously offered and I was enormously relieved when they accepted my terms and agreed to go.

# CHAPTER 22

After that little confrontation everything seemed rather anti-climatical, a little empty and hollow. This feeling lasted for what must have been all of thirty minutes until the loos started to back up. From one load of shits to another, I thought. In fact, it was no joke as nearly three quarters of the loos on site ran off a proper mains drainage system, complete with large bore pipes and flushing cisterns. It was at one of the many junctions that the problem had occurred, threatening to close down the entire system. This was a potentially disastrous situation. With the showground hosting a virtual city whose population was even larger than that of Bath, sanitation was without doubt one of the most important aspects.

Luckily help was at hand. It arrived in the unlikely form of a Royal Naval Commander, who, as a member of the Bath and West Society Committee, had come along to see for himself exactly what a 'Pop Festival' was all about and a member of the audience named, I believe, Malcolm. Malcolm, being exceptionally public spirited and with previous experience of drains and all that sort of stuff had volunteered his services, without necessarily knowing what he was letting himself in for. Donning full-length waders, the Commander and Malcolm were soon up to their waists in effluence. They did a superb job and within an hour or so the blockage was cleared and things were back to normal. I didn't dare ask them how they did it. But whatever it was, it didn't seem to worry them unduly as they agreed to stay on for the rest of the weekend to make sure that there were no further problems. It is one of those strange consequences of a festival, rather similar to a natural disaster or a war, that people are thrown together for a short period of time, develop a close bond and then part never to see each other ever again. So it was with Malcolm and the Commander. In my opinion they really were the unsung heroes of the Bath Festival.

Due to the continuous pressure in the admin office, my visits backstage were very infrequent and I was quite happy to leave the administration of the groups and all the hassles that it entailed in the very capable hands of Brian and Tony. I think I only actually made it on to the stage once over the entire weekend. In fact, apart from the trouble with the Hell's Angels, the only other time I visited the backstage area was to sort out a problem with the backstage caterers. It appeared they were mistakenly charging the groups for the complimentary drinks that Coca Cola had so generously provided. Unfortunately, it wasn't the only problem we were to have with them as we found out after the event.

Throughout the crazy, long weekend, I saw little of the artists or managers involved in the event. Apart from The Byrds that is, who lost and confused were dumped in the admin office by a rather disorientated driver. Of the managers, it was Peter Grant who bothered to track me down and brought the boys over to say hello, lifting me off the ground and smothering me with an enormous bear hug when he finally found me.

One other manager who took the trouble to come over was Herb Cohen. We were sitting in my office talking when we were interrupted by a knock on the door and a young girl who had obviously escaped our rather unreliable security screening entered the room.

'I have lost my scarf, ' she announced rather dramatically.

'Fuck off ', said Herb Cohen emphatically. 'Can't you see this man's busy running this festival. He certainly hasn't got time to worry about finding your fucking scarf.'

After I had shown the highly embarrassed young lady to the enquiry desk, I returned to my office to find Herb still seething with indignation. It was all I could do to keep him from yelling at my entire admin team. He just could not get over their lack of concern.

'But you pay them don't you?' He kept muttering in a perplexed manner. No wonder Herb and I became such good friends.

Early on Sunday morning, around 2-3 am, things gradually started to quieten down. Feeling a little frazzled, I decided some fresh air would do me good and I decided to go for a walk. The uncertain weather we had been experiencing all weekend still hadn't made up its mind. It wasn't exactly raining but moisture was heavy in the air. As I walked slowly along behind the stockade that housed the stage area, I suddenly heard the most astonishing sound. It was truly breathtaking - voices of a mass choir and keyboards entwined. I stood still and listened. I really couldn't think who it could be and then it dawned on me - it was Pink Floyd performing Atom Heart Mother. I found out much later that it was the very first time they had played it live. What made it all the more extraordinary was, from where I was standing, I couldn't see a single solitary soul, yet less than a hundred yards away there were over 130,000 people sitting, listening with rapt attention. Returning to the office feeling a lot better I remember thinking 'only another day to go'. In fact, it was a further 36 hours before I would get any sleep.

Sunday morning was marked by a short service and an address given by the Bishop of Bath and Wells - well I really did owe it to him after so inconsiderately standing him up. After this, things in the admin office started to hot up again. Lost children, lost dogs, lost friends, lost property, lost hair - no of course that was mine. Complaints about catering prices, loos, transport, the lack of food, water, alcohol, contraceptives (I never thought of that one), bad acid. You name it there was a complaint or enquiry for or about it. Amazingly there were no complaints about the programme running order. Everyone

showing just a few of the 1,000 tents that we supplied

seemed to understand the problems we had been experiencing and were sympathetic or at least philosophical. It helped of course that all the groups had eventually turned up and were actually on site.

Later on Gene Parsons of the Byrds paid me a visit. Gene it seems had been appointed spokesman for the group to discuss some problem that could not be resolved by the backstage management. Whatever it was he came to see me about could not have been too important because taking one look at my rather pathetic state he decided to go and bother someone else. The incident obviously stayed in his mind because on hearing that I was writing a book about my experiences he sent me the following.

'I can't help but recall again the first time I met you Fred. It was in the temporary office at the Bath Festival. The rest of the band had sent me to ask you for something or other. I think the Festival had already been going for two days? There were tons of crazy, wonderful and excited people everywhere, Led Zeppelin was blasting away on stage and it was trying to rain. Anyway, I knocked on the door and heard you say, (weakly); 'Come in'. I opened the door and stepped in. You were sitting behind a desk at the end of the room with your head in your hands. I stood there for what seemed a long time. Slowly you looked up and I could tell you hadn't slept for days. I thought; 'I'll bet this poor trouper hasn't left the site for days and God knows what torture he's had to go through organising and making sure everything was right and everyone had what they needed even before the festival opened. You looked at me with very tired but very friendly eyes and said in a soft tone; 'Is there something I can do to help you?' I knew I had just met a very kind man. I realised that whatever it was I was going to request really was not necessary, considering the state of things at that moment. I think I said something like. 'The band sent me to ask you for something but I think I'd rather not. When was the last time you got any sleep?'

During the seventies we worked with the Byrds a great deal and Gene and I became great friends. A friendship that has lasted up to the present time. Initially I only knew Gene as the drummer of the group. However, as I got to know him better I found out that he had started out on his musical career playing guitar and banjo, then electric bass before finally taking up drums. He was, in addition to being an all round musician, an outstanding songwriter having written Gunga Din and Monument amongst many others. Before becoming a professional musician Gene had trained in his father's workshops as a machinist and it was this love of things mechanical that formed the basis of our friendship

The last major problem of the festival came late on Sunday evening or to be strictly accurate, early Monday morning, when the Moody Blue's manager came over to see me to explain that because of the bad weather the band were unable to play. He was understandably anxious to find out whether, in the circumstances, they would still be paid in full. Initially I wasn't exactly overjoyed at the thought of paying them to simply go home. However, when I found out from Brian that they had been waiting patiently all day and were really desperate to play, as they did not want to disappoint their many fans, I started to relent. It also appeared it was not just the danger of electrocution because of the driving rain that bothered them but the fact that they were experiencing technical problems with Mike Pinder's Melotron because of the weather. In the end I really couldn't see any grounds for withholding payment and agreed to pay them their fee. It was at this point, I found out later, that the Byrds turned the bad weather to their advantage by playing an acoustic set, which was so well received that it helped to establish their reputation in the UK as one of the truly great live bands of the seventies.

# CHAPTER 23

With a loud bang the door of the admin office burst open revealing an indescribably angry young man waving a large iron bar. How, I thought, could I be all on my own with over 130,000 kids outside and a dozen or more staff in the adjoining room? The boy advanced across the room, iron bar now poised and raised, ready to strike. Where was everyone? And what the hell had I done to provoke him? Scared stiff but determined not to show it, I tried to engage him in conversation. Nothing, not a word. It seemed he was only interested in braining me. As he brought the bar down I grabbed it with both hands and let out a loud yell for help. As I struggled with him, I was suddenly aware of running footsteps and two of our staff charged in. The cavalry had finally arrived. We never did find out his reasons for attacking me as he was totally and most comprehensively out of his skull. The nearest thing to an explanation was when he looked at me and muttered half to himself that I was the devil. I mean, I know promoters have a bad reputation but this really was ridiculous. While all this was going on someone, unbeknown to me, had sent for the police. When they arrived they asked if I wished to press charges and when I declined they very helpfully offered to drive him the couple of miles to Evercreech Junction, the temporary railway station British Rail had set up for the event. As the festival was now officially over I thought this was a good idea - anything to get him off site. Within thirty minutes he was back in our office. This time he had abandoned the violence and aggression and just sat staring malignantly at me, his eyes following my every move. Once again our two helpful policemen drove him to the Junction and this time they actually saw him onto a train. He still managed to beat them back to the office. More weird and crazy than ever, he prowled around the room like an avenging demon. This time the long-suffering police actually waited until the train, with him on board, pulled out of the station. It was, thank God, the last time we ever saw him.

At last it was all over. Although by now I was totally shattered, I decided I really had to tour the showground before grabbing some much-needed sleep. It was a pretty depressing sight that greeted me - litter everywhere, missing and damaged fences including most of the jumps used in the equestrian centre. Worst of all, about five hundred of the small tents had been stolen or vandalised. Inwardly wincing and mentally adding up the cost of the damage, I continued my inspection of what I was now referring to as the disaster area. By mid-morning I couldn't stay awake any longer and slowly and with great care drove back to our rented house.

# CHAPTER 24

Early next morning, just as we were finishing breakfast, a deputation from the Farmers Union arrived. They hadn't wasted any time in tracking us down and wanted to discuss the numerous claims for damage that had already been drawn up by their members. Still not fully recovered, we did not wish to be drawn into any arguments without first having the opportunity to view the damage for ourselves. In the circumstances, controlling my urge to tell them to go to hell we told them to contact our insurance company and take matters up with them. Worse was to come. On arriving at the showground Lord Darling had also wasted no time and had already given Mike Good an enormous list of things that would have to be put right. My initial reaction was to leave our insurance company to deal with this claim as well. However, when I found out after a telephone call to our brokers that we were liable for the first £100 of each and every claim and that the insurance company insisted on treating separately every damaged section of fence, every individual jump, or even a slightly damaged window or door on the same building, it became obvious that it would be much more economic if we could carry out this work ourselves.

At this point I really started to feel worried that the festival was going to show a fairly heavy loss. So I was really relieved when Lord Darling indicated that the Bath & West Society were prepared to let Mike and our team repair the damage rather than insisting on bringing in specialist firms who would have charged considerably more. However, my relief was short lived when I suddenly remembered the missing and damaged tents. Panic stricken, I rang our brokers again to be told that they were covered under a different policy- thank God! Late on Tuesday afternoon, leaving Mike to finish restoring the showground to its original condition, we left the site never to return.

On arriving home, we found a message waiting for us from Bill Thompson, asking us to call him at a hotel in Switzerland. When we finally got through to Bill he wanted to know if we would like to join him and his wife, Judy, for a few days in Europe. After the stress of the last few weeks we both thought it was a good idea to take a short break, especially as Ian had now recovered and could take care of things in the office. We set off the next morning with Steve Heffner, a young, American student friend, who had been staying with us and had worked very hard assisting with the festival. We met up with Bill later that evening and spent the next few days touring around Switzerland and France before ending up in Nuit St.George. It was here that we met up with Marty Balin from the Airplane, who, with his father, was also touring Europe. Along with Grace Slick, Marty shared the vocal duties in the band and turned out to be an intelligent and thoroughly engaging person. It was easy to see why he was the one out of this most charismatic group that attracted so many of the female fans. After spending a couple of nights in Paris, Wendy and I decided it was time we headed for home, especially as our car was starting to play up. We shouldn't have been experiencing problems with the car as it was less than eight months old, but it had been troublesome from the day we got it. It was a Lancia Fulvia 1.6 HF, basically a slightly detuned rally car. Great while it was running but horribly difficult to start and totally unreliable. On this occasion, as we were driving into Paris, the alternator had stopped charging, the brakes had developed an air lock in the hydraulics, coupled with a slow leak and to cap it off the exhaust had fallen off, just after the manifold pipe. Saying our goodbyes to Bill and Judy, we headed towards Calais hoping to arrive home before the battery finally ran flat. Just past Charles De Gaulle Airport, travelling in the outside lane of the Autoroute at around 65 to 70 MPH, the car I was just about to overtake appeared to edge towards me forcing me to move to the left and causing my left front wheel to drop into the shallow gutter than runs alongside this particular stretch of road. Without thinking and without slowing, I just gently pulled the steering wheel to the right. Suddenly I found myself snaking towards the car I had been about to overtake. I instinctively hit the brakes. Nothing happened. I frantically pumped the pedal and suddenly the front wheels locked up and in the middle of one of the straightest roads in France the car spun through 360 degrees and headed for the gently sloping verge, where it proceeded to destroy itself in a number of loops and rolls ending up on the roof with its wheels in the air. Not wearing a seat belt I had actually popped out of the drivers window landing miraculously on my feet.

Steve, who was so scared of travelling in cars that he made my equally nervous mother in-law seem like Nigel Mansell, was securely strapped into the passenger seat and was totally unscathed, but of Wendy, who had been travelling on the rear bench, there was no sign. Panic stricken, I started searching through the long grass. I finally found her about sixty or seventy feet from the car. I was certain she was dead. She was unconscious with a bad cut to her head and her eyes were open, wide and staring. Distraught and totally hysterical, I just did not know what to do, when suddenly she moved. By now a sizeable crowd had gathered, but no one offered to help. Eventually two policemen in a Citroen DS19 Estate Car arrived and communicating with them in my faltering French, I learnt that an ambulance was on its way. Fifteen minutes later and still no ambulance I could stand it no longer. Gesturing at the two policemen to lower the rear seat of their estate car, and against all medical procedures, we gently slid Wendy onto the metal floor. The hospital turned out to be less than five minutes drive away. The ambulance men who had still not arrived by the time we left were obviously having a coffee break. When we finally got to the hospital we were both placed on gurneys and left in a hallway while a doctor was found. Wendy, who had recovered consciousness but was still in a state of shock, caused a great deal of confusion amongst the very attentive nurses by saying to them 'Je suis mort'.

After an extensive examination and numerous X-rays, the Doctor explained to me that Wendy had broken her back splitting three vertebrae in the process. She had been extremely fortunate, he said, as the damaged area was only a couple of millimetres from her spinal cord and she could have been, so easily, paralysed. He went on to explain that she would be sent to a hospital in central Paris with better facilities for this type of injury and, in the meantime, we would be admitted to his hospital overnight. At around 3 am, I was woken up and taken to an operating theatre by three young doctors, who if they weren't actually stoned, were giving a pretty good impression. They had had obviously just seen the film of M.A.S.H., and the hip repartee, or at least what passed for it in French, was flowing fast and furious. The general idea was to clean and stitch up the rather large gash over my left eye. Whether they were successful in their endeavours is open to debate, as three or four weeks later, my brow started to swell and my doctor discovered grass seed germinating in the wound.

The next morning we were transferred by ambulance to the hospital in central Paris. On our arrival I couldn't believe my eyes. It was just like something out of Orwell's 'Down and Out in Paris'. Finding a phone box I called the British Embassy for advice and was told although there was a British Hospital in Paris, the American Hospital was by far the best. When I got through and explained our position, they told me, much to my relief, that they would send an ambulance within half an hour to collect us. The American Hospital was a revelation. Situated in Neuilly, a fashionable suburb of the city, it was every thing that I had hoped for - modern and extremely well staffed and equipped. To top it off, they allowed me to stay in the same room as Wendy without incurring additional charges.

If I was impressed with the hospital, it was nothing compared to the two doctors assigned to Wendy. One male, one female, both unbelievably good looking and sophisticated, their white house coats setting off to perfection their expensive sun tans, both of them simply oozing charm as only the French know how. There has to be a down side to every thing of course and in this case it was the physiotherapist who bullied and cajoled Wendy for the next 14 days. I am sure she acted on the instructions of the medical specialists. However, as she was the one who actually made Wendy get up and start to exercise just 48 hours after the accident, she was the one, of course, who took the brunt of Wendy's bitter resentment.

As soon as we were ensconced in our room, I made contact with Ian to explain what had happened and to arrange for him to fly over. I felt that we could discuss what needed to be done to finalise the festival and at the same time he could bring a few necessities such as a tape player and tapes. Before Ian could arrive, we had an unexpected visit from a representative of Tony Elliot's company, who unsurprisingly, I suppose, wanted to be paid for producing the programme. Unable to collect a cheque from Ian, as we had the chequebook with us, and not prepared to wait another couple of days until we could organise things, they decided to send someone over to Paris to hassle us. At least you couldn't accuse them of hypocrisy.

'I've come for the cheque' was the limit of their envoy's conversation. Not a word about the accident, not even a polite if meaningless enquiry about Wendy's condition.

Fortunately our next visitors were entirely different. David Odie and his wife, who were in Paris for a few days holiday, had heard about the accident and had called Ian to see where we were. David was one of my favourite agents - always in a good humour and someone with whom it was always fun to do business. Extremely astute, he also managed Rory Gallagher of Taste. After the trials of the last few days it was heartening to see some familiar, friendly faces.

At last, after what seemed an eternity, Wendy was considered well enough to travel. Ian had arranged seats on a BEA flight. However, as her specialist insisted on her travelling prone on a stretcher, they would only accept her if we purchased first class tickets. The journey to the airport in a small, private ambulance was a nightmare with the driver throwing the vehicle around like a sports car. Looking at each other we decided he was probably on commission from the hospital. I tried to tell him that we had already had the accident and could really do without another, but I don't think he understood or if he did, he certainly didn't slow down. On our arrival, we drove straight to the aircraft and Wendy was lifted up to the cabin on a hydraulic platform where she was carefully laid across three seats. There was another ambulance waiting for us when we arrived at Heathrow and this time it was, thank God, a less frantic journey home.

# CHAPTER 25

To quote my all time favourite rock musician Frank Zappa 'the torture never stops' and the first visitor we received the very next day was Caroline Coon of Release, all smiles and flowers. Unfortunately, the smile wilted somewhat when she learnt that apart from paying the previously agreed expenses we simply could not afford a generous donation to her charity, however worthy the cause.

The correspondence and notes we found waiting for us made depressing reading. Apart from scores of small invoices, there was a simply swingeing bill from the backstage catering company, which, I felt, could not possibly be correct. In addition, there was a letter from the tent hire firm explaining that the missing and vandalised items came to a total of around £15,000. The worst and probably cheekiest claim was from a local farmer who said, although fed their normal amount of food, his pigs failed to put on their normal weight gain because they didn't like the music. If only I had known about this beforehand I would have asked him if they had any particular favourites we could have played for them.

Our argument with the backstage caterers continued for some time before they eventually served us with a writ. We were delighted when at the pre-trial hearing the judge dismissed their case out of hand, citing the fact that in the catering business nothing was ever rounded up to the nearest pound as their invoices had been. The claim for the lost tents was every bit as traumatic but for an entirely different reason. Topliss and Harding, the loss adjusters, who had been appointed to deal with the claim, finally agreed a figure of £15,000 with the tent company, an amount the insurance company also considered acceptable. We all heaved a big sigh of relief until a few days later we received a phone call from Norman Hawes, the family friend who took care of our insurance.

'The cheque for the tents is being sent to you day,' he said, 'express clear it as soon as it arrives - the insurance company is going bust.'

Wendy followed his advice and took it to their bank in person. Two days later the newspapers carried banner headlines announcing the closure of the company. It appears ours was virtually the last cheque to be honoured.

On a more positive note, Gentle Ghost the company that had filmed the festival invited us to view the rushes. They were excellent, with very acceptable sound quality. Unfortunately, in an overdrive of artistic creativity, they had solarised several of the clips that we were shown. It was, of course, very trippy but personally I would have preferred to see the bands as they actually appeared on stage. The best of the lot, and definitely not solarised, was one featuring Dr John and his backing vocalists. They were playing Gris Gris, slow, moody and hypnotic, everyone totally relaxed. Halfway through the number, Dr John decided to bring the microphone nearer to his guitar. He moved it this way and that for perhaps half a chorus before finding a satisfactory position. Happy at last, he closed his eyes and promptly forgot to play the guitar. It was a wonder that they made it on stage at all considering they had to wait nearly 48 hours before they could appear. Add to this the fact that when their dressing-room trailer was finally moved our team found more syringes underneath than the local hospital would have used in a month, it really was a tribute to their endurance that they not only appeared, but also played an absolutely blinding set. Unfortunately this screening was the last time we had any contact with the filmmakers, rather annoying really as we still own the rights to the film and would very much like to know what happened to it.

It took another four or five weeks before we were finally finished with the festival but at last it was done. Whereas the '69 event had been easy and unexpectedly profitable, the 1970 festival had been a real ordeal. We had never worked so hard and for so long in our lives and for so little. We made less than a quarter of the previous year's event; about £5,000 and certainly not the half a million pounds so often quoted in the papers. And if you feel this is just promoter's bullshit perhaps the fact that we never attempted a multi-day event again should be sufficient proof. Anyway, we finally decided after a great deal of discussion that if, and it was a big if, we were ever to run a festival again, it would have to be a one-day event.

Slowly, sometimes painfully slowly and sometimes just painfully, Wendy continued her recovery and by the beginning of November she was pretty much back to normal and could walk again unaided. TWA as a sort of 'thank you' for the charter flight had given us two return tickets to Hong Kong with unlimited stopovers. As we had nothing planned for the immediate future, it seemed an ideal time after eighteen extremely fraught and hectic months to enjoy a long relaxing holiday. Before we left, because of the fabulous reception they had received at the festival, we started negotiations for a tour by the Byrds to start early in the New Year. So, leaving Ian to keep an eye on things, we departed. It was a great holiday - just the break we needed. It started in Athens and ended in Rome with a beach holiday in Thailand, a tour of Ceylon and a shopping spree in Hong Kong in between. We arrived home six weeks later, a couple of weeks before Christmas, fully rested and raring to go. While we were away we had decided to go ahead with another festival and had decided once again to attempt to stage a really good Folk Concert.

# CHAPTER 26

As soon as Christmas was over we started to look for a suitable site. It was while we were away that I had come up with what I thought, rather immodestly, was a brilliant idea to help us in our search - an advertisement in Farmers Weekly. Much to our surprise it actually worked and we received a dozen or so replies. Most were unsuitable but one we thought had possibilities. It was a small estate of around three hundred acres called Tupholme Manor Park, with a large empty Georgian house ideally positioned to act as the backstage and admin area. Its biggest drawback was the fact it was situated in Lincolnshire, not exactly near the population hotspots. However, in its favour was the fact that the estate was situated in beautiful and rather mystical country and had very few neighbours. Also, of course, Lincolnshire was renowned for its folk music. Summing up everything, we decided that the good points far outweighed the bad and decided to enter into negotiations.

The estate was owned by William Hardy who, in addition to Tupholme Manor Park, near by farmed a further 1500 acres. A really tough and capable character, he had not always been a farmer, having previously owned a company exporting second hand lorries, engines and tyres to countries in the Eastern European bloc. He was pleasant and businesslike to deal with and it didn't take long to work out an arrangement that was satisfactory to both sides and we were once again in business.

At the beginning of February we decided to have a party. Herb Cohen, who was in town with Frank Zappa for the filming of 200 Motels, was amongst those invited. Arriving late, it was immediately apparent that he was in a furious temper. Apparently Herb had just come from the Albert Hall where the booking manager, Miss Herrod, had told him that the Albert Hall management were cancelling the live performance of 200 Motels because they considered it obscene.

''What the fuck do they know?', he spluttered indignantly.

It seems he had tried to reason with them and had even offered at one point to delete the lyrics altogether and just play the music. However, it was no good. Their middle class, moralistic minds were made up.

'Where can I find a solicitor?' he asked me.

Always happy to oblige, I led him across the room and introduced him to an intelligent and easygoing friend named David Cooke, whom I had known since my teenage years. Herb wasted no time in explaining his grievance and finally in order to reinforce his argument pulled out of his pocket a rather crumpled copy of the contract. David sat and read the document for ten minutes or so and then gave his considered opinion.

'I am afraid it looks as if they are quite within their rights', he said and around four years and many thousands of pounds later David's spot assessment was unfortunately proved to be absolutely correct.

While we were busy putting the Lincoln Folk Festival together, I got a phone call from Peter Grant. Led Zeppelin wanted to get back to their roots and play some club dates and would really like to play the Pavilion Bath again. Could I set it up? Could I! The band by now was amongst the biggest in the world and the thought of putting them on in the Pavilion was both exciting and challenging. In keeping with the general philosophy of the tour, the deal was to be exactly the same as it had been on their last visit to the Pavilion way back in 1969 - £75 guarantee against 60% of the gross. As a special thank you to their fans the admission price was kept down to a most reasonable 10/- (50p). For the first time ever in Bath, in an attempt at fairness and to stop total chaos on the evening of the show, we sold tickets in advance.

As soon as I arrived at the Pavilion on the day of the show, Clive, one of the band's road crew, pounced on me. He claimed I owed him money for some service or other that he had performed at the previous year's Bath Festival. I didn't know what the hell he was talking about and told him so. An hour or so later, while Zep were sound checking, I found myself alone with Clive in their dressing room and he once again started hitting on me for money. This time I'd had enough and really let rip, telling him exactly where he could go, what he could do, and what I felt about him and his antecedents in general. When I finally stopped, I was surprised to receive a round of applause and loud cheers. Turning round I found Peter and the boys standing in the doorway with big grins on their faces. Thank God they thought it funny. Peter actually called it a virtuoso performance. Clive really needn't have bothered trying it on because within two years he was looking after Bad Company for Peter Grant and earning a great deal of money. Later that night it was Jimmy Page and the rest of Led Zeppelin that really put on a virtuoso performance to a packed and wildly enthusiastic audience. The boys it seemed had achieved their objective.

The bookings for Lincoln were coming along rather well. We had now received confirmation from a number of American artists including James Taylor, Tom Paxton and Buffy St Marie. These, along with a number of top English acts, meant the programme was looking quite promising. However, I wasn't altogether convinced. What we really needed to make quite sure of attracting a reasonable crowd was another headliner, I thought.

'Why not try the Byrds?' someone suggested.

'Great idea,' I said.

However, as we were just about to start a national tour with them I wasn't quite sure if they would be prepared to come back to England quite so soon, particularly as it would be only five or six weeks after the finish of the European leg of their tour. Still, there was no harm in asking.

When we first discussed the Byrds tour with CBS they were keen to give the support slot to a band called Trees, for whom they had high hopes. I was quite happy with this, as they were very competent and their music would compliment the Byrds nicely. Unfortunately for them, Clarence White had the hots for Rita Coolidge and we ended up with her instead. By a strange coincidence, several years later I discovered that a good friend of mine, David Costa was actually playing guitar with Trees at that time, although it was to be some years before we met. David is a brilliant graphic designer having produced artwork for George Harrison, Genesis, Elton John and Eric Clapton etc. - the list is endless. He was also responsible for some of our best festival poster designs, which is how we met.

When The Byrds flew in at the beginning of May - sorry I'll rephrase that - When the Byrds finally arrived; they brought with them their agent, whom, for the sake of the narrative, I shall call Bob. Anyone less like the members of the Byrds was hard to imagine. Thin, quick talking and neurotic he was almost a caricature of a New York agent. As soon as he had booked into his hotel he informed me that he intended to accompany his 'boys' throughout the entire tour and would require a secretary. Hastily ringing around the various secretarial agencies, we managed to arrange interviews for the next day. After seeing four or five girls, Bob finally found one that was suitable. I had already heard him mention that the young lady would have to accompany him on the tour. However, I couldn't believe it when, with a perfectly straight face, he went on to explain that due to the tours limited budget she would also have to share a room with him. Expecting ructions I got ready to take shelter underneath my desk and was totally dumfounded when, without a moment's hesitation, she agreed.

The tour kicked off at the Colston Hall Bristol on the 3rd of May and was a great success, every date selling out well in advance, including the last date at the Albert Hall, London. The only small glitch on an other wise perfect tour was that, at each show, The Byrds' tour manager, Jimmy Seiter would stand on stage next to Gene, beating out the time on a cymbal with a borrowed drumstick. This used to send Gene wild but being an incredibly nice guy he didn't say a word until finally, towards the end of the tour, he snapped and, handing Jimmy a tambourine, he invited him to go and shake it elsewhere. The final bonus as far as we were concerned was that the band agreed to play Lincoln.

# CHAPTER 27

The 1971 Lincoln Folk Festival was a pleasure to set up. The local authorities, especially the police, were most co-operative and the local people charming. The only major problem was British Rail. The festival site was some seven or eight miles from Lincoln and I thought it would make things easier for our patrons if B.R could arrange for trains to stop at Woodhall Spa, a fairly easy walk from the site, rather than bringing them in by coach from Lincoln station. Although they had arranged something similar at Evercreech Junction for the last Bath Festival, this time they were being singularly unhelpful.

After my last abortive conversation with the Passenger Services Manager Northern Area, I was sitting at my desk quietly fuming about the stupidity and general lack of co-operation shown by BR when Ian handed me a phone.

'It's Richard Marsh,' he said with a grin.

At this time Richard Marsh, later to become Lord Marsh, was the Chairman of British Rail. Ian was full of these little tricks and I never actually found out how he got me put through. However, always the opportunist, and without any real hope of success, I explained my problem.

'Err' he said a little diffidently, 'I am not actually responsible for the day to day running of the railways. I just sort of help nudge it in the right direction. You really should speak to one of the operations managers.'

With that, I was back to square one. In the end, of course, we used coaches.

We were more successful with Securicor, who because it was a Folk Festival, as opposed to a pop festival, agreed to provide overall security for the event. This was probably the only time in the company's history that they agreed to such a thing, which was a pity, because they did a fabulous job. I have fond memories of several of their uniformed staff using flying rugby tackles to catch gatecrashers who had just climbed over the fences. Despite this, their men were really not at all heavy handed and got on well with the crowd. It was just reassuring, for once, to feel that you had people totally on your side, particularly as this time we needed every penny we could take. It was our own fault entirely. After the difficulties we experienced running the previous year's Bath festival and, more especially, after the sensationalised publicity generated by the Isle of Wight festival, we deliberately kept a low profile. No full page adds in the music papers and no national P.R. This way we hoped to run the perfect, non-controversial event. Unfortunately, it backfired in the biggest possible way. Just three weeks before the event we had sold less than 5,000 tickets. Looking at the projected ticket sales leading up to the event, we realised if we didn't change our tactics we were going to loose our shirts. We immediately started placing full-page advertisements in the music papers and, as an act of desperation, placed a number of TV advertisements with Anglia Television. Miraculously, our new campaign started to work and ticket sales started to pick up dramatically, culminating in a huge walk up on the day of the concert. Whilst this was good news, it still left us with serious problems. Deposits for the groups were due two weeks before the event and, of course, if these where not received on time rumours that the event was not going ahead would start to spread like wild fire - something we obviously wanted to avoid at all costs.

Whilst we actually had enough income to cover the deposits, the money still had to be transferred from our various ticket agents scattered around the country. We sent the cheque for the deposits anyway, thinking we had three days before it would clear, time enough to transfer all the funds. Unfortunately, The Harold Davison Agency express cleared it. The very next day we received a phone call from Tom Gilbert, our bank manager, to say the cheque was there but not the funds to meet it. Instant panic! What the hell were we going to do? Wendy tried to explain that the money was on its way. However, Tom didn't seem inclined to phone over fifty ticket agents for confirmation.

After a minute's contemplation and, for us, nervous waiting, he finally said,

'If you give me your word that you will come in some time and sign a personal guarantee I'll let it through straight away.'

They don't make bank managers like that anymore!

After this little drama it was a relief to actually get on site and check on what progress was being made. Mike Good, after the excellent job he had carried out for us the previous year, was once again our site foreman. Although the event was considerably smaller than the Bath Festival, there was still plenty to do. We certainly missed the flushing loos of the Show Ground and, instead, had to rely on a number of Portaloo mobile toilets that we rented and old fashion wooden crappers that Mike and his crew manufactured on site. This time there was no attractive farmhouse to rent. Instead we stayed at a hotel in Lincoln some seven miles from Tupholme Manor Park. We normally worked on site until about ten in the evening and finding somewhere to have supper that was open that late in Lincolnshire in 1971 was always something of a problem. On the evening before the concert we were tired and hungry, having worked non-stop all day and as we were going to be up all night, at about eleven pm, decided to find somewhere to eat. One of the guys working on site suggested we try Bardney, a village about five miles away that had a fish and chip shop that stayed open reasonably late.

We set off with Ian at a scorching pace. It didn't take long to get there. Bardney, when we arrived, was larger than we thought. We decided to ask the way but to the fish and chip shop. However, at that time of night, Bardney was closed - not one person was to be seen. Suddenly, like a vision, I saw two people bathed in a tiny pool of light, sitting on the pavement opposite a zebra crossing, backs against the door of a shop and they were eating fish and chips. Braking hard, Ian, who must have been as hungry as we were, was out of the car almost before it had stopped. He was rather longer coming back. When he did, he explained that the couple eating fish and chips had turned out to be Linda Lewis and her record producer boyfriend. At that time, Linda was having a fair amount of chart success and had obviously come up to watch the festival. By a strange coincidence, the following week we shared a double page review of the concert in Melody Maker with an interview given by Linda. And oh yes, we found the fish and chip shop and it was still open.

# CHAPTER 28

The day of the festival dawned with every promise of good weather. We had learnt a lot from the second Bath Festival and our general organisation was much improved. Of course, it helped that we were dealing with a far smaller crowd and, of course, a far smaller area. The reduced numbers attending also ensured that the roads were less congested, making it easy for the bands to arrive on time. However, the big advantage as far as I personally was concerned, was the fact that my office was actually part of the backstage area. Now I could really keep a close eye on all aspects of the festival.

Charlie Watkins was once again employed to look after the sound but this time we had engaged a very experienced stage manager, Hugh Price, to make sure everything ran as smoothly as possible. Hugh was a very large and fit young man who, probably because of his size, commanded instant respect. Rather unsubtly, I used to refer to him as Huge Price. However, never, of course, to his face. He did an outstanding job and kept the programme running pretty much to time throughout a long day, coping with the odd artistic temperament superbly.

By mid morning I was beginning to feel that my decision to run a folk festival was fully justified. Things were running smoothly - the weather was pretty good and we were selling a lot of tickets. Better still, in Tupholme Manor, I was back in the centre of things and I really started to enjoy myself. We used the main entrance hall as a general hospitality area and every one seemed to hang out there at some time or other. Happily for me, it was right next door to my office and although it could get somewhat crowded, it gave me the opportunity to talk to the press, assorted liggers and, of course, the artists, all of whom, thank God, seemed to be having a good time. I remember being particularly impressed by Buffy St Marie. Small, dark girls were just my thing and she was a real charmer. Leading up from the hall was the main staircase that led to the various dressing rooms. Walking up these stairs and along the corridors was like a journey through musical styles. Everywhere you went you could hear people rehearsing or simply warming up. We had given Sonny Terry and Brownie McGhee a large room on the second floor. As I was a very big fan and had been for many years, I was in and out of their dressing room all day. I must say there didn't seem to be a moment when they were not performing for, or with, their fellow musicians.

'Just keep the whisky coming,' they said and I was more than happy to oblige.

This fabulous music, combined with the faded elegance of the eighteen-century building, helped to create the most magical backstage atmosphere of any event I ever promoted.

I realise that there are number of cruel, unthinking people in the world. However, I never expected to find them back stage at Lincoln. From my office window I had a commanding view of the area immediately in front of the house. As it was fenced and guarded, it was very much an extension of the backstage area and contained loads of invited guests avoiding the crush of the house. Glancing out, I noticed Tim Hardin staggering and lurching around, totally out of his head and clearly in need of help. With all the debris and old marble statues and stone urns that were lying on the ground, it appeared that he was in danger of hurting himself quite badly. Expecting a dozen or so people to rush to his aid, I was amazed when people started to laugh at him, pointing and jeering. Before I could rush out and help, someone from his management company finally arrived and led him away. Tim was a fine artist and a brilliant songwriter and certainly deserved better than that, I thought. How could people show so little compassion?

One of the big surprises of the festival, well to me any way, was Dion. To be very honest, I had only put him on the bill as a favour to Herb Cohen, who had explained that he was no longer the drug addicted rock 'n' roller he had been with the Belmonts, but a mature and responsible singer songwriter. He was right. Dion still had a great voice and played excellent guitar. I thought some of his material was a little weak - nevertheless he was a great revelation.

I must say I was a little taken aback by Tom Paxton's appearance when he arrived. I was standing at the top of the rather grand flight of steps that led up to the front door when a large chauffeur driven car pulled up and out leapt what I thought was some rather self important record company executive. He was wearing a formal grey suit and carrying a briefcase. Of the obligatory long hair, there was no sign.

'Who the hell is that?' I asked Ian who happened to be standing close by.

I really thought we had a gatecrasher. I also happened to be around when Tom emerged from his dressing room to go on stage. However this time he was one of the boys wearing a football shirt, blue jeans and a saucy little cap on top of his shoulder length hair. I was more than a little disillusioned. Until then I had never thought of folk singing as a business. It didn't stop him getting a rapturous reception, though.

By now, The Byrds were old friends - as laid back and amiable as ever. Nevertheless, they still managed to give me kittens when they got on stage. After the success of their acoustic at the Bath Festival, I had thought it would be good if they could recreate the same magic at Lincoln. However, Roger McGuin, canny as ever, realised that after all the laid back music earlier in the day, an electric set would make a bigger impact. I needn't have worried. Opening with 'So You Wanna Be a Rock 'n' Roll Star', they brought everyone to their feet. The audience were fantastic with, it seemed, very eclectic musical tastes - just the sort of people I hoped I would attract when I put the programme together. Keeping to their agreement, the Byrds alternated between acoustic and amplified guitars and, in my opinion, stole the show. After the Byrds and James Taylor it was the turn of Buffy St Marie. By now it was getting dark and, of course, colder. Some of the audience decided that they would rather be warm than enjoy the rather primitive facilities that we had provided and promptly set fire to the loos. The effect was dramatic - almost as if it had been stage-managed. Intensified by the leaping flames, Buffy's strong vibrato and dramatic persona made an absolutely unforgettable impression. Dave Swarbrick and Martin Carthy brought the festival to a close with some amazing reels and jigs. Suddenly it was all over, leaving me as fresh as if I had been attending the event rather than organising it and quite convinced that a one-day concert was the way to go.

By mid-day on the Sunday most people had departed except for fifty or sixty kids that we employed to help with the clearing up. In fact, by Monday afternoon, Mike Goode and his merry men, combined with Bill Hardy the landowner and his farm hands, had already made huge inroads into restoring the estate to its original condition. We even had time for a gossip and, talking to Ian, I discovered I had missed seeing Brit Eckland backstage. Very remiss of me - I must have been busier than I realised.

Before we returned home late on Monday afternoon, I called the editor of the Melody Maker. After the terrible slagging off they gave us for the Bath Festival, I wanted to see what sort of review Lincoln would receive. Luckily the two journalists he had sent along to review the concert had really enjoyed the music and better still, they liked the park and the atmosphere it created and had no complaints about the actual organisation of the event. In fact, when the review came out at the end of the week, it could not have been better if I had written it myself.

On our way home Wendy and I had a disagreement. Neither of us can remember what it was about. It was nothing serious - just the sort of pathetic bickering that most married couples indulge in from time to time. Now I can bicker with the best of them and still drive a car. However, not it seems bicker and watch the petrol gauge at the same time. We ran out of petrol just outside of Welwyn. It caught me totally unawares on a small stretch of dual carriage-way and I had no option but to park rather prominently on a nice grassy roundabout. Still bickering, we set off to find a garage. It wasn't until we returned to the car clutching a full can of petrol that we realised that we had left all the Securicor cash boxes containing around £30,000 neatly piled up

The Lincoln Festival -1971 Tupholme Manor, stage and part of the audience.

127

on the back seat and had forgotten to lock the doors. Which, of course, started us off bickering, all over again.

By the time we finally finished working out the accounts, we were surprised to find we had made a profit nearly three times larger than in 1970 for about an eighth of the outlay and a lot less work and hassle. I was convinced that this was the way forward and we were keen to repeat the festival the following year. However, Bill Hardy had other ideas and immediately and rather greedily, I thought, invited me to run another festival at Tupholme Manor Park later that summer. When I tried to explain this was just not feasible, he wouldn't take no for an answer and was so insistent that he became known in the office as 'Bill the Foolhardy'.

Eventually he entered into negotiations with a company, formed by Lord Harlech and the film actor Stanley Baker and although they also failed to run an event later that summer, they did out bid me for the site the following year, which rather pissed me off. They were the worst sort of amateurs - rich ones! The next year they ran an event they called the Great Western Express. Running a festival over four days at the end of May was asking for trouble and they got it in the shape of an injunction and bad weather. After all the good press our rather laid back folk festival had received, they probably misjudged the reaction of the local authorities, who I feel must have panicked at the dreaded words 'pop festival'. Whatever the reasons, the upshot was the courts upheld the injunction and the festival went ahead under fairly stringent conditions that could have seen Lord Harlech and Stanley Baker going to jail if the festival was deemed to have caused a nuisance. Looking back at old advertisements, it really wasn't such a bad programme. With acts such as The Beach Boys, Joe Cocker, Genesis, the Faces with Rod Stuart, Status Quo, Sly and the Family Stone, Humble Pie, Sha Na Na, and Roxy Music, they should have really drawn more people than they did. Whatever the outcome, and I believe the promoters lost quite a lot of money, we could never use Tupholme Manor Park again and it was once again back to the Farmers Weekly and a new search for a site.

# CHAPTER 29

A couple of weeks after our Lincoln Festival, I received a phone call from Bill Thompson. Bill had very skilfully negotiated a deal with the Airplane's record company, RCA, for them to fund an independent label that would give the band greater control over their own affairs. It also allowed them to sign and record any artists that they felt warranted their encouragement. They called the label Grunt Records and ironically, in view of my cynical opinion of record companies, asked us to be their Grunt Records European representatives. It took me all of two seconds to agree. If I had thought about it a little longer then perhaps I wouldn't have been quite so enthusiastic. In addition to large amounts of administrative work, it meant regular meetings with RCA UK and although I came into contact with many thoroughly pleasant individuals, it only served to confirm my view that record company executives were, in the main, philistines, only interested in preserving their position within the company and with no great love of music or insight into the workings of a creative musician's mind. It was at times extremely hard work and very, very frustrating but it was an extremely interesting experience.

A few weeks later we flew out to San Francisco for the Grunt inauguration party. Bill had invited us to stay with him and Judy at their house in Mill Valley and was waiting for us at the airport. The party was being held a couple of days after our arrival in an old ballroom situated on the coast, just south of the city. We certainly needed a couple of days to recover from jet lag. However, more importantly, Wendy required this extra time just to get ready. Even then, it was a close run thing. She had taken the party as an excuse for a shopping spree and was all prepared to have fun. When we finally arrived at the party it was everything you would have expected from the Airplane and San Francisco at that time. Weird lighting, oil slide projection, waiters and waitresses on roller skates with long hair flying, zipping up and down the hall delivering drinks and food, plus of course the distinctive aroma of patchouli oil and dope pervading every corner of the room. Great though it was, I couldn't help feeling that San Francisco and all it stood for was becoming slightly un-hip. Amongst all the freaks, the record company people from New York seemed uncomfortable and decidedly out of place. At last the Airplane took to the stage. This was what I had really been looking forward to - the opportunity to see this great group in a small hall. As they finished their first number I was really impressed, although I was quite surprised at the lack of interest shown by the rest of the audience. At the end of the second number, there was still a noticeable lack of enthusiasm and after the third, some of the crowd actually started to heckle the band. I just couldn't believe it. These were friends, relatives and local Airplane freaks. Grace couldn't believe it either. She was the American equivalent of gob smacked. With a slightly bewildered look on her face, she put everything she had into the next couple of numbers until at the end of their set, the band had won everyone over and left the stage to tumultuous applause. I realised then that what set them apart from other bands was not just their musical ability, but their general awareness and determination to succeed, even at what was, to all intents and purposes, a family gathering.

For the rest of our stay we alternated between business meetings, where we met the people working on the Grunt project, and enjoying ourselves sightseeing in San Francisco. I particularly enjoyed Chinatown as I have a great liking for Chinese food and there were a huge number of terrific restaurants to choose from. I was also impressed with the Airplane house on Fulton St. It was, as you can imagine, extremely large, at one time accommodating the entire group. Now it was used as the Airplane offices. It had survived the famous earthquake of 1906 and once, reputedly played host to the great Carouso, the legendary opera singer. However, the most striking feature was the large Tiffany stained glass window situated on the first floor landing. Whilst we were there, Bill told us about an incident that had happened the previous week. He had received a phone call from a garage in Los Angeles asking him if he would confirm that it was in order for them to supply Jorma Kaukonen with a rather expensive car. It appeared he had done this on a previous occasion and Bill was just about to confirm the order and arrange payment when Jorma walked into the office. It turned out that the young man trying to order the car had severe psychiatric disorders and really believed he was Jorma. A couple of days later he turned up at the Airplane house demanding to be allowed in. According to Bill, it took them the best part of two days before they could convince him he wasn't Jorma and get him to leave.

Bill, like so many Americans, was very sociable and made sure we met all the various band members, as well as the road crew and loads of friends. He also took me along to several recording sessions, where, if my memory is correct, the Airplane were putting the finishing touches to 'Bark', their first album to be released on Grunt Records. On our second visit, we left the studio around 5.00 a.m. in bright morning sunshine. The roads at that time of day were comparatively deserted and as we swung down hill onto the Golden Gate Bridge, I started to pick up signs of distress from the engine. Looking at the speedometer, I saw we were cruising at a comfortable 55 m.p.h. as we had been for several miles. It wasn't until I checked the rev counter and saw that the needle was in the red that I realised the car was still in second gear. Bill was quite happily chatting away, very relaxed - a little too relaxed, I thought. It was then that I made a fundamental error of judgement. I pointed out that he still had three more gears to go and invited him to try third. Wham! And the peppy little BMW shot off like the proverbial scalded cat and was soon exceeding 75 m.p.h. Luckily, as the end of the bridge approached, Bill seemed to regain his concentration and the rest of the journey turned out to be pretty uneventful.

# CHAPTER 30

Back in England, it wasn't long before we were once more in the thick of it. Herb Cohen had asked us to book a European and UK tour for Frank Zappa, starting in November. We had never arranged anything this comprehensive before and it meant that we had a lot to learn about carnets, border procedures, what countries banned lorries travelling on a Sunday etc and not least, the most competent and trustworthy promoters in each country. Herb, who was vastly experienced in these matters, gave us a lot of advice. Nevertheless, it was a steep learning curve.

The tour kicked off in Stockholm on November 19$^{th}$. Being pretty conscientious, I would normally have travelled out with the band to make sure there where no foul-ups. This time, for some reason, I didn't. It could have been quite simply Herb telling me it wasn't necessary, or it could have been the fact that I don't like very cold weather. Whatever the reason, I was in bed comfortable and warm when one of the Zappa road crew phoned complaining bitterly about the two articulated trucks we had rented on their behalf. Overnight, the brakes of both trucks had frozen and a cab window had fallen out leaving the drivers very cold and extremely irritable.

'We asked you to instruct the hire company to prepare them for sub zero temperatures. Why the fuck didn't you?' one of the road crew asked me.

In fact, we had. However, the hire company had forgotten to act on our request. They were sufficiently contrite to arrange for a Swedish depot to carry out the necessary work. After that, things started to settle down until a few days later when I received a phone call from Dick Barber, the tour manager. Dick was a great guy, very laid back, as you would expect from someone who was happy to play the part of an industrial vacuum cleaner in the film of 200 Motels. So when he said in a matter of fact way there was a problem I wasn't exactly expecting to hear that the Montreux Casino had burnt to the ground. According to Dick, one of the audience who had been sitting in the balcony had apparently let off a firework while Frank and the band were on stage and the fire had spread like, well, wildfire. It was a miracle that no one was killed or seriously injured.

Frank, it appears, had been his normal cool self, conducting the evacuation from the stage until he too was forced by the dense smoke to leave the hall. Several of the road crew, attempting to salvage what they could of the equipment, had their escape route cut off and had to leave through a window, one cutting himself quite badly in the process. Talk about going out in a blaze of glory! The final outcome was that the equipment, with the exception of a couple of instruments and a cowbell (probably borrowed the day before from some Swiss cow) had been totally and most comprehensively destroyed. It was ironic that for the first time ever Frank and the band had decided to take out insurance against such an eventuality, once again courtesy of Norman Hawes, who was by now beginning to think that any dealings he had to do with us and music were jinxed.

Wendy and I were quite convinced this was the end of the tour, so we were rather surprised when Herb called to say that Frank wanted to play the UK dates and gave us a great long list of equipment that we would have to hire. By the time the band arrived in London we had everything together including a rehearsal room. There were only a couple of days left before the first of four sold out Rainbow Theatre gigs, just time for some pretty hectic rehearsals.

Frank was particularly keen to play the Rainbow, possibly because, at that time, it was the new, trendy, London venue or perhaps because the whole idea to turn this old cinema into a rock venue had been conceived by John Morris an American who also managed it. At that time, the Rainbow was not available for hire as John insisted on promoting all the artists himself, so we were effectively agents for the London shows.

A sound check had been arranged for the afternoon before the first show and Herb and I went along just in case there were any more problems. The Rainbow, formerly the Astoria, Finsbury Park was probably one of the finest example of 1930's cinema architecture in the country - a real peoples' palace, all over the top tiling and elaborate metal work. Unless you are directly involved in a sound check they are normally stullifyingly boring so I spent sometime wandering around admiring all the features of this amazing building. It wasn't until I was standing in the main balcony that I noticed the orchestra pit, situated just in front of the stage. It looked like some medieval moat only without the water. Hurrying down to the stalls for a closer inspection, I was appalled to see close up it was even more daunting. It must have been eight to ten feet wide and just as deep with what looked like a bare concrete floor. Appalled, I went in search of a representative from the Rainbow management who, when I finally found one, assured me that mattresses had already been ordered and would be in place before the first performance.

As I have already mentioned, I am a complete Zappa freak and as I wasn't directly involved in the running of the show, I decided to watch from the main balcony. It was a great performance from what I still think was the best of Frank's many bands. Aynsley Dunbar, the British drummer whom I had used so many times in the past with both Retaliation and Blue Whale, had stepped up to a new level and was at that time, in my opinion, one of the five best rock drummers in the world - truly awesome. Although I know not everyone agrees, I also felt Mark Volman, the ever so slightly overweight, ex member of The Turtles made a noticeable contribution, with his subtle humour and good taste. Oh My God what am I saying, he was gross!

It was just as the band finished their last number and Frank was actually in the process of removing his guitar that I noticed a man running towards the stage from the central aisle in the stalls. Standing helpless, in stunned amazement, I watched as he cleared the orchestra pit and in a single, effort-less, bound landed on stage. Without a moment's hesitation, he spun around in a graceful pirouette, which put him in an ideal position to hit Frank in the small of his back with the flat open palms of his hands. The effect was dev-astating. Frank was lifted off his feet, flying like some huge, ungainly bird straight into the orchestra pit. Continuing his pirouettes, the assailant leapt once more across the orchestra pit and disappeared into the audience. Not waiting to see anything else I shot down the back stairs straight onto the stage.

Herb was already there peering apprehensively into the pit. Frank was lying on the concrete floor unconscious, his neck bent at an ominous angle. There was no sign of the much-promised mattresses. Checking with Herb that an ambulance was on its way, I went to see how the band was coping. However, before I could walk the short distance to where they were standing, huddled together at the back of the stage, the two quick thinking stewards who had grabbed the attacker as he tried to leave the theatre, suddenly appeared with him as if to display their prize trophy. They were, I discovered later, actually on their way to the manager's office where they planned to hold him until the police arrived. It was a monumental error of judgement. Herb, as if by some sixth sense, suddenly arrived next to me.

'Is he the fucking son of a bitch that did this? I'll kill the bastard,' he snarled.

I had no doubt he meant it and even less doubt that he was capable of such an act. Drawing his fist back, he prepared to launch his attack. Quickly looking around for assistance, I realised I was on my own. There was only a split second for me to do something. Yelling, 'Don't do it Herb' at the top of my voice I did the only thing I could and grabbed his arm with both hands.

The stewards, reacting to my screams, pulled Trevor Howell, the attacker, out of the way and with me still desperately hanging onto his arms, Herb missed his target altogether and unable to stop, punched the back wall, his fist connecting with a sickening crunch. As the back wall was at least ten to fifteen feet further down stage, you can imagine the sort of force involved. While Herb was attending to his injured hand, I finally caught up with the band. After the additional drama they had just witnessed, they were in a worst state of nerves than ever. However, as soon as it became clear that Frank was not going to die, their recovery was remarkable. Mark and Howard in particular took full advantage of the situation to comfort Herb's extremely glamorous wife Suzanne, cuddling and mauling her in a way that would have got their faces slapped if she hadn't been so distraught.

Their euphoria didn't last long as it suddenly dawned on them that they were out of work. It was obvious, even at that stage, that Frank's injuries were serious enough to keep him from playing for some considerable time and it was right here on the stage of the Rainbow Theatre that I think the seeds of a great new group 'The Florescent Leech and Eddie' led by Mark and Howard, were sown.

Frank was taken to the Royal Free Hospital, which in 1971 was still situated in the Holloway Road. It was housed in a decrepit Victorian building, which did nothing to raise the expectations of the medical care available inside. When we arrived we went straight to the emergency department only to find, as it was Friday evening, the staff were rushed off their feet - in fact it was just like Bedlam. Leaving Wendy, Suzie and myself in the waiting room, Herb went to find Frank. Before we could find somewhere to sit, the entrance doors were thrown open dramatically and like something out of a really bad TV sitcom, a young man was dragged into the room by two friends.

'Oh my balls,' he was shouting at the top of his voice over and over again, whilst clutching his testicles with both hands. They were obviously regulars as they dispensed entirely with the formalities at reception and instead dragged him straight to the examination room where they swung him like a sack of potatoes up onto a bed. I could still hear him complaining about the state of his goolies some thirty or forty minutes later.

I could see from Herb's face, when he returned some time later, that he was angry. It appeared that the doctor attending Frank was supercilious and patronising, in a way that only the English at their worst can be and hadn't been exactly helpful. Herb asked me to speak to him as he thought there might be a little more rapport between two Englishmen. There wasn't. The doctor was just as rude to me. Even so, he did unbend sufficiently to tell me that so far they had discovered that Frank's injuries comprised a crushed larynx, a fractured rib, a fractured leg, a paralysed arm and head injuries and although they were short of beds they would keep him in overnight for observation. Wow, I thought, the man's a saint. The following morning Herb arranged for Frank to be transferred to The London Clinic!

The next day, around lunchtime, Wendy and I were sitting in the kitchen having just finished lunch, still trying to come to terms with the events of the previous evening, when the phone rang. Answering it, Wendy discovered it was Tony Dodds, who had been the driver of the coach transporting the Zappa band around Europe. Sounding unusually subdued, he asked her if she would send any money we still owed him to his wife as he was going away.

'Anywhere nice?' Wendy asked him cheerfully.

'Not really,' he said rather evasively, ' I'm just going away and never coming back.'

By now a little worried, she asked him exactly what he meant and after a great deal of tactful persuasion, he finally told her that on arriving home he found a letter from his wife explaining that she was leaving him for another man. He was totally devastated, as he had absolutely no idea she had been having an affair. Over the next few days he tried to find her to see if he could persuade her to return, but without success. Now all he wanted to do was end it all. The longer he talked to Wendy the more slurred his speech became until he finally admitted that he had already taken a large number of pills. What they were he wouldn't say, nor, more importantly would he give her his address. We had no idea where he lived, apart from the fact it was somewhere in South London. I decided the only thing to do was phone his employers and obtain the address from them. Not wanting at this stage to get Tony into trouble with his employers, I made up what I thought was a good reason for wanting his address. Unfortunately, it wasn't good enough.

'Sorry we do not give out personal information.' was the rather surly reply.

So I had no option but to tell them the truth. Armed with the address, we called the police who were surprisingly sympathetic and within minutes sent a car round. When they arrived, we found out later, they had to break the door down as Tony had taken the precaution of nailing the front door and all the windows shut. He was unconscious when they found him, but soon responded once he was taken to hospital and his stomach was pumped. Whether he was grateful for our prompt action we had no means of telling, as we never heard from him again.

Later that afternoon, as we drove over to the London Clinic to visit Frank, we asked ourselves a number of agonising questions about the last two or three weeks. Where any of the problems directly our fault? Was there anything we could have done to prevent such awful things happening? Would Frank ever work with us again? In fact, would any one work with us again? Maybe it was my eternal optimism that encouraged me to carry on. But if I had known then what the future held for us over the next ten years, I think I would have gone out and got myself a proper job.

# PART 2

# THERE MUST BE A BETTER WAY

# Knebworth House

*Home of the Lytton family since 1492*

# CHAPTER 31

'Fuck it. I'm going home.'

Getting into the car, I was half way to Chippenham before I started to calm down. Even then it took another couple of miles driving at breakneck speed before Wendy finally convinced me that I was doing the wrong thing.

'The Who aren't going to give a damn that you've thrown a tantrum,' she said, 'You're the one who is going to look stupid'.

Still seething with what I saw as self justified outrage; I reluctantly turned the car round and headed back towards Bath. It should have been a great day. It was certainly one to which I had been looking forward. After several years of enormous success, The Who, like Led Zeppelin a few months earlier, had decided to return to their roots and play some club dates and The Pavilion, Bath, scene of many of their earlier triumphs had been included in the tour. Arriving really early on the day of the show to make sure that the load-in went smoothly, I was appalled to see that the road crew had already set up banks of speakers, lights and mixing desks on the floor of the hall. Finding the head roadie, I had tried to explain as reasonably as possible that the positioning of the equipment was in breach of safety regulations. It was also cutting down the capacity of the hall by at least twenty five percent, an important point I thought, as The Who were being paid a very large percentage of the gross take. It was a total waste of time, rather like talking to an extremely aggressive brick wall and as the argument progressed, I found myself surrounded by the rest of the roadies who made it clear, in their typically friendly fashion, that they would rather die than move one piece of equipment. I guess I should have expected this from a road crew that had grown used to setting up for monster gigs in giant venues. It was at this point that I had split. Ironically, when I arrived back the Hall Manager had pointed out the errors of their ways and the whole problem had been resolved. His pronouncement 'clear up or clear out' had, it seemed, won them over.

Later that evening, to a packed and highly appreciative audience, The Who literally tore the place apart ending their show, as so often happened at this time, with the destruction of guitars, amps and a final explosion of drums and cymbals. Sadly, it was to be our very last club date.

# CHAPTER 32

Our first major tour of 1972 was with Captain Beefheart and his Magic Band. How we initially got involved with them I just cannot remember. Frank Zappa and Captain Beefheart, aka Don Van Vliet, had been friends from their school days so it was probably through a recommendation from Herb Cohen. Whatever the reason, we ended up with a 15-date tour, starting in Birmingham and ending up in Paris. On the first night of the tour I got a taste of what to expect when the beautifully gift wrapped present that a fan had asked me to give Don turned out to contain some magic mushrooms and a dead rat!

The following evening we played the first of two sold out nights at the Albert Hall. It was here that I first found out that Don could at times be a little difficult. We had employed a well-respected and thoroughly competent sound company to provide the PA system throughout the tour and all had seemed well on the first night. It was only when he saw the size of the hall and the large stage area that he started to get paranoid about monitors. It seemed at times during the sound check that there was more power going through the monitors than into the main speakers. It was just as bad during the show. Don, clearly unhappy with the sound, managed to get through three or four microphones during the course of the evening, at one point dropping one deliberately on the floor while looking at the guys at the mixing desk, saying slyly 'Well did you see that?' The audience, thank God, seemed blissfully unaware of these little dramas and gave him a fantastic reception.

After the show, as I was escorting him and his wife Jan to their car, I saw his better side. Emerging from the stage door I was amazed to see the size of the crowd waiting for autographs. I immediately regretted not bringing any stewards. However, as every one was well behaved and Don, it seemed, was happy to sign anything and everything placed in front of him, I relaxed. After what seemed forever, I at last got him into the car. Just as they were finally moving off, a rather strange looking young guy who had been hanging around all evening thrust his head into Don's open window, forcing the limo to stop. By now I was even more anxious to get the pair of them away, as even Don was starting to look a little impatient. I gave the fan a couple of minutes and then started to explain that it was time for Don to go. The boy's reaction was as swift as it was unexpected. Swinging away from the car, he launched an all out attack on me. Don, who was perhaps more used to the peculiarities of his rather more idiosyncratic fans, was out of the car before I had even hit the ground. His intervention and curt instruction 'Leave him alone. He's a friend of mine.' certainly saved my hide.

It really wasn't my evening as later, when I attempted to rejoin Wendy and some friends who had gone on ahead to one of our favourite Indian restaurants, I was greeted at the door by the manager who explained they were now closed and handed me my supper neatly packed in a large bag.

A couple of days later the tour played the De Mountfort Hall, Leicester, which like all the UK venues on the tour, was a complete sell out. On this particular evening the band were really delivering and the audience was enjoying every minute, whooping and hollering for more at the end of every number, so much so that Don sent one of the hall stewards to fetch me.

'I think there's going to be a riot' he explained, looking apprehensively at the audience 'You look after Jan,' who was sitting unconcernedly at the back of the stage, 'and I'll cool them out.'

Taking out his Soprano Sax he proceeded to let rip with seven or eight minutes of some of the most inept musicianship I have ever heard, leaving the audience totally stunned. It certainly did the trick. It took another couple of numbers at least before they recovered most of their earlier enthusiasm. Luckily the rest of the concert passed without incident.

'You know I never had a lesson in my life', Don whispered to me, as he finally left the stage.

Our first European date of the tour was in Groningen City, in the north of Holland, called appropriately enough the 'city of students'. At least I thought, we were going to be assured of an audience. Arriving in good time for an 8pm performance, we found the hall dark and deserted. It seemed the local promoter had forgotten to tell us the show had been put back to midnight. When the time finally came for the band's performance, they rather belatedly realised that there were no curtains. This was a problem as their entry called for a darkened stage. Normally they would set up behind the curtains and the stage lights would be switched off when they were ready to go. The solution was to kill the lights both on stage and in the auditorium. This was fine as far as it went. However, it still left the problem of getting them into place without them colliding with each other, or falling over the equipment. The solution was simple. I was handed a torch by the stage manager and told to get on with it. Feeling rather like a cinema usher, I had the band line up behind me, each with a hand on the shoulder of the man in front and like something out of a scene from the first world war, led this bizarre crocodile of eccentric musicians out on stage.

The tour at last drew to a close in Paris and after the show Don, Jan, Wendy and I went out for supper. Don, who was in a high, good humour, entertained us with stories of his early days after he left school. My favourite was about the time he tried his hand at selling vacuum cleaners door to door. By his own admission he wasn't the best salesman in the world and his grasp of the technicalities of vacuum cleaners decidedly limited. One day during one of his routine calls, he was surprised to be invited in to give a demonstration by a man who, rather unusually, actually seemed to want to buy a machine. The man turned out to be Aldous Huxley, author of amongst many erudite works, A Brave New World and Doors of Perception, the essay that influenced Jim Morrison so much that he named his band after it. Huxley it seemed agreed to buy a machine if Don showed him exactly how everything worked. Can you imagine the scene? Aldous Huxley, by this time nearly blind and Captain Beefheart down on their knees trying to work out the intricacies of a vacuum cleaner.

Over coffee I became aware that, for the last few minutes, Don had been staring with rapt attention at a middle age Frenchman who was sitting at a nearby table with a young female companion. Such was his concentration that I was sure the man would take offence, or at least think Don was a private detective engaged by his wife. It wasn't until Don passed me a sheet of paper that I realised that he had surreptitiously been making a sketch. It was excellent - a neat and economic representation of the subject. Up to that time I had taken Don's claim to artistic genius as pure bombast. Even when two large crates of paintings had turned up at our house I wasn't totally convinced, especially as he claimed he could turn out two or three an hour if the demand was there. The paintings had immediately been sent on to the Bluecoat Gallery in Liverpool for his first ever exhibition anywhere in the world. They were sufficiently well received, as you can see from the various reports printed below, for Don to concentrate on this aspect of his many talents, eventually becoming as well known in America as an artist as he was as a musician, with his paintings fetching very substantial sums.

# Exhibition Reviews

Liverpool Daily Post April 5<sup>th</sup> 1972
Merete Bates: Beef Art.

"Captain Beefheart, the American rock singer, who scored a great success with the Magic Band at Liverpool Stadium on Easter Monday, opened an exhibition of his paintings at The Bluecoat Gallery yesterday. The exhibition of 15 canvases lasts for two weeks, even though Beefheart has gone to Newcastle for the last show of his British tour.

He says he did thirty paintings in a day 'I was just exercising my arm, like an ass swishing its tail'.

Even so, the paintings are often compelling and stark with their shades of black and grey."

The Guardian April 15<sup>th</sup> 1972.

Captain Beefheart, what is he? His paintings, great black and white daubs, some that catch, some that miss are left like a trail behind him on the walls of Liverpool's Bluecoat Gallery.

# CHAPTER 33

While all this was going on, Barry Dickens mentioned that the Osmond Brothers would really like to play an open-air concert. At that time, young Donny was one of the biggest 'scream age' acts in the world. Well, I thought, it might not be the greatest music but it would sure as hell help pay the bills. The trouble, once again, was where to find a suitable venue. This time I tried a change of tact. Instead of the Farmer's Weekly, I used as our bible a book listing all the stately homes in Britain. It wasn't until I reached L for Longleat that I remembered that the Marquis of Bath, the owner of this magnificent estate, had allowed a Rolling Stones concert in the grounds way back in 1964. Firing off one of my flamboyantly illiterate letters, I was surprised to receive a reply almost by return, inviting me down to Longleat to discuss the matter. Lord Bath was a pleasant surprise. Tall, raffish and very approachable, with all the charm and confidence you would expect from someone whose family had lived in the same house for over four hundred years, he also turned out to be extremely well informed about popular music. Piling into his rather decrepit mini, he drove Wendy and me around the park, pointing out what he thought would be a suitable location for the concert. Once back at the house, the negotiations took less than an hour and a deal was done. We could use Longleat. Just over a week later, the manager of the Osmond Brothers flew in. The next day, accompanied by Barry and security specialist, Don Murfitt, he drove down to Longleat. It was a typical late winter's day, bitterly cold and pouring rain by the buckets. No matter, he loved it and a date for the concert was set.

It was on the way back to London that I began to have second thoughts. I had always had reservations about access to the park and seeing the local road system once again, long, narrow and miles from any really main road, the doubts came flooding back. However, what really concerned me was the safety of the kids. Not only might we have the problem of young girls, having been denied permission by their parents to attend the concert, simply running away and hitching lifts from places as far away as northern England and Scotland, with all the attendant dangers, but what worried me even more was the problem of dealing with upwards of 60,000 screaming hysterical girls, all crowding to the front of the stage to be as near to their heroes as possible. The image of girls being trampled underfoot in the melee was just too terrible to contemplate.

The next day I called Barry and told him my decision. As I expected, he was not happy with my change of mind or my timing

'You could have given it a little more thought before you dragged their manager halfway around the world,' he said. However, he respected my decision.

Two years later, a fourteen-year-old girl was killed and dozens of others injured during a David Cassidy concert at the White City, London, so perhaps my fears were justified after all.

# CHAPTER 34

Like a large number of successful managers that we dealt with, Led Zeppelin's manager, Peter Grant, had a great interest in collectable cars and I would often meet him at the auctions that were held at Alexandra Palace in North London. We would frequently walk around the cars together deciding if there was anything worth buying. On one occasion I remember enthusing over a simply superb and very imposing Issotta Franchini town car. It required a full restoration but was a very rare car that would, I was sure, prove to be a good investment, as well as a joy to own. I told Peter to buy it and rather to my surprise, he did. Several days later I received a phone call from him inviting me out for lunch. It seemed he was thrilled with his new purchase and was grateful to me for pointing it out. When I arrived Peter had a present waiting. He knew I collected motoring books and he had found a truly mint copy of Hoopers the Motor Car, a History and Souvenir. It was first published in 1908 and was an enormous leather bound tome. Where he had found it I really don't know as I had been looking for a copy for years. This sort of behaviour was very typical of Peter. It wasn't just his generosity, but the fact he went to endless trouble to obtain something truly appropriate.

Our next tour was with a group that, until December the previous year, had been the Mothers of Invention. After the disaster at the Rainbow Theatre, the Mothers, with no immediate prospect of work, had decided to go it alone. Adding guitarist Gary Rowles to the line up of Mark Volman, Howard Kaylan and bass player Jim Pons, all from the Turtles, plus Don Preston and English drummer Aynsley Dunbar, they became, in effect, the reborn Turtles. Because of contractual problems, they called themselves The Fluorescent Leach and Eddie, which was soon abbreviated to Flo and Eddie. Mark and Howard were ideal front men. They both sang brilliantly and had the same zany, off-the-wall sense of humour, with Mark perhaps compensating for being just slightly overweight by being totally outrageous, both on and off stage. If Frank and the Mothers were my all time favourites, Flo and Eddie were a close second - tight, musicianly and highly entertaining. Without doubt the short tour of mainly university gigs we arranged for them, was the most enjoyable of the many that we organised. To celebrate the end of the tour, we all went out to dinner in a Mexican restaurant in Sloane Square. Although it wasn't intended to be an excuse for a total piss-up, given the circumstances, I suppose it was inevitable that this was the way it turned out. Wendy, who would normally only have had a couple of glasses of wine at the most, had, at this dinner, taken a great liking to Tequila Sunrise. Unaware of it's potency, she had already had four or five glasses and when she reached out to refill her glass from one of the conveniently placed pitchers, she didn't notice that the voluminous sleeve of her blouse was draping into one of the lighted candles that were placed at regular intervals along the huge table. Seconds later it burst into flames. She still didn't notice. Fortunately, Aynsley Dunbar, who was sitting next to her, did and immediately set about dousing the blaze. Unfortunately, he was also just a little wasted and was so intent on saving Wendy that, as he bent over the table gallantly attempting to extinguish the flames, he also failed to notice the candle. Seconds later his hair was on fire.

Now Aynsley's hair was his pride and joy, worn long and bouffant in the style so popular with English pop stars of that time. It was one of his principal assets in his never ending pursuit of willing young girls. Reacting quickly, I started vigorously hitting the top of his head with the flat of my hand and to make doubly sure that the flames were definitely out and would stay out, tipped a jug of water over his head. The hurt and bewildered look on his face will always remain in my memory.

'What did you do that for?' he said plaintively. 'I was saving your wife'.

When I pointed out the reason for my actions, he suddenly realised the implications. Clasping his hands to his head, he gave out a loud yell and rushed off to find a mirror.

'It's all right Aynsley,' one of road crew said rather insensitively, I thought 'You've got too much hair anyway.'

# CHAPTER 35.

It was just after we got back from a trip to New York to see Bill Thompson and RCA that Peter Grant rang.

'Me and the boys have an idea we want to talk over with you. Why don't you fly out to New York to see us?'

'But I've only just got back,' I complained.

'That's all right,' he said, 'It's not that far. It'll be fun. The boys would really like to see you.'

Highly flattered, I agreed. Three days later, Wendy and I were back in New York. Peter had arranged for a limo to meet us at the airport and take us directly to Nassau Colosseum in Nassau County, where the band was playing the last of two dates. We arrived just before Zep was due on and we were given two seats in the special guest enclosure, right in front of the stage. Wendy, rather tired after all this jet setting, stuffed cotton wool in her ears and promptly went to sleep. I on the other hand wasn't that tired and really enjoyed the band's performance. Seeing them in full flow from only ten or fifteen feet away was really exciting. I couldn't get over the size of the Colosseum. It probably held around twenty thousand people and was quite the biggest hall I had ever seen. However, large as it was, Robert held this enormous crowd firmly in the palm of his hand. After the show, we returned to Manhattan in a Limo that we shared with John Bonham. During the trip he told us how important the 1970 Bath Festival had been to Zeppelin and how it had helped to break them in the UK. By the time we reached their hotel, the very glitzy Waldorf Astoria, I was thinking that this was already shaping up to be a great trip. Unfortunately, this was as good as it got. After giving every one time to shower and change, Peter took us up to a suite where the boys were relaxing. With Wendy present they were all on their best behaviour and really quite chatty. However, after a couple of drinks, we returned to our room, leaving them to more interesting past times. At breakfast the following morning, the only person who was around was their tour manager Richard Cole.

'When do you think we will get to see Peter?' I asked.

'Dunno. He's got a lot on at the moment,' Richard replied. 'I'll keep in touch with you.'

This went on for three days with Wendy and I either sitting in our room waiting, or making sporadic shopping trips. Finally, Peter and Richard turned up for the eagerly awaited meeting. They were aware that we were planning a concert at Wembley Stadium with Jefferson Airplane and Peter told me that Led Zeppelin were really keen to play the concert as well.

'We'll do it for nothing,' Peter said.

'Oh yeah,' I said, 'What's the catch?'

'No catch,' he replied, 'We just want to appear at the end of the show unbilled and unannounced. Just think of the impact that would have,' he added.

'And just think how thrilled the Airplane would be, ' I said, 'They wouldn't allow it.'

'Do they have to know?' asked Peter.

'Well, as their European representative, I would have to tell them,' I added rather pompously.

And that was it. A 7,000 mile round trip for nothing.

A mutual friend told me some time later that Peter and the boys thought it would be a great idea to have some fun with me. However, the fact that I had brought Wendy had spoilt their plans. Knowing their reputation for the ultimate in rock 'n' roll excesses it seemed like I had a narrow escape.

## CHAPTER 36

By one of those strange coincidences, the very next tour we arranged after Flo and Eddie was with Frank Zappa. Although confined to a wheelchair for the best part of nine months, following his brutal assault at the Rainbow Theatre, he had still found the energy and enthusiasm to produce three albums - 'Just another Band from LA', featuring Mark and Howard, 'Waka/Jawaka' and 'Grand Wazoo'. The latter was very different from anything he had previously written. For a start it was scored for a twenty-piece band, including a large brass section and was mainly instrumental. It seemed that Frank, off the road for almost a year, was getting bored and decided a short tour of seven or eight dates with Grand Wazoo was just the thing to get him back into action. Herb Cohen gave us the job of setting up three European dates. This wasn't quite as easy as it initially appeared. Although European promoters were queuing up for dates on Zappa and the Mothers, a twenty-piece band, with all its attendant expenses and its rather avant garde music into the bargain, was a different matter.

After many phone calls and much haggling, we finally ended up with three shows on three consecutive days in three different countries. All tightly clustered around a weekend, on Friday the 15th of September we played Berlin, on Saturday the 16th, an outdoor show at the Oval Cricket ground in London, promoted by Ray and Ron Faulk, organisers of the Isle of Wight Festivals, and on Sunday the 17th, the Hague in Holland.

Logistically, it was something of a nightmare. How the hell were we to get the equipment to each venue in time to set up and sound check without resorting to the expensive, and thoroughly impractical arrangement of renting two lots of equipment? The only option appeared to be to charter a couple of aircraft to fly the musicians and equipment between the gigs. Using a broker to obtain competitive quotes, we finally settled on a four-engine, turbo prop, Vickers Viscount for the musicians and various other members of the party and a Bristol freighter for the equipment. Everyone loved the Viscount. However, the road crew had strong reservations about flying in the Bristol Freighter. The prototype had first flown in 1945, so I suppose it was getting a little long in the tooth, although I think it was the appearance of the pilot that really put them off. He was the nearest thing to an old sea dog I had ever seen - sixty years old with a swaggering walk and with so much ash spilt down the front of his uniform, it looked like he had just cremated his mother. He and the plane were a perfect match. He could, however, really fly this difficult and noisy old aeroplane, as he proved over the next three days and turned out to be a real asset, personally supervising the loading and stowage of the freight and always departing and arriving on schedule.

For the first date in Berlin, Wendy and I flew on ahead by a scheduled flight to make sure there were no problems. It wasn't until we arrived at the airport where the band were due to land that we both remembered, virtually simultaneously, that we had forgotten to apply for permission for the two aircraft to fly through the air corridor, between East and West Germany. Total panic set in. We had visions of both planes being shot down by the Russians who controlled this stretch of airspace. Hurriedly putting in a phone call to our office, we were relieved to find that Ian Tilbury had already taken care of the problem.

Rushing back to London for the show at the Oval, we were pleased to find that the weather was fine and really quite warm. We had all been a little worried about playing an outdoor show in England so comparatively late in the year. There is nothing worse for the performers and audience if it's cold and wet, especially in the case of 'Grand Wazoo', whose members used loads of different instruments where the tuning was very sensitive to temperature changes.

Frank was due on stage around 7pm and at 6pm Wendy and I went to the promoter's office to collect the fee. In accordance with the terms of the contract, a copy of which we had brought with us, payment was due in cash before the performance commenced. According to one of the Faulk Brothers, it seemed that they hadn't taken enough cash on the door to pay us. Would we take a cheque? Would we hell! Herb Cohen was sent for. Would Herb accept a cheque?

'What the fuck do you take me for?' he snarled.

A typical rock and roll stand off developed. After a half an hour or so of ever more heated argument, I had a thought.

'If we took a cheque' I enquired 'would you be prepared to offer some security to back it up?'

After a short discussion, they said that they wouldn't. However, their principal backer might. He was sent for.

'Exactly what sort of security had you in mind?' he asked.

'Well, your house would do nicely,' I replied.

He winced slightly but after a few minutes deliberation and to his everlasting credit, agreed. A contract was drawn up and signed and a few minutes later 'Grand Wazoo' took to the stage.

Conveniently, the band was set up in one of the grandstands and I watched the performance from the back, standing next to Ruth Underwood, the percussionist. The standard of musicianship was a revelation. How Ruth could stand casually chatting to me then instantly pick up the most intricate patterns and rhythms is beyond my comprehension. It wasn't just Ruth. Every one of the musicians was outstanding. I later discovered that even the contractor, Kenny Shroyer, the man who booked the musicians and had come over to make sure everything went smoothly, had played bass trombone on recording sessions for Mel Torme and Ray Charles.

After the show, I went to fetch some papers from my car, which was parked in a quiet part of the backstage area. Sitting, searching through a file, I was suddenly aware that I had company. Standing in front of the car was a burly young man wielding an iron bar. Terrified, I sat motionless as he raised the bar prior to smashing the windscreen.

Suddenly, in the distance I saw Herb Cohen and winding down the window I yelled, 'Herb help me,' at the top of my voice. I had a feeling of déjà vu.

Mercifully, he saw me and came racing over. After a moment's hesitation my assailant took off at top speed. It could well have been a coincidence. However, I have always wondered if this little incident would have happened if I had accepted a cheque without any security.

The next day, instead of flying to Holland with the rest of the party, Herb decided that it would be better if Wendy and I stayed in England ready to get to the bank really early on Monday morning. He reasoned that although we may have had a surety in the form of the house, there was no guarantee that it would stand up in court. As the fee was a substantial part of the tour budget, it was really important that we were first in line to collect it, especially as it looked as if the company would be going into liquidation.

Monday morning found us waiting anxiously outside a private bank in Mayfair. As early as we were, the backer was there before us. After what seemed a lifetime, the doors opened and he signalled for us to wait, then shot into the manager's office. Ten minutes later he emerged, looking greatly relieved and led us over to a teller who gave us the cash.

# CHAPTER 37

The start of 1973 saw us no closer to finding a suitable festival site. I wondered whether I should lower my standards or go back, cap in hand, to the Bath and West Showground, who seemed quite keen to discuss another show with us. Of course, it could have simply been that we were kept quite busy with tours and one off shows and my enthusiasm had waned a little. Whatever the reason, we seemed to be getting nowhere fast.

Our first tour of the year was with Roy Harper, plus American singer songwriter, Judee Sills playing support. It was an interesting mix, both from a musical and personal viewpoint. Both were accomplished performers who wrote great songs. However Roy was a cynical agnostic, while Judee was a born again Christian - an explosive mix. It began to show itself early on in the tour when Roy's fans started heckling Judee. Roy didn't make it any better by saying, both on and off stage, that she was going to have a really hard time when they played the Albert Hall, where he expected enormous numbers of his hard core fans. I think that if I had been Roy, I would have kept my mouth shut. When the tour reached London, Judee, with God on her side, received a standing ovation and Roy was the one who got heckled. Some of her fans even going so far as to sing the odd hymn in between his songs, with one fanatic pointing a crucifix in the general direction of Roy as if to ward off the devil.

All in all it was, as far as I was concerned, a fairly traumatic tour. It wasn't helped when at one of the shows Roy, who was still suffering the after effects of a serious illness he had contracted in 1972, played a long rambling introduction to one of his most popular numbers and after three or four minutes stopped and confessed to the audience that he had forgotten what song he was supposed to be singing. Nor did it exactly fill me with confidence when Judee, who used to travel between gigs with Wendy and me in our car, told us that she had been to jail for armed robbery. It seemed she made a speciality of holding up garages. However, she was, she assured us, a reformed character, having discovered 'The Lord Jesus Christ'. Unfortunately, she seemed to have lost Him a few years later, as she died in the late seventies from a drug overdose. The loss of any life is always tragic. In Judee's case it was made worse because she had a truly great talent that was never fully realised.

# CHAPTER 38

Later on in the year, Herb Cohen called me from Los Angeles.

'Frank is pretty much back to normal and wants to do a full tour of Europe and the UK,' he said.

Great, I thought, another opportunity for a little paid sightseeing. Working in conjunction with Danish promoter Arne Warso, we put together a tour that started in Copenhagen and ended up twenty-three dates later in London. This time everything ran like clockwork. That is, until we reached Italy. Our first show was in a sports stadium in Bologna. I should have had my doubts as soon as I saw the lorry loads of armed soldiers sitting in the car park. When I asked the local promoter why they were there, he just shrugged and explained they sometimes had a little difficulty keeping the fascists and the communist elements apart, but it was of no consequence and I really shouldn't worry. How very reassuring, I thought.

Problems started as soon as the band set up. The crew were experiencing a series of enormous power surges, which had almost totally fried one of the synthesisers and threatened to put most of the keyboards out of action. Looking around at what was obviously a pretty new building, the crew sent me to see if the stadium was fitted with a voltage stabiliser. Finding the promoter, I asked him to check with the stadium manager whether they had such a device. It turned out that the tough looking guy he had been talking to when I interrupted was the manager. A lengthy conversation ensued, which eventually turned into a screaming match, hands gesticulating, noses just inches away from each other. A fistfight, it seemed, was inevitable. Eventually they stopped and the promoter came back to me.

'Well,' I said,' Do they have one?'

His answer this time was short and to the point.

'Yes' he said.

I was invited to follow them to a building, the inside of which resembled the Houston Space Centre control room. The stadium manager turned a switch and, in an instant, we had stabilised electricity.

'Why,' I said to the manager, 'Didn't you turn this on earlier?'

'Because,' he replied,' You didn't ask.'

Later that evening, the crowd went wild with more than 15,000 happy Italians getting their rocks off. Zappa it seemed, because of his Sicilian ancestry, was their absolute hero.

As soon as the band came off stage, the local stewards split, leaving Herb and me to guard the entrance to the staircase that led down to the dressing rooms.

'It's OK,' Herb said, 'There's a fifteen-foot fence between the crowd and us'.

At that moment, almost as if they had heard him and were rising to the challenge, several hundred crazy Italians started to swarm up the wire mesh fence like pirates climbing the rigging and promptly engulfed us. Luckily, they were less menacing than they looked from a distance and were quite happy to stand and wait, hoping to catch a glimpse of Frank and the possibility of an autograph. It was at this point that Herb decided to go and see the band and check if there was another way out of the dressing rooms. Leaving me totally on my own, with what seemed half of Bologna, I felt appropriately enough like Horatius defending the bridge against the Etruscan hordes. By now, the crowd were getting a little restless, which wasn't helped when they discovered that there was indeed a back way out of the dressing room, of which Frank and the band had taken advantage. Providentially, at that point, seven or eight hefty stewards turned up otherwise I think I would have been lynched.

The next day Zappa was booked to appear at an enormous sports hall in the suburbs of Rome. The sound check was uneventful. This time there was no problem with the voltage stabiliser. However, when we returned for the performance, our coach couldn't get near the stage door for the large and decidedly unruly crowd blocking the way. God! I thought, Frank is really big here. When the coach was eventually manoeuvred into place and every one started to get off, it transpired that they couldn't give a toss about Frank, but made it clear in a concerted and well organised rush on the door that their sole interest was in gaining free admission to any concert.

It was a scene of total chaos and very dangerous. Wendy, Herb's wife Suzanne and Ruth Underwood were all knocked to the ground and if it wasn't for Herb and some of the musicians, they would have been quite seriously hurt. Even Frank wasn't immune to the violence, getting vigorously shouldered aside by the leader of the mob - a tall, well-built, young man, who, I later learnt, was a well-known communist agitator.

With his repeated chant of 'Avanti, Avanti', he spurred on the rabble, the words ringing out like a war cry.

In the end all their efforts came to nothing as the hall staff, who were evidently used to this sort of thing, linked arms and valiantly stopped the crowd from breaking through. When we were all safely inside the compound, Herb strolled up to the gate and beckoned to the leader, who after a moment's hesitation, came over. Herb, rather conspiratorially, beckoned him nearer as if he had something of great importance to impart. By now, thoroughly intrigued, he brought his face close to the widely spaced iron bars of the gate and at just the right moment, Herb let him have it with one of the best aimed right jabs that I have ever seen, in or out of the ring. He went down as if he had been pole- axed. I just hope he didn't get any blood on his beautifully tailored, Armani overcoat that all Italians, whatever their politics, seemed to wear. After Italy, the rest of the tour was something of an anti-climax.

# CHAPTER 39

Shortly after the Zappa tour we set out for San Francisco to see Bill Thompson and to catch up on the latest developments at Grunt Records. It was great checking out the new signings, attending the occasional live date and meeting all the people that handled the different aspects of the label. After four or five days of this, Bill's wife, Judy suggested that we took a break.

'I'm off to the Renaissance Fair tomorrow. Why don't you come with me?' The fair was held on a huge site in very pretty countryside, five or six miles from the city centre. Everywhere you went there was something different to see, hear or simply experience. In one leafy glade we came across the San Francisco City choir, a hundred strong. In another area, a barbershop quartet were singing lustily, not quite sixteenth century but great fun and in every corner of the fair you found wandering minstrels playing guitars or occasionally the more esoteric lute or lyre. There were also plays, medieval dancing and craft stalls. Whatever your feelings about Americans, the one thing you have to give them credit for is enthusiasm. The stalls were a particularly good instance of what I mean. Many were constructed to look like bowers, using totally natural materials such as hazel twigs and saplings - no plastic sheeting here. The articles they displayed for sale were as diverse as the people selling them including tie dyes (remember this was 1973), hand made candles, stained glass, ceramics and pottery, wood items, metal works, enamels, hand knits and weaves. Not only were these articles for sale, you could also see how they were made. People had brought along ovens and kilns, weaving looms, spinning wheels and were happy to give demonstrations of their skills, or indeed let you try for yourself. One enterprising fellow had set up an entire forge complete with furnace, bellows and anvil.

As we walked around, I was surprised to see just how many of the visitors had made the effort to dress in period costumes. From talking to them, it seemed that the majority had researched the subject and made the clothes themselves. Everyone seemed to be having such a good time and to top things off, the food and drink was superb, rich and imaginative with numerous spit roasts and other delicacies. We were totally captivated.

'This is what I want to run,' I said.

Already a little disillusioned with the grasping, greedy people on the fringe of the music business that I had dealt with for three festivals, this type of event seemed refreshingly different.

Driving back from the fair, Judy pointed out The Cow Palace, the late Bill Graham's famous San Francisco venue.

'That reminds me', she said, 'Elvis is on tonight. We've been given some tickets. Do you want to go?' At that time, Elvis was distinctly out of favour and, instead, we chose to go to a restaurant in China Town.

On our return, I immediately started looking for a place to hold the fair. I felt it should be as close as possible to London, with its eight million population, or at least in the Home Counties.

Unlike our search for a festival site, finding a suitable location for this type of event should be easy, I thought. As usual, it wasn't. Despite an ad in Farmer's Weekly, nothing suitable was offered. This time I was the one being fussy. I knew precisely what I was looking for. I wanted a large pretty parkland area that had plenty of undulations and features with good access to a main road. Close to giving up altogether, I unexpectedly received a phone call from someone who had seen my advertisement.

'I don't own any land myself,' he said, 'But I have a large number of contacts and I am sure I can find you something suitable.'

As good as his word, he started taking us to various estates owned by friends. They were all most impressive. However, none exactly fitted our criteria. Not at all disheartened, he made further enquiries and called us again.

'I'll collect you in the morning. We're going to Hertfordshire to Knebworth House,' he said.

Driving up the A1M, he told us a little about the estate. It was owned by Lord Cobbold, a former Governor of the Bank of England and Controller of the Queens Household and was administered by his eldest son David. What he didn't mention was the fantastic access from the motorway, which I was shortly to see for myself. As soon as we drove into the park, I started to get excited. It was large, attractive, undulating and, with the adjoining road system, was just what I had been looking for. We were rapidly introduced to the Estate Manager, a charming and helpful man called David Condy. I told him all about the renaissance fair we had visited in California and exactly what it entailed and how we would really like to stage it at Knebworth. He thought it was a great idea. However, he would have to put my request to David Lytton Cobbold. Reassuringly, he said he could see no problems, as it was just the sort of event the estate was keen to encourage. It wasn't until we were leaving the estate on our way home that I noticed an area of the park that appeared to be a natural amphitheatre.

Nudging Wendy, I said quietly 'What a great place for a rock concert.'

The very next day we came back on our own. At this time of the year, the park was officially closed. However, finding the gates open, we drove straight in, hoping we wouldn't bump into David Condy or any one else connected with the estate. I was, as the expression goes, totally gobs-macked. The park was just what we had been looking for to stage a one-day concert and to come across it in this way, after searching for over two years, was just unbelievable. Not only was there a gently sloping arena, but there was also a huge area of flat land nearby for car parking. As an added bonus, there was even an excellent internal road system in place that ran around the entire periphery of the park. With all thought of a renaissance fair put on hold, I rang Peter Grant.

'Have I got the site for you,' I said, 'Only twenty eight miles from London, a huge park, a natural arena and access straight off a motorway.'

'Funny you should ring. The boys were thinking of playing a festival this year. If it's as good as you say, I'll come and look at it,' he said.

Less than a week later, we met Peter and drove him to Knebworth. To avoid any embarrassment, we had told David Condy, the estate manager, that we wanted to look around the park again and were bringing a friend with us. Now here was the tricky part. We didn't want to tell Peter that we hadn't yet obtained permission to use the park for a rock concert and we certainly didn't want David Condy to know who the hell Peter was.

It should have been a simple matter of showing Peter the park and leaving. Unfortunately, the first person we met on our arrival was the estate manager. Charming and helpful as always, David offered to drive us around in his Land Rover. We had no alternative but to accept and for nearly thirty minutes Wendy and I carried on this bizarre conversation with the two of them totally at cross-purposes. Somehow we carried it off. On the way back, Peter agreed that it was an incredible site and we started to talk about provisional dates. All we had to do now was to persuade David Lytton Cobbold that a rock concert was a good idea.

A couple of days after our visit we received a phone call from David Condy.

'David Lytton Cobbold thinks a renaissance fair is a great idea and is very happy for you to go ahead.'

'Great,' I replied. 'However, there has been a slight change of plans. What would he think of a rock concert instead?'

There was a long pause. I thought at first that he had hung up.

Are you serious?' he said at last.

'Totally,' I replied. 'Would you put it to him? Obviously I could offer a lot more money, somewhere in the region of £10,000.'

Reluctantly David Condy agreed. He called back the next day.

'Well he didn't turn you down out of hand. In fact, he wants to meet you.'

I don't know exactly what I was expecting - from my preconceived and highly prejudiced notions of the English nobility, probably some silly ass, weak chinned wonder. What I found was an extremely tall man a couple of years younger than me, worldly, amiable and very shrewd. After grilling me for thirty or forty minutes, he told me he would think it over and let me have an answer in a week or so.

Although David and I had got on very well and the meeting had ended amicably enough, one or two issues had been raised that I had found difficult to answer so I wasn't entirely sure what the outcome was going to be. The next few days passed slowly as I anxiously waited for a decision. Eventually I received the phone call I had been waiting for. We were in.

The next phone call was from Peter.

'I've talked to the boys and we are interested. Why don't you come down to discuss it?'

Peter had, a little while earlier, moved into Horselunges Manor and apart from discussing Knebworth, I was really keen to see the house - from all I had heard, it was quite something. When we arrived the stories proved correct. Horselunges Manor was an impressively large timber frame Wealden House, set behind a wide moat and boasting an attractive Georgian addition. Peter told me it had been built in 1487 for Sir John Devenish of Hellingly, the local Member of Parliament. Inside was even more impressive, with a huge timbered hall that Peter had turned into his sitting room. While we were looking around, we were shown the garages, which contained his two beautiful Pierce Arrow motorcars. The garages still had plenty of room, I noticed, should he want to expand his collection still further.

The meeting, when it finally got under way, was short and to the point. We had already agreed the terms; it was just a matter of choosing a date, which was easy. We had a festival.

# CHAPTER 40

The next thing was to book a support programme. I started to look around for an American group that hadn't been seen in this country or at least hadn't been seen for sometime and came up with the Allman Brothers, at that time reputedly America's biggest live draw and a really great southern, boogie band. A week later, the Doobie Brothers joined the bill, then Van Morrison and the New Caledonia Soul Express. The support programme was beginning to look good, perhaps too good. Just as I felt on top of things, I got a phone call from the late Ray Coleman, the editor of The Melody Maker.

'I hear Led Zeppelin are playing at Knebworth,' he said. My heart sank. How the hell did he know this? An official announcement was still a couple of weeks away.

At first I denied it. However, it was no good. Someone with inside knowledge had obviously tipped him off. I knew damned well if the story broke before Peter Grant OK-ed the announcement, the gig was off, as he had made quite clear during one of our numerous phone conversations. I tried to bluff it out, but without any success. In the end I tried to appeal to Coleman's better nature. Unfortunately, he didn't have one, even though I told him Zeppelin would pull out if he ran the story. I then tried to work out a deal, giving him total exclusivity on the announcement and coverage of the festival if he would just hold off for another week. Again he refused to even consider it.

'What,' I said, 'is the point of announcing that Led Zeppelin will be playing if you know because of your article they won't be? You will be just disappointing your readers.'

I should have saved my breath. He wasn't going to change his mind. The following Thursday the Melody Maker carried on its front page, in huge letters, the headline 'Together for just one show Zeppelin, Allmans!'

Joint equals. Oh my God, that's it. I knew that Peter didn't consider any band to be Zeppelin's equal, let alone The Allmans. Bracing myself for the wrath of Grant, I called him straight away. Ominously, he was not available. The next week The Melody Maker carried, buried inside on page four, a small piece stating that Led Zeppelin were in negotiations to play a concert at Knebworth in Hertfordshire and that the Allmans had also been approached. It was all somewhat different from their blazing front-page announcement of the previous week. The next day we received a telegram from Peter Grant thanking us for our kind offer but explaining that recording and film commitments prevented them from accepting. Oh yeah!

Feeling well and truly fucked, we pondered our next move. Do we fold the whole thing? A ruinously expensive operation as we had by now reached an agreement with the Allmans and had, in addition, exchanged contracts with the rest of the bands. It would also mean that we risked losing our fantastic new site. Or should we go ahead with what was basically our support programme, albeit a very strong one? As must by now be fairly well known, we chose the latter, scaling down the size of the event and reducing the facilities in line with our lower expectations. It was a harder job than I imagined. We still required a decent size stage and cutting down the number of loos and reducing the overall number of stewards saved a lot less than we had hoped. The weather didn't help. It rained continuously for nearly four weeks, right up to the day before the show. I can remember getting out of bed each morning, pulling the curtains and seeing a picture of unrelieved gloom. We should be building a bloody Ark, I thought, not a stage. It certainly didn't help ticket sales, which while initially pretty good had now slowed down to a worrying trickle. It didn't help either when I received a phone call from the Allman's agent.

'Some of the road crew are flying in for a quick look at the site. It would be a really nice gesture if you could pick them up in a limo and take them up to Knebworth.'

What a waste of money I thought. However, it turned out to be a good investment. Driving out to Heathrow in solitary splendour in the back of an enormous Daimler limousine, I felt a little like the Queen if not a queen. However, my mood changed abruptly when I saw the roadies. There were four of them, large and I do mean large, Southern boys. My first reaction was 'I hope to God they'll all fit in.' They turned out to be less intimidating than I feared and by the time we arrived at Knebworth, a working relationship had been established. What really made me warm to them was their enthusiasm for the location and the facilities that were being constructed.

'Why the hell can't they build stages like this back in the States?' one of them said.

It was time well spent. When the four of them eventually flew in with the band for the actual concert, they were already friends and we had no trouble whatsoever with either the musicians or crew - they were simply terrific from beginning to end. However, I must say when I first saw their rider, I feared the worst. It was pretty demanding, stipulating that they had trailers complete with telephones, several kinds of American beer as well as mineral water, which as far as I can remember was to be obtained from a small spring situated in some remote part of Georgia. Also included was a stipulation that we provided equipment capable of cleaning 90 square feet of oil coated steel in not less than thirty minutes. The mind boggles! Thankfully, Polydor, their UK record company, took the whole matter off our hands. Rather than fly everything in from America I think they finally found every thing they needed

The Allman Bros

in a US Air Force base in Germany. In exchange we allowed them to display four huge 'Capricorn Records' banners on the front of the stage.

Unlike any of our later Knebworth Festivals, we did not apply for a licence. As the event only lasted for one day, we did not think it necessary - a conclusion that was disputed by the local licensing officer, Mr Pruett, who only heard about the event from his daughter reading about it in Melody Maker. He was rather pre-empted by the fact that the festival was only two weeks away and decided that this time at least, if we co-operated, he would waive the requirements and help all he could. All in all we found the local authorities very helpful, especially the police. One of the senior Stevenage policeman at this time was Chief Superintendent Oliver, a policeman of the old school, tall, ramrod straight with a bull neck and tough as old boots, who must have put the fear of God into the local villains whenever they saw him. It shows that appearances can be a little deceptive because he turned out to be a thoroughly pleasant, efficient and understanding man with whom I got on very well and who gave us a great deal of help and a lot of good advice. His main worry, as it was with every senior police officer with whom I subsequently came into contact, was basically how many people were we expecting and were they likely to riot? At first I thought they were just over-reacting until I found out that the local police force was financially responsible for any damage caused by rioters. This explained quite a lot.

Meanwhile, the weather continued to do its worst. On the day preceding the concert, it rained so hard that I was forced to carry out a lot of the final meetings and discussions in my car. If I were religious I would say that night I prayed for a miracle. I didn't, but someone must have, because the day of the concert dawned dry and sunny and it stayed that way virtually all day. Although there were muddy patches, particularly near some of the entrances where the vehicles of various contractors had chewed up the grass, the vast majority of the arena was completely unaffected by the previous few weeks of rain, a great tribute to the draining properties of Knebworth Park. Great though it was to see the sunshine, I was sure it was too late to help ticket sales. However, once again someone up there must have liked us because we ended up selling over ten thousand tickets on the day of the concert. Not quite enough to get us out of trouble, but it certainly helped to minimise the loss.

As this was our fourth outdoor event I was determined to make it the best-organised one so far. Unfortunately, even the best-laid plans can go awry and owing to one or two technical problems, by the time Tim Buckley finally took the stage, we were already an hour behind schedule. To add to my worries, the water bowsers were late. One of the minor drawbacks of Knebworth is that is suffers from low water pressure and to overcome this we

'Van the Man' enjoying his birthday

had arranged for all the water taps, strategically placed throughout the arena, to be hooked up to enormous bowsers that we could replace as required throughout the day. After a few frantic phone calls they eventually turned up, forming an impressive convoy as they drove into the park. It seemed they had been held up in traffic!

By early evening we were running more than two hours late and as no one else wanted the job, I was asked to get Van Morrison off the stage. After a slow start, he was really starting to cook and encouraged both by the audience reaction and compere John Peel, had substantially exceeded his allotted time.

'I'll soon put a stop to that' I said.

When I arrived on stage, a jubilant Van Morrison greeted me.

'Thank you Freddy for allowing the extra time' he said. 'It's really great, especially as it's my birthday.'

Ouch. Low blow. What can you say to that? So he played two more numbers before triumphantly retiring undefeated. Ironic, as he nearly didn't play at the festival at all. His contract was so outrageous that I was going to replace him. It even contained a clause that stated he did not have to perform if he did not like the look of the audience. In fact, it was so one-sided that our lawyer said it wouldn't hold up in court, so we let it stand.

Watching at the back of the arena, I was impressed by the quality of the sound. The NME in their 1st of June edition stated:

"A feature of the event will be the special P.A. system, which, says Bannister, will provide the finest sound quality ever heard at an outdoor event in Britain. It weighs about 12 tonnes and is being built by the Showco Company of Texas. It is being specially flown in from the States, complete with five technicians to operate it."

This was obviously going to be for Zeppelin and was cancelled when they pulled out. The sound system we eventually ended up with was actually supplied by IES, a London based company. Dave, a visitor to the festival, confirmed that the sound was exceptional and recently had this to say:

' The organisers had seen fit to provide one of the best outdoor PA systems that I've ever heard at a festival and given this was 26 years ago, it must have been state of the art for the time. A massive stack of speakers, which were directed through huge horns, ensured that the sound was crystal clear whilst being also very loud, (apparently they could be heard miles away) so wherever one was in the audience, one got a great sound. This was nowhere more evident that during the Mahavishnu Orchestras set, where the sound quality was just stupendous.'

John McLaughlin and Jean-Luc Ponty

Two of the stipulations that David Lytton Cobbold had made when he allowed us to use the park were no alcohol and no glass. A great pity I thought, as profits from a beer licence would go a long way to bridging any shortfall in the gate money. As it was, I could only look on as the kids brought trolley loads of booze onto the site.

As the demands of the event quietened down, I was able to spend more time on stage. Our curfew was a self-imposed 11pm and I wanted to make sure we stuck to it, if it was humanly possible. With Van Morrison eventually coming off stage around 7pm, we only had four hours to put on the final two bands. Both liked to stretch out and as the Allman Brothers had stipulated a three-hour set, it looked as if I had an impossible job. The Doobie Brothers got on stage with the minimum of fuss and played a great set that was extremely well received. Up until now the atmosphere, both back stage and on stage, had been very good, spoilt just a little by one of the Doobie Brothers' roadies, a truly huge guy with a mouth to match. I could see that he had been getting on the nerves of the Allman's roadies for most of the day and as soon as the stage was finally theirs, they celebrated by heaving him off the back. Because of the way the ground sloped, it was nowhere near as high as the front, which was around 12 foot off the ground. Nevertheless, it was high enough for him to get the message.

It was a pity we had lost those two hours earlier in the afternoon because towards the end of the set, people began to leave to catch their coaches and trains and also to meet up with prearranged lifts. They must have found it really frustrating as by midnight the Allman Brothers were just getting into their stride - one of the all-time great bands.

As soon as they came off stage close to 1am, we had one of those familiar festival situations with every one trying to leave at once. We had set up a one way system for cars. However, not everyone was willing to sit and wait patiently for their turn to leave and a couple of hot heads decided to take a short cut off the grass and onto a part of the road nearer the exits. Unfortunately, they didn't realise, although we had clearly marked the area with orange and red striped tape, that there was an extremely nasty hidden ditch into which they dived at some speed. Amazingly, no one was hurt but they had to wait until daylight before the Estate's tractor could pull them out.

The pedestrians were just as impatient and instead of following the well signed and lit path, they took the more direct route through a tenant farmer's wheat field, destroying three or four acres of wheat and wrecking several expensive fences in the process.

The next morning, as soon as it was light I stood and looked at the aftermath. I didn't think it was possible for forty thousand people to leave so much litter behind. Clearing up was a daunting task, which if the truth be told, we hadn't really given as much thought to as we should have done. However, slowly, with a lot of hard work and with the assistance of the Knebworth Estate, the park was returned to its former glory.

We waited with some trepidation for the following Thursday when the music paper reviews would be out. Our hearts sank when we saw the headlines of the double page spread the Melody Maker had given us 'Knebworth: Great music but a non-event.' Rapidly reading through the report, we relaxed. The reviewer, Michael Watts, had actually enjoyed the festival but felt that outdoor events had lost their way. The reasons he gives are I think even more pertinent today than they were in 1974. As we move ever further away from the politically driven days of the early gatherings I can not help but wonder what he makes of today's festivals, where for large sums of money large companies are allowed to install special grandstands, marquees and other facilities for the exclusive use of their guests, who would probably prefer to be at the races anyway.

Report: Michael Watts; Melody Maker

Rock festivals come these days without loud trumpeting and laying on of hands without, in fact, the blah and hoo-hah that attended the Isle of Wight's and the events in Hyde Park of three or four years ago. Conceivable all this prevalent gentility maybe welcomed by many, but to my mind it is vaguely dissatisfying that everyone is now so contained in their enthusiasm artists, public and music business alike. These events have become so highly institutionalised that pretty soon one fully expects the kids to be playing croquet, as well as throwing Frisbees, in between sets. Maybe the high tea atmosphere of The Crystal Palace Garden Party will be the first to feature it. This is not a denigration of such festivals, merely a reflection on how they've ceased to be events of much significance, and excitement, as often as not monopolised, like cricket matches, by the topic of the weather. Dark clouds on the horizon offer more of a threat than a mega-death guitar solo, it would appear. So the spirit of Woodstock, cliché though that be, has evaporated, and therein partly lies the explanation for the low-key nature of the current festival scene. The times have changed. The sixties are dead. And the focus of energy is on the pop charts and all, which that entails of 'product' and contrivance, not on large personalities and extravagant musicianship. Besides, where are those large personalities, artists with the magnetism of Hendrix and Cream, who can render transcendental a day and night spent in some farmer's hired field? They can be counted on the fingers of one hand and even then a couple of them are dead.

Rock music, you must see, is never just about music and neither are rock festivals. They're very much to do with people, and the people around at rock festivals these days have lost some capacity to be surprised and enthralled by what's presented to them. We've all grown accustomed to the best; our imaginations find it easy to encompass the larger than life and so we settle for a pleasurable ambiance: sun on our backs, adequate facilities and a few square feet on the grass. A socio-cultural becomes a picnic. Last Saturday's Knebworth Bucolic Frolic bathed as it was in sun, and blessed with good organisation, was an extremely pleasant occasion, but I doubt if it will be remembered for much other than the first appearance in this country of The Allman Brothers Band a group which fully lived up to its reputation.

The rest of the music papers were less philosophical and even more complimentary. Knebworth, it seemed, was a hit. We may have lost money, we may have been broke but at least, we consoled ourselves, we had hope. However, next year was a long way off.

# CHAPTER 41

The rest of 1974 was rather bleak for us. In September my father in law, Steve Duman, died. He had been ill with cancer for some time and although he bravely made the effort to help us with the Knebworth festival, he was not at all well and on the day of the concert itself, unable to cope, had to be taken home. Steve and I did not always see things the same way, especially in the early days when I first met his daughter. However, over the years our relationship slowly improved. Steve was always there with sound advice and offers of help. An extremely intelligent person with a strong personality, both Wendy and I were going to miss him tremendously.

Although we were kept quite busy throughout the autumn with various one-off concerts and short tours, the only gigs that really stick in my mind were John Entwhistle from the Who, also known as the Ox (great band…poor ticket sales) and The Bee Gees at the Festival Hall with the Royal Symphony Orchestra. This was some time before 'Saturday Night Fever' and although they still had their fans, it was bloody hard work selling out the show.

It was because of Steve's illness that we had taken over the running of a disco that he promoted at the Ship Hotel in Weybridge. It was to be a temporary measure until he recovered sufficiently to once again run it himself. The DJ was Mike Allen, who very deservedly went on to great things with Capitol Radio and LBC. The disco only occupied one evening a week and was fun to run. The only problem was that, in the chill winter months, standing on the door, my feet would freeze up. One morning, after a particularly cold session the night before, I found that the big toe on my right foot was turning black. Highly alarmed, I shot round to my doctor who was not at all reassuring.

'Could be a heart problem. You should really see a specialist,' he said.

The specialist was more sympathetic and carried out every test imaginable. When he finally wrote to me with his conclusion he said, 'As I originally suspected, it was frostbite.'

Ye gods, frostbite in Weybridge! That had to be a first. For a cure, he suggested a pair of fur-lined boots.

# CHAPTER 42

All the time we were working, my mind was fixed on the next summer. At any period there were only a limited number of suitable acts that were capable of filling an arena the size of Knebworth and at one point Yes seemed to be ideal. I arranged a meeting with their manager, Brian Lane to discuss the possibility of their appearance. I had met Brian several times before, but didn't know him well. We had arranged to meet at his office in Notting Hill and when I arrived Brian suggested we had lunch at Geales, a fish restaurant that he used regularly, as it was just around the corner from his office. As we were being shown to our table, Brian stopped to speak to someone.

'Who was that?' I asked when we sat down.

Brian gave me a dirty look.

'For God's sake,' he said, 'it was George Best.' Adding in disgust, 'I can see we don't have much in common.'

Actually we did. Brian, I discovered, was an enthusiastic collector of by Norman Rockwell artwork, the man whose paintings graced the pages of The Saturday Evening Post for nearly 47 years and who was one of my favourite illustrators. Unfortunately, nothing came of the meeting because I think the band had other commitments during the summer.

We considered quite a few bands including The Who, The Stones, Dylan, before narrowing it down to Elton John and the Pink Floyd, two very diverse acts. Elton John was at this time really hot and as we were good friends with his agent, Steve Barnet, we made him an offer. However, the band we really wanted was Pink Floyd.

When we first started promoting, finding out which bands were popular was easy. I just talked to the kids at the gigs we ran regularly in halls around the country. This way we had an unrivalled view of what was happening. However, when we stopped our grass roots promoting, it was not quite as easy. Sure we knew, as most people did, who the really big pop acts were, but before we put ourselves on the line financially we wanted to know that the average kid in the street liked the sort of bands we were considering for Knebworth. We arranged a survey. We prepared a form with questions like 'Who is your favourite band?' 'Who would you like to see at a festival?' and our particular favourite 'Place the following groups in order of popularity.' We then paid a dozen or so students to go out one Saturday onto the streets of London, Birmingham and Manchester and try to get young people to answer our questionnaire. In fact, it wasn't that difficult because once the youngsters realised what the survey was about they were keen to take part. When it was analysed we found rather unsurprisingly that David Bowie and the Stones were amongst the most popular, along with Queen and Status Quo. Beafheart and JJ Cale also did well, but out in front by a country mile were Pink Floyd.

Keeping our fingers crossed, we sent their manager, Steve O'Rourke, a letter outlining the advantages of Knebworth and also included what we thought was a generous offer. Several days later we returned home after being out for the day to find that Steve had been leaving numerous messages both at our home and our office for us to call him urgently.

'Well,' said Wendy in a matter of fact manner, 'We've got Pink Floyd then.'

When I got in touch with Steve I found out he was leaving for New York the next day and wanted to make contact before he left. The Floyd, he told me, was definitely interested in playing Knebworth and we arranged to meet when he came back from the States. Steve at that time was living in Esher and on his return we sat in his kitchen and over a cup of coffee worked out a deal. Instead of a guarantee, the band was to receive a substantial percentage of the net amount remaining after all expenses were deducted. It was a great deal all round. If the Floyd drew them in, as I was sure they would, then they would receive considerably more than we were prepared to guarantee. For us, there was no risk at all meaning we could relax and really concentrate on organising the event.

Or could we? Although there had been very few complaints after the Allman Brothers' event, the North Herts Council had decided, in consultation with Mr Pruette the Licensing Officer and, of course the police, that we would require an extension to Knebworth's existing licence, which was limited to 15,000. An application was duly made to increase the numbers for the concert to 40,000. On the evening that the application was to be heard, David Condy, Wendy and I decided that we would attend the meeting and sit in the public gallery to hear exactly what was said. The proceedings started off promisingly enough with the very capable Chairwoman putting a fair and precise summary of the application to the body of the council. Then Mr Pruette was called to give his report. Although critical of some aspects of the event, mainly the sound levels and the time we overran, he was surprisingly upbeat and supportive. It was when the matter was put to the council for open debate that things started to deteriorate. I was quite surprised at the amount of opposition we faced, mainly from people who I learnt later had not even attended the concert to see for themselves what it was like. As someone with strong socialist views I couldn't believe it when a labour Councillor got to his feet.

'What I really want to know, he exclaimed, 'Is where the vast profits from these concerts go? Is it right that they should go into one man's pocket?'

Does he mean the loss we made last year I thought?

The Chairwoman immediately pounced on him. 'We are here to discuss the issuing of a music licence. Your question is totally irrelevant.'

Someone else, another labour councillor, I'm afraid, asked with rather more relevance was it right that the local ratepayers should bear the cost of the police and other incidental expenses. It was at this point that I became aware of a strangulated hissing noise coming from my right, accompanied by regular prodding's to my ribs.

'Tell them we will pay the police costs,' said a by now almost apoplectic Wendy. Trying to catch the Chairwoman's eye wasn't easy. However, she finally noticed me.

'Have you something you would like to say?' she asked and to her ever-lasting credit she invited me to address the council.

Standing at the back of the chamber, with most of council members swivelled in their chairs to see exactly what this upstart looked like, I explained that we had already had meetings with the police to discuss matters for the next festival and we were prepared to pay their costs.

'In addition' I said, 'we are also be prepared to make a contribution to the council's out of pocket expenses.'

The atmosphere started to thaw but we still weren't out of the woods yet as there was still the final vote to take place. We finally won by a reasonable majority. However, it was interesting to note that most of the young labour councillors voted against us and virtually every one of the little old Tory ladies voted for us. Not at all what I was expecting.

After the meeting, elated but absolutely emotionally drained, David, Wendy and I retired to the nearest pub to celebrate.

The next thing to do was book an interesting support programme. Never an easy task, it was made even more difficult by the members of Pink Floyd insisting we book Linda Lewis and Roy Harper, both excellent performers but not my first choice for such a large outdoor event. Steve Miller, I thought would be ideal, his recording of The Joker being a particular favourite of mine and I reasoned, a good boogie band is always safe and would keep the crowd happy. He very nearly didn't accept the offer as he had just split up his band but he really seemed to like the idea of playing a British stately home and in the end he put a band together just for Knebworth. Beefheart also formed a band especially to play at the festival. He had just been working with Zappa and the Mothers and was being looked after at this time by Herb Cohen. When I called Herb to see if Don was available he told me that the Magic Band had just broken up so it was going to be difficult.

'How much are you offering,' he asked.

'$15,000,' I replied.

There was a moment's silence, 'We'll put a band together even if it means my mother will have to play.'

We would normally have booked five supporting acts, but as a sop to the local council we had agreed to limit the total number of groups to five to avoid the over-running that had so hampered us the previous year.

To add a little more spice to the programme, I thought it would be great to book a top rate comedian so that, in addition to comperes like John Peel and Pete Drummond, there would be someone to fill in those boring gaps between changeovers. I approached Frankie Howard's agent to see if he could be persuaded to appear. A few days later, somewhat to my surprise I received a phone call from Frankie Howard himself - very business like but still with all of his mannerisms intact full of 'ooh's and aah's' and 'No but really'. It seemed he was very tempted by the opportunity of working with a much younger age group than his usual audience, but he was very worried that they would reject him and he would be booed off stage. I tried to reassure him and explained that the kids would love him and be right on his side. At one point I thought I had him. However, after thirty minutes or so of my cajoling, his natural caution asserted itself and he decided against appearing. A great pity because I think he would have been a great hit.

The next comedian I tried was Barry Humphrey better known then, as now, as Dame Edna Everage. Perhaps it was the nature of the request. However, once again, instead of a call from an agent, I received a call directly from the comedian. By one of those strange coincidences, I dealt quite frequently in those days with a record company guy also called Barry Humphrey. When a call came in, Wendy, quite convinced that it was Barry from the record company, put it straight through to me.

'Hi,' I said rather familiarly, 'how's it going then?'

There was a slight pause and a rather pompous voice said, 'There are one or two questions I would like to ask you about this festival you wanted me to appear at.'

'What the hell are you talking about?' I said, 'the only place you're likely appear at is the Old Bailey.'

Then the penny dropped. Christ, I thought, he's supposed to be the funny man. Briefly explaining my mistake, I apologised. Like Frankie Howard, he was intrigued. It was something he had never tried before and after a number of searching questions, agreed to appear. Unfortunately, a couple of weeks later I received another phone call, this time from his agent so I knew it was going to be bad news explaining that something had come up that prevented Barry from appearing.

The late Graham Chapman

Of course, we ultimately booked Graham Chapman from Monty Python's Flying Circus, who turned up on the day with a friend, who looked to me suspiciously like Michael Palin.

At this time we were living in the country about forty-five miles south of London. Although very pleasant, it was not exactly practical when it came to running a large scale festival and we decided to rent temporary offices in town. What we ended up with and I am not quite sure how, was a four bed roomed house in Waterford Rd, just off the lower end of the Kings Road. It also had an enormous room suitable for use as an office situated on the first floor, above a triple garage. It was absolutely ideal. The house was owned by Piers Weld Forester, who, I later discovered, was a member of the Guinness Family and had been a regular escort of Princess Anne. I also found out that he raced motor cycles and up to a short while earlier had been sharing the house with his chum, two times world champion Barry Sheen.

Just as we moved in I received a phone call from our part time assistant David Campbell. He wondered if we could find a job in the office for a friend of his from Australia, a young lady called Jenny. It appeared she had come over to England to marry a Warwickshire farmer but had changed her mind. Apparently he had looked O.K in the Australian sunshine, but was not nearly as attractive set against the Warwickshire mud.

Jenny, when she arrived at our office was something of a surprise. Not only was she extremely attractive, well I had expected that from David's description, but more importantly she was hard working and efficient, in fact, a definite asset. She also turned out to be something of a raver. Coming in rather late one Monday morning, she explained that she had met this distin- guished middle-aged man in a pub who had promptly taken her to Paris for the weekend.

'He claimed to be an actor' she said. When Wendy asked his name she answered Anthony Steel adding that she'd never heard of him. But both Wendy and I had. Anthony Steel was a British matinee idol who had starred in a string of adventure films for the J. Arthur Rank studio in the fifties. However, his sole claim to fame as far as I was concerned was that he had married the blonde Swedish bombshell Anita Ekberg. This man was now in his fifties and still pulling them. Lucky old Anthony, I thought. One of Jenny's jobs was to mail out publicity photos of the bands to various newspapers and magazines. Sitting at her desk, sorting through a pile of photographs, she came across one of Steve Miller.

'Oh,' she exclaimed, 'he's nice.'

One of the other girls in the office came over to have a look.

'He's horrid,' she said, 'fat and ugly.'

'I don't care,' Jenny said defensively,' I'd like to marry him.'

'Strange girl,' I thought.

# CHAPTER 43

It was probably around seven or eight weeks before the festival when I thought history was going to repeat it's self. Steve O'Rourke had told me to leave the announcement to him and the story had not yet been given to the press. Walking into the Ship Hotel for one of the weekly discos, I was stunned when Mike Allen came up to me.

'Congratulations Freddy' he said, 'I hear you've got the Floyd.'

'Where did you hear that?' I said anxiously.

'Someone in the Floyd's office told me,' he replied.

Oh my God, suppose a journalist gets to hear, I thought. However, I needn't have worried. These things didn't bother Steve in the same way as they did Peter Grant.

It wasn't long before we started work at Knebworth. Our site manager was Barry Turner, a tough, capable guy from Bristol whose only qualification for the job appeared to be that of deep-sea diver and boat builder. Nevertheless, Barry did a terrific job for us at every one of the seven festivals we staged at Knebworth; working ridiculously long hours to tight deadlines never once complaining as ever more responsibilities were put on him.

For the Pink Floyd concert we decided to increase the size of the arena to accommodate the larger crowd that we anticipated, and to reposition the stage slightly to improve the sight lines. Positioning the stage was always one of my least favourite jobs, a real responsibility - get it wrong and it would have serious repercussions on the day of the concert. This year, the stage was to be even bigger than the one that was constructed for the Allman Brothers. The overall width was close to 150 feet and the performing area was an unobstructed 50 feet wide by over 40 feet high to accommodate the huge circular screen that was fundamental to the Floyd's performance. It gave the stage a rather odd appearance. However, it was still pretty impressive.

In the midst of all this frantic activity Frank Zappa and Herb Cohen arrived in London for the case they were bringing against the Albert Hall. The hearing was held in the Royal courts of Justice in the Strand, before Mr Justice Mocatta, an elderly, and as I was to see for myself extremely unworldly man, who didn't seem to know what a long playing album was, let alone a groupie. I am sure that that Judge was totally impartial. However, it did not help to give this impression when on one occasion he rose from the bench and waved to a man entering the court as if he were a long lost friend. He probably hadn't seen him for at least a couple of days, not in fact I presumed since they last met at their club. The man turned out to be Sir Louis Gluckstein, the President of the Royal Albert Hall.

In the cross-examinations, Frank was more than a match for his inquisitors. However, instead of a simple case of breach of contract, the opposing barristers attempted to turn the hearing into what Frank rather perceptively described as a 'bogus obscenity case'. Predictably Frank lost the case. The judgement succinctly summed up (by Frank) on page 137 of his Real Frank Zappa Book was as follows

[1] The material was *not* obscene.
[2] The Albert Hall had, in fact, breached its contract. *But*
[3] As the Albert Hall is a *Royal* institution, it would be improper for an American musician to prevail in a case like this, so Yankee, Go Home.

In fact, what I understood from the Judge's summing up, apart from the fact that he had taken a rather strong dislike to Herb Cohen, was what was considered acceptable at a venue such as the Rainbow theatre, or the Odeon Hammersmith was simply not acceptable at the Royal Albert Hall - in my opinion, a very prejudiced interpretation of the law.

After all this legal argument, it was a relief to return to the general hassles of setting up a festival. By now the stage was virtually finished and the Floyd's crew were busy rigging the large model aircraft that was used at one point during the performance. For maximum effect it had to fly over the heads of the audience before crashing into a corner of the stage. To achieve this effect a cable had been rigged between a crane with a sixty-foot jib and the stage. I happened to be on stage while some of this work was being carried out talking to Bill Harkin, our stage designer. Deeply engrossed in our conversation, I couldn't believe it when I was rudely and none too gently pushed to the floor. I know promoters aren't exactly popular, I thought, but what the hell have I done now. Suddenly, there was a high-pitched whistling noise followed by a loud explosion. Looking at the back of the stage, I saw that two of the huge tour cases had been virtually reduced to powder. It was only then that I realised the cable that was being tensioned had snapped. With a dozen or more people on stage, it was a miracle that no one was injured. The speed with which the cable whipped back could have quite easily cut a man in half.

The Pink Floyd had decided that as sound quality was so important they would supply the PA system themselves. Also, and perhaps for the first time by anyone at a festival, they would install quadraphonic sound. This would entail building extra PA towers at the side and rear of the arena. The week before the event these had still not been built and the Floyd technical crew, who were waiting to install the speakers and ancillary equipment, were giving me a very hard time. The people responsible for the construction of the

'Pink Floyd's projectile ready to go'

towers and other work to the stage were a specialist-rigging company from Wales, referred to by our staff for reasons of easy identification as the Welsh Wizards. Bill Harkin had been responsible for choosing this company, explaining to me that they the were the only people in the country prepared to take on the more hazardous aspects of hanging equipment in the roof of a stage some sixty feet above ground level. I asked Bill if he would find out why the work hadn't been completed and was eventually told that the crew hadn't been able to start on the towers as they were behind on the stage work and were tired and dispirited. If I wanted the work done immediately, a sharp injection of cash was required to help raise their energy levels.

Rather reluctantly, I agreed. I always tried to avoid these sorts of demands as exhortation seems to be highly contagious in festival situations and before you know where you are every one is after more money with potentially disastrous consequences for the event. The one stipulation I made was that all the work to the PA towers was to be completed in twenty-four hours. The next morning I was in the arena around 6am to make sure that the work was being carried out. Of course, there was no sign of the Welsh wizards. I decided the only thing was to go and find them. They had set up home in a quiet part of the park, pitching their tents either side of a track. Driving into the enclave, I was intrigued to see an attractive young woman come out of a tent stark naked. As soon as she noticed me, instead of running back inside, she shot across the track squealing loudly all the time, before disappearing from view into another tent. What's the matter with her, I thought? Hasn't she seen a fully clothed man before? Everyone of course came out to see what all the commotion was about and I, ever the opportunist, managed to nab my workers.

# CHAPTER 44

We were at home when we received a call from Chryssie Lytton Cobbold.

'I have just had a phone call from Lady Bowes Lyon. Her son, the Lord-Lieutenant of Hertfordshire and his wife are holding a chamber music recital by their lake on the evening of your festival and as their property is very close to Knebworth, they would very much like to meet you to discuss any potential problems. Would you be kind enough to phone them?'

Wendy rang and arranged for us to see them the following week. When we arrived, Lady Bowes Lyon, who we had discovered was the Queen Mother's sister-in- law, met us. Her son, it appeared, was running late but she wondered if we would care for coffee. Sitting in the kitchen she turned out to be an extremely charming, relaxed woman. Her son, when he arrived, was very different - tall, courteous, cold, very correct and I could tell without any great difficulty that he was not exactly a fan of pop festivals. What the family wanted was for us to suspend our concert for an hour while their string quartet performed. They explained that as Luton Airport was only a few miles away and they were under the flight path, they had also written to air traffic control asking them to suspend flights during the performance. I can just imagine what the reply would have been to such an arrogant request, especially at the peak of the holiday season. Making vague promises, we left.

Ten days before the festival a bombshell struck. Mr Rourke, the owner of the herd of deer that was kept in the park, had obtained an injunction stopping the festival from taking place because he complained the safety and general welfare of his herd was at risk. Panicking somewhat, I drove straight up to Knebworth for an emergency meeting with the two Davids. I looked at the agreement between the estate and Rourke with total amazement.

'Good grief David!' I exclaimed, 'You've given your park away.'

In fact, it wasn't quite that bad. However, it did appear that Rourke had a large say in what events could be held in the park. There was nothing else to do it seemed but fight the injunction in court.

So to this end we instructed our solicitor Stan Beller to set up a meeting with a prominent barrister. There was a certain amount of confusion on our arrival.

'Which one of you is the solicitor and which one the client?' asked the barrister who seemed genuinely confused.

For a minute I couldn't understand the reason for his question. Then the penny dropped. Looking at Stan, I saw he was wearing a brilliant white raincoat and sported day-glo socks one green, one orange and a simply outrageous tie whilst I was wearing a very conservative suit.

An early morning view from the stage. Note Pink Floyd's giant screen
ready to be swung into position

The barrister was very positive. He felt that in view of the importance of the event, a judge would order that some compromise was reached and that is exactly what happened. On the morning of the hearing at the Law Courts in the Strand, close to the scene of the Zappa debacle, a deal was thrashed out. Rourke it seemed did not want to stop the festival from taking place. He just wanted the welfare of his deer to be taken seriously. Certain safeguards were given and the injunction was lifted. After our court appearance, it didn't help my peace of mind that tickets were selling so well that it looked as if we would be substantially in breach of the licence. I could definitely do without further court appearances, I thought and for the first time ever we announced that the festival was sold out and asked people to stay away. A hard decision for a promoter to make and against everything I held sacred. However, if I thought everything from now on would be smooth sailing, I was wrong. We had mentioned in our pre-event advertising that there was only a limited amount of camping space. However, nobody had taken any notice and it was obvious that by around 10pm on the Friday evening prior to the event, the two fields we were using for camping were going to be full. Our only alternative was to obtain permission from one of the Estate's tenant farmers to use his fields that adjoined our campsite. Why are farmer's natural negotiators? I haven't found one yet, simple souls that they are, that hasn't run rings round me when it comes to extracting the last penny for the use of their land. Of course, it could just be whenever I meet them I am always in a desperate situation, as I was with David's tenant farmer Tommy Young. True to form, he held out for a substantial sum but at least when we finally left his house we had permission to use his three fields.

The first couple of hours at the start of a festival are always rather fraught and at Knebworth it always seemed a little worse than normal. Perhaps this was because the campsite area was about three quarters of a mile walk from the arena and the fanatics, who were determined to nail a place right in front of the stage, tended to get extremely frustrated by about 6.30 a.m. Although we always advertised the fact that the gates opened at 10am, by 7am the stewards and police were hard pushed to hold back the heaving multitudes. As soon as the outer gates were opened, there was always a mad dash along the internal road in the park. Luckily, by the time they reached the entrance to the arena even the fittest, after carrying knapsacks full of beer for nearly a mile, were pretty pooped and normally filed in without any trouble.

At noon, pretty much on time Linda Lewis opened the festival. Unfortunately, the PA, running somewhat under its full potential, did not do justice to her superb voice and she had a rather hard time trying to project beyond the first few rows.

Before Roy Harper made it to the stage we had our first drama of the afternoon. It appeared that Roy or at least one of his retinue had forgotten to take Roy's stage clothes from the boot of his chauffeur driven car, before it was removed to a place of safety. Another story goes that he was rather annoyed that he couldn't ride his horse that he had brought to the festival, onto the stage. Whatever the reason, Roy, predictably enough I suppose, had thrown a moody and at our expense smashed up his dressing room. He had obviously enjoyed himself so much that he was starting on a second one when fortunately he was restrained. After having his fun spoilt in this way he did the next best thing and had a fit of the sulks refusing to leave his caravan.

When she heard this Jenny, who was working with me in the admin office offered to assist.

'No worries, leave it to me. I'll make sure he goes on stage.'

I don't know what she did. In fact, I'd rather not know. However, whatever she did she was as good as her word and thirty minutes later she lead a rather sheepish Roy Harper out of his caravan and onto the stage.

Beefheart was next on with a Magic Band that contained all the old favourites who had played for us before, either with Don or Frank. People like Elliot Inger, better known as Winged Eel Fingerling who had been one of musicians I had led on stage in Holland and Jimmy Carl Black who had featured significantly in 200 Motels, one of my favourite films. Well, I never claimed to be mature.

For all his idiosyncratic ways, Don if he was in the mood, could really work an audience. However, this time his performance was just a little flat, as if he had other things on his mind. Towards the end of his set he did finally succeed in getting a large part of the audience up on their feet with a stirring harmonica solo during a hard driving 'Gimme dat Harp Boy'. But I have to say, having seen him perform many times previously, his heart just didn't seem to be in it.

Some twenty-six years later Herb Cohen told me an interesting story about Jimmy Carl Black and his appearance at Knebworth, which I'm sure he won't mind if I repeat it. After their performance the band, with the exception of Jimmy Carl Black, left to return to their hotel in London, as they had just came in for the one gig and were returning to the States on a mid-day flight the next day. Jimmy, who obviously had another sort of performance in mind, had quietly disappeared with a very attractive girl who had been hanging around the band all day. Herb remembered her well if only because they shared the same surname. The following day Jimmy arrived at the airport just in time to catch the plane and Herb forgot all about the incident until 21 years later when he was sitting in a bar in L.A and heard a young lady, with an English accent at the next table telling her friends that her real father had been a rock musician named Jimmy Carl Black, whom her mother hadn't seen since the summer of 75 and who unfortunately had died not so very long ago. Of course, Herb being Herb, at this point butted in.

' You must be Michelle Cohen's daughter,' he said. Total consternation. However, worse was to come. 'Actually, your father's not dead but very much alive and living in Germany,' he went on, 'If you hang on a moment you can have a word with him.'

Herb then used his mobile phone and called Jimmy in Germany.

'Are you ready for this Jimmy?' he said, 'I've got your long lost English daughter here and she'd love to speak to you.'

Roy Harper with Trigger

# CHAPTER 45

Ever the professional, Steve Miller had chartered a helicopter to bring the band to Knebworth. It wasn't strictly necessary because, despite the traffic jams that stretched at times 6 miles north and 10 miles south, we had worked out a back street route for the bands and their guests that led directly to the private entrance to Knebworth House. In this way we managed to avoid the nightmare problems that we had experienced in 1970 at the Bath Festival. It was really left to Steve and his band to finally bring the festival to life with an hour and a half of 'up and doing it' boogie.

With every one by now in a happy and relaxed frame of mind, it was a good time to bring on the Floyd. However, technical problems with their Hammond Organ and the general inefficiency of the stage crew that we always seemed to suffer at festivals saw the poor long suffering audience in for another long wait. We had been asked to book two World War Two Spitfires for the Floyd and I had contacted the late Neil Williams to supply them. Neil, a former RAF pilot, had been British Aerobatics Champion three or four times and had loads of experience flying Spitfires, plus practically everything else with wings. The general idea was just as Pink Floyd started their performance, the Spitfires would fly in at treetop height and, crossing over, would pull up into a vertical climb just as the band struck their first chord. The timing was going to be critical. We had already, of course, obtained permission for the stunt and our local contact was Luton Airport. One of the air traffic controllers had agreed to liaise between Neil and myself. Sitting in my office, the upper of two Portacabins, I had a terrific view of the stage area. Barry Turner had arranged for a phone line to be rigged up between the office and a point backstage and we had a GPO phone line installed on which I could call Luton. Sitting there with a phone to each ear, I was enjoying myself. About ten minutes before the start of the Floyd's performance I made contact with Neil, courtesy of our friendly air traffic controller.

'When exactly do you want us?' he asked.

I checked with the Floyds co-ordinator

'We've got a problem. It'll be another ten minutes,' he said rather abruptly.

Ten minutes later, when I checked back with him, I was told my assistance was no longer required.

'Just have the aircraft cross the stage in ten minutes,' he said, 'Make sure it's ten minutes to the second.'

Passing on his message, I sat in the office and waited. A couple of minutes before the Spitfires were due I dialled the talking clock. The pilots

The Pink Floyd aftermath

B.T.'s answer to communication for 80,000

timing was impressive. Just as the pips went so the two Spitfires appeared crossing behind the stage and pulling up with perfect symmetry into a vertical climb, the Rolls Royce Merlin engines making the sort of noise that make the hairs on the back of your neck stand up. Unfortunately, The Floyd didn't start playing until a minute and a half later, but as they say 'It's only rock 'n' roll'.

Wandering into the arena at the beginning of the Floyds' set, I was pretty impressed. The sound quality had improved dramatically. The volume had been increased and the satellite speakers switched on. I can't guarantee that it produced quadraphonic sound or if it did it was only for the lucky two or three thousand sitting in exactly the right position. However, it was about the best I'd heard at an outdoor festival. Unfortunately, it didn't stay like this throughout their set. The crew, it seemed, were tired after the extensive American tour they had just undertaken and most of the bands equipment had not arrived at Knebworth until the Friday, giving them less than 24 hours to assemble a very elaborate sound system as well as the groups stage equipment. I suppose it was only to be expected that they experienced the occasional technical problems. The worst ones were with the generators the crew had booked. They were not stabilised and this affected the keyboards, as the band were to find to their cost. Why the crew didn't leave us to book the generators I am not quite sure, as I am certain the problems we had experienced in Italy with Frank Zappa at the Bologna Sports Stadium would have made us aware of this point. Nevertheless, these set backs did not seem to affect the way the band were received. After a slow start, they picked up the pace and by the end of their show they had everyone on their feet, cheering wildly. The specialist effects were quite brilliant and the fireworks spectacular. Unfortunately, despite the care taken by the pyrotechnics company in positioning the fireworks to make sure they exploded behind the stage, one of the rockets fell back into the arena hitting a young man in the eye. He was lucky in one respect that the pyrotechnics company, the Floyd and we all carried third party insurance covering such an eventuality. However, I am certain that whatever compensation he received, it was not nearly enough to compensate for the trauma he suffered.

Once The Floyd were on stage our crew set about dismantling the fencing along the side of the arena, where the main entrances were situated. A lot of nonsense has been talked about removing the fences to make more room in the arena but the truth is that it was simply a safety measure to avoid hurting people when such a huge crowd started to leave en masse at the end of the festival. If we started a little early it was because there was a lot of corrugated iron fence and scaffolding to dismantle and remove by young men who had been working flat out for at least twenty four hours and were literally out on their feet. We had discussed this problem with both the police and the council who thought it an excellent idea and we followed this policy at all of our subsequent Knebworth events.

Driving around the park just before the end of the Floyd's show I noticed a commotion in the Red Cross tent. Intrigued and nosey as ever I parked and went to see what was happening. Sitting in the centre of the marquee, looking extremely embarrassed, was an obviously naked young man partly covered by a blanket, surrounded by seven or eight highly amused young nurses. Apparently, in no fit state to be wandering around, he had gone looking for his friends and in a quiet corner of the park, a long way from the arena, had fallen into the Estate's slurry pit. He had been discovered walking around stinking to high heaven and taken to the medical centre where he had been instantly stripped and washed by the nurses. We should charge extra for that I thought, making a mental note for the future. The only problem was that his clothes were now unwearable and had been thrown away. Luckily I was able to provide a shirt and spare pair of trousers that I kept in the boot of my car for just such an emergency. I would love to know who he was. Just think, by now he could possibly be a rather pompous head teacher or bank manager. What a depressing thought. 'And what did you do at the festival Daddy?'

As soon as the Floyd came off stage every one started to relax a little. Jenny, as active as ever, was spotted coming out of the bushes with one of the group's managers giving a whole new meaning to PR and I wondered, a little anxiously, just how public her relationships were going to be.

That year, the police had decided to take charge of the traffic arrangements, not just on the roads leading to Knebworth, but inside the park as well.

Early morning in the arena 1975

To be fair to them, they probably weren't expecting as many people as eventually turned up. That said, they probably had a pretty good idea of what to expect when a week or so before the event, we announced via the BBC that all tickets had been sold and advised any one without a ticket to stay away. We had limited the ticket sales to around 80,000. If we hadn't, I think we could have easily sold a further twenty or thirty thousand such was the popularity at this time of the Floyd. Getting everyone out was a nightmare as the entire park was grid locked. David Lytton Cobbold, in an attempt to ease the situation, opened the private entrance and had some of the staff from his estate direct people out. The police were furious. An argument developed and at one point David was nearly arrested. The police, it seemed, felt that if anyone was going to cock things up it was going to be them and not some well meaning civilian, even if he did own the whole bloody shooting match.

It wasn't until 4 or 5am that things finally started to quieten down. By then I was quite ready to call it a day and Wendy and I retired to our room in the Roebuck Hotel for some much-needed sleep. We were back on site less than five hours later to see what damage the park had suffered. Surprisingly, in view of the enormous attendance, it wasn't too bad. The worst damage was to a wooden rail fence just outside the park, which had been systematically destroyed and burnt by our happy band of campers to fuel their campfires. What really alarmed me though was the simply unbelievable amount of litter left in the arena. How the hell where we going to shift this lot? One of the more inspired members of our staff came up with the answer in Captain Olley, an ex army officer who ran an industrial cleaning company that specialised in litter clearing. Even he was taken aback when he saw the size of the problem. Still, undaunted, he soon worked out a price that included hand picking and machine finishing and promptly, thank god, got on with the job.

It was on the Monday morning that I got a phone call from Jenny.

'There's not a lot for me to do at the moment,' she said, 'so would you mind if I took a few days off. Steve Miller's asked me to go with him to Paris.'

'Good God!' I thought,' How does she do it? She'll soon know the place better than Jane Birkin.'

Anyway, she not only went to Paris with him but also back to America and her wish came true. She married Steve Miller.

Wendy and I waited impatiently until Thursday when the reviews in the music papers were published. A good review would, of course, make it considerably easier to book a major attraction the following year. The Melody Maker's reporter, Chris Charlesworth, dismissed our organisation of the event in nine words (not counting the hyphens) 'It was a reasonably well-organised one-day festival'. That's it, I thought, four solid months work

Pink Floyd and their crowd

dismissed in those few words. No wonder I didn't like music journalists. Generally, it seemed to me they were frustrated musicians jealous of the success of the bands they reviewed, self important beyond all reason and very aware of the influence they had on their readers. They seemed to think that access to all the restricted areas was theirs by right. If they had come to review the show, I felt, then why not sit in the arena and experience it as one of the audience? Maybe I was wrong. However, I always put the kids before the press. To be fair to Chris Charlesworth, the rest of his review was quite objective and he took into account The Floyd's many technical difficulties when assessing their performance. However, he just couldn't resist adding at the conclusion of his piece that he was one of the privileged few allowed on the stage during the Floyd's performance and I quote:

'My last recollection, apart from the two hour wait to move my immobile motorcar through the insane traffic jam, is dancing with a total stranger, an intoxicated coloured girl, on the stage while dry-iced circulated around my feet and lower shins. Ever looked down and wondered where your legs are? Yes, Knebworth happened.'

The NME review was even worse. Although it ran to a very generous two pages, they spoilt it by using one of the most insensitive headlines I would have thought possible in a music paper. 'All aboard for the Belsen Express.' To compare the short journey on a packed train from Kings Cross to Stevenage with the journey to the Belsen concentration camp that ended in death for so many hundred thousands of people, was gratuitously insulting.

The NME had actually sent two journalists to review the festival. Like the police, they always seem to travel in pairs. There's safety in numbers, I suppose - 'It's a dangerous job but someone has to do it'. In common with most of the other reviewers, they seemed to enjoy the Spitfires and Steve Miller and not much else although they did seem to be impressed by the musicianship of guitarist Chris Spedding and drummer Bill Bruford, both members of Roy Harper's band Trigger. Thank goodness they ignored the administrative aspects of the festival completely so we lived to fight another day. Although, in general, the journalists didn't seem to enjoy the Floyd's performance, I doubt that anyone in the audience who was there that evening has ever forgotten their spectacular show.

I was really upset that the reviews had not been better because The Pink Floyd had been exceptionally easy to work with. Also, the financial arrangements had allowed us to come out with a profit without the enormous worries that a huge guarantee imposed. In addition, Steve O'Rourke had turned out to be amongst the very best managers I have ever worked with - intelligent, amusing, and a car nut like myself. I just wish all the Knebworth Festivals could have been as much fun to promote.

# CHAPTER 46

Later that year, we decided to move back from the country to London. The novelty had more or less worn off and I was getting a little tired of endless views of fields and cows. It was also rather inconvenient having to make a round trip of over a hundred miles every time we had a meeting. After a long search, we finally found a house in Chester St, West London that was both large enough to live in and provide room for an office. More significantly, it was available on a short lease at the sort of figure we could afford. Putting in an offer we waited anxiously to see if it would be accepted. In fact, it was during a Beefheart concert that we were organising at the New Victoria Theatre, just around the corner from Chester St, that we received a call from the agent telling us our offer had been accepted

The moment contracts had been exchanged we rushed over to our new acquisition to check what work was needed before we moved in. On arriving, we found that all the door furniture and light fittings had been removed. Nothing was left, not even a light bulb. Complaining bitterly to the agents, we were told that the vast majority of the fittings would be returned but it would be up to us to refit them. When the previous owner, a rather pompous middle aged man, came to return the missing items he explained that if we ever had the service lift repaired we would probably find a number of wills belonging to his clients at the bottom of the lift shaft.

'Don't bother returning them' he said 'The money's all gone'.

We found out later that he was a solicitor who had used a great deal of his clients' money and assets to speculate on the stock market and had come rather unstuck when he made one to many bad investments.

As soon as the New Year arrived we were once again faced with what was now becoming a regular problem. Who would headline the next Knebworth Festival? As usual, we approached a number of bands, sending off to their agents or managers presentations which consisted of a large album showing flattering photographs of the two previous festivals, a full colour Brochure of Knebworth House and a letter containing our financial offer. If my memory is correct, in 1976 we sent offers to Led Zeppelin, Queen, Bob Dylan and the Rolling Stones. The first to come back were Led Zeppelin. Wow, we thought, maybe this time they'll appear. A lunch meeting was arranged with Richard Cole, Zeppelin's tour manager, an old friend of ours from way back, and Carol, Peter Grant's secretary, who we also knew very well. It was a great lunch. However, once again it turned out that Peter wasn't sure if it was the right thing to do and nothing came of it. The next call we received was from John Reid, Elton John's long time manager and at that time also manager of Queen.

'I got your offer,' he said, 'I have talked it over with the band and they would really like to play Knebworth this year.'

I was really pleased as Queen was really popular and would, I was sure, present a spectacular show.

A few days later Sally Arnold called from the Stones office. Sally was the personal assistant to Peter Rudge, who, although not officially the Stones' manager, was carrying out that function in everything but name.

'I thought I should let you know that the Stones are interested in playing Knebworth,' she said, 'They are going to talk it over and give you a definite answer in the next few days.' Bloody hell, I thought, the Stones at Knebworth would be really something. Several times more popular than Queen, they would totally guarantee a sell out crowd, even allowing for the fact that they would be playing a national tour a few weeks before Knebworth. A week or so later Sally called again.

'Peter would like a word,' she said. I had known Peter from the time he had first started working in the music business. He had been a social secretary while up at Cambridge and was a highly intelligent and ambitious person.

'I've got good news,' he said 'The Stones will do it, but Mick doesn't want to announce it through the music papers. You have to come up with something different.'

When I got off the phone my jubilation turned to panic.

'What have I done?' I thought,' I've just double booked two of the biggest bands in the world.'

The first thing to do, of course, was phone John Reid. When I got through I explained that there was a problem and, reluctantly, I would have to cancel Queen's appearance. My words were greeted with a rather scary silence that seemed to last an eternity.

'You had better come over to my office and tell me just what's going on,' he said coldly.

This was one meeting that I was definitely not looking forward to.

When we finally met, John surprised me by immediately asking, 'Who is this band that you've blown out Queen for.'

This put me on the spot. If I told him and he passed on the name of the band to the press, then like Led Zeppelin back in 1974 I was probably going to loose the Stones. Knowing there was no real option, I tried to explain that I had been sworn to secrecy. From the look on his face I realised I had made a tactical error. Facing the inevitable I said 'It's the Stones'. He immediately seemed to relax a little.

' Well,' he said. 'That's the only band in the world I would have accepted.'

Ever since this meeting I have always had the greatest respect for John. He didn't say a word to the press or, as far as I know, to anyone else.

Although we now had an agreement in principal with the Stones, it was by no means certain that they had definitively decided to play Knebworth, whatever Peter said. I found this out a few days later when someone called me from the Stones' office.

'The band have some questions they would like to ask you,' I was told, 'Could you see them at one of the Glasgow shows?'

Driving up to Glasgow, I wondered why they couldn't have chosen somewhere a little closer to London. However, I consoled myself that, at least, we had tickets. A Stones' gig was always worth seeing or at least it would have been had I actually been able to see them and not just the large pillar I was sat behind. After the show we were taken back stage only to be told 'now wasn't a good time'. Hoping this wasn't a bad sign, we drove the 300 miles home. However, talking to Sally later that week, it seemed they had finally committed and were definitely planning to do the show - that is until Keith crashed his car on the M1 driving back from a gig at the New Bingley Hall, Stafford. Unfortunately, when the police arrived they found some marijuana and cocaine in his car and promptly charged him with possession. The first we knew of his bust was when Sally called and told us what had happened.

'It could cause problems,' she said, 'Not just with Knebworth but also with the rest of the tour. I'll let you know as soon as we have any more news.'

Luckily the police didn't consider it a really serious matter and, in due course, Keith received a fine.

Meanwhile, the Knebworth estate had already obtained a licence for the event and this time it was for 100,000 people. Of course, there were the normal conditions that applied to sound levels and sanitation etc. There was even talk, although it was not written into the licence, of us footing the bill for a fully fledged contra flow system on the A1M to avoid the hideous traffic jams we had caused the previous year.

Everyone, the police especially, were anxious to hear whom we had booked. As the story had not yet broken, we were very reluctant to tell anyone. However, eventually we realised that we had to give the police as much advance notice as possible, to enable them to plan for the event. Swearing both the police and Mr Pruette the licensing officer, to secrecy and explaining the likely outcome if the story should come out, we told them. The effect couldn't have been more devastating if I had said I'd planted a bomb in the Houses of Parliament.

'Oh my God,' the Chief Superintendent said, turning a little pale.

What they thought was going to happen I'm not quite sure. It's true that in the early days the Stones had a reputation amongst the middle aged and elderly as being the spawn of the devil, rather than the happy geriatrics they have become at the start of the 21$^{st}$ century. However, in 1976, the Stones, whilst maybe not quite considered part of the establishment, were, nonetheless, hardly the enemy of the State. Calming them down, I suggested that the best thing would be for them to see the band in action and at the same time check out what sort of an audience the Stones' attracted. So that is how I came to be at Earls Court with two burly policemen and a slightly built licensing officer. I can't say that they enjoyed their outing. However, they were genuinely impressed with the Stones' fantastic production and the behaviour of the crowd, so the trip had undoubtedly been worthwhile.

I can't think why I complained about the distance to Glasgow as the next trip we were asked to make to see the Stones was to Germany. This time we weren't even offered tickets to their show. Instead we had to hang around their hotel for two days. The only time I met any of the band was when I bumped into Bill Wyman and Charlie Watts in the restaurant while we were having breakfast and they certainly weren't in the mood to discuss Knebworth, as they made abundantly clear.

In fact Charlie's, first remark on seeing me was, 'I didn't know we were even thinking of doing Knebworth.'

I must say as far as Charlie Watts was concerned it was loath at first sight. In fact, it wasn't first sight at all, as we had of course used the Stones a lot in the sixties when we were running clubs. However, Charlie had changed. He was now a lippy, sneering ego. I was really surprised. After ten or twelve years in the limelight you expect people to change a little. However, you also assume that over such a long period of time members of a band as famous as the Rolling Stones would begin to get used to their position and learn to keep their egos under some sort of control. In the end we had a thirty-minute meeting with Peter Rudge and discussed various ways of announcing the event. We also discussed the general theme for the festival. Mick was keen to keep the atmosphere light and laid back, so he suggested we call it the Knebworth Fair and employ jugglers, clowns, fire eaters, jousters etc to entertain the crowd.

We found out later that the Stones were going to turn down our offer until Prince Rupert Lowenstein, the band's financial advisor, pointed out that coming right at the end of their UK tour, when all of the expenses would have been well and truly covered, the enormous fee we were offering was an added bonus. The fact that there were still a large number of disappointed fans that had been unable to buy tickets for their sell out tour had also helped, of course.

# CHAPTER 47

The next problem was how to announce the story without involving the music press. Giving the matter some thought, I decided to release the story over a complete weekend so by the time the music papers picked up on it the story was already out. We started in a in a low-key fashion. David Campbell, who was working in our office at this time, produced a very neat drawing of a leaping clown over the legend 'Stones Knebworth' and the date. We then had it printed on to paper squares and turned it into a flag by attaching them to short green garden canes. We also had a couple of thousand balloons printed with a similar design. When everything was ready we rented a 1920's charabanc from the Beaulieu National Museum and filling it with clowns, fire eaters and jugglers, sent it out around central London, stopping every so often to give a show and hand out the flags and balloons to the tiny tots who stopped to watch the performance. The effect wasn't quite what we expected. Most of the parents seemed to think we were advertising Stones Ginger Wine. However, slowly the older kids started to catch on and a nice little buzz started to develop.

Our next stunt was to be a much higher profile event. It was the Wimbledon men's tennis final that weekend which guaranteed virtually blanket coverage on television and an ideal opportunity, I thought, to get some national exposure for our announcement. The idea was to find two young acrobats, dress them like clowns, provide them with a large banner with our slogan 'Stones at Knebworth' printed on it in large letters and at an appropriate moment have them invade the court. It was left to our tour manager Chris Cooke, who when required would also lend a very capable hand in the office, to put the whole thing together. He found two suitably qualified young men, acquired centre court tickets, including two in the front row and, accompanied by his solicitor just in case things turned nasty, set out for Wimbledon.

The final that year was between Bjorn Borg and Ilie Nastase, two formidable characters. As soon as the two players took a break at the end of the first set, Chris signalled to the boys to start. Peeling of their tracksuits to reveal two rather splendid clown costumes, they tumbled onto the court. For several minutes they entertained everyone with a great display of acrobatics, before unfolding the banner and waving it in front of the cameras. They finally brought their performance to an end by rushing over to Borg and Nastase and rather pushed their luck, I thought, by presenting each of them with a red rose.

While our clowns were giving their all, the two BBC commentators, possibly glad of something to talk about during the pause in play, speculated aloud about what it could all mean. For quite three minutes the talk was all about the Rolling Stones and what on earth Knebworth meant? What they didn't know, and come to that, nor did we, was that Lord Cobbold, the owner of the Knebworth Estate, was watching the match from the Royal Box. He was at that time Lord Chamberlain to the Queen and a very distinguished figure having also been Governor of the Bank of England. I found out later that he had been none too pleased with us as apparently the other occupants of the Royal Box thought that he had arranged the whole thing.

As soon as they had finished their show, our two heroes couldn't decide on what to do next. We had all presumed they would be removed immediately and possibly arrested. However, as no one seemed to be taking any notice of them, they returned to their seats. It was only then that a policeman appeared.

'If I was you,' he said in a kindly fashion. 'I would leave now'. Taking his advice and what was left of their dignity, they left.

In fact it was Mick Jagger who had put the idea of gate crashing Wimbledon in my mind. A few days before the tournament started Peter Rudge had phoned me.

'Mick would appreciate it if you could supply him with a couple of Centre Court tickets, front row seats if possible,' he said.

As usual, centre court tickets were as rare as hen's teeth and we had to phone around the touts to find them. In the end it was Stan Flashman, king of the scalpers, who came up with them, charging us a rather swingeing £240 for the pair. I had heard that Mick Jagger was very careful with his money. However, it was only when some one from his office rang to thank us on his behalf that I realised just how careful.

'Mick asked me to thank you for the tickets,' she said, 'He really enjoyed the match' she continued, 'but he really couldn't believe how much he had to pay for a portion of strawberries.'

We were on television again later that evening when BBC2 broadcast live a stock car race meeting. A friend of Chris Cooke's was racing there and Chris had arranged for him to place several large 'Stones at Knebworth' stickers on a potentially front running car that was entered in one of the televised races.

I watched eagerly when the programme was broadcast and although you could see the stickers if you looked hard enough, it didn't last long as the wretched car turned over at the end of the first lap.

Much more successful was the diversion we arranged for Sunday afternoon. As a motor racing fanatic I have always, rather unfairly I suppose, considered cricket to be stunningly boring. In the seventies BBC2 carried hours of it at the weekend, so I decided to do my bit to liven up the game. All we required to bring about an immediate improvement were a couple of naked girls. These were easier to find than I thought. A couple of phone calls to an agency, a decent fee and a guarantee that we would pay any fines or legal costs and we were in business. The match being covered that weekend was at Hove. Once again Chris stepped into the breach. This time he didn't require any prompting, nor did his solicitor who by now seemed to be really getting into the swing of things. Once inside the ground, the girls stripped off and with each of them holding a large sunshade painted neatly with the magic words, 'STONES AT KNEBWORTH,' set off at a canter for the cricket pitch. The television cameras, as I had hoped, zoomed in on them. However, when they saw that the girls were au natural, the director, rather than embarrass their rather staid viewers continued to zoom and showed a close up of our message on the sunshades. Very satisfactory and for two or three minutes the game actually came to life.

While Chris was looking after the stunts, we were arranging for Terry Slater, without doubt the godfather of London fly posters, to place large banners about 10ft long by 2ft 6ins deep on selected sites in Central London. He started late on Sunday evening so that the young commuters flooding into London on Monday morning could receive the benefit of our campaign. To his credit he carried out all the dangerous work himself, climbing up several huge cranes to attach the banner along the boom some 80ft above the ground - quite scary I would have thought, especially in the dark. His piece de resistance was to place a banner on the arch at Hyde Park Corner. According to Terry, he was standing on a ledge, no more than six inches wide, about twelve feet above the ground, frantically searching for somewhere to attach the banner when he heard a door open just below him. Looking down, he saw a large policeman step out. Now although Terry thought he knew London better than anyone, he had no idea that there was a police station contained in the arch. If he had, I guess, he would have asked me for danger money. The policeman had obviously heard a noise as Terry had climbed up the building and using his flashlight made a thorough search of the area. Luckily, he didn't think to look up. If he had, he would have seen Terry with his back to the wall, arms outspread with the banner hanging from his mouth looking like a character from a Peter Sellers' film. As soon as the copper went back inside (now there's a Freudian slip) Terry finished fixing the banner and very quietly left. I was up really early on Monday morning to admire Terry's handiwork and the banner was still in place at 8am. By 9am it was gone.

Once their tour was over communication with The Stones improved dramatically. Mick Jagger even found the time to come round to our house to discuss, in detail, the concept and general arrangements of the show. I have to admit I was impressed. He was very shrewd, knew just what he wanted and, unlike Charlie Watts, was very level and easygoing. His arrival at the house caused something of a furore. At the time we had six or seven girls working for us, both in the office and handling the ticket postal bookings and they all, of course, wanted to see him. The meeting was held in our sitting room and over the hour or so that the meeting lasted, every one of the girls managed to find some pretext or other to come in and take a look at him. When he left, I discovered half a dozen cans of beer, numerous cups of coffee, sandwiches, note pads etc strategically placed where he had been sitting.

The meeting was really useful in that we now had a clear idea of Mick's requirements. However, very worrying in terms of escalating costs. When we had made the original offer, we had presumed that we would be providing the standard type of stage that we had used previously at Knebworth. Now it seemed we were being asked to build a gigantic structure that would transform into the Stones tongue logo, plus additional sound and lighting and a number of extra projection screens as well as the medieval style tents used in the film Anne of a Thousand Days. In addition, Mick wanted us to employ a film set designer to co-ordinate all the various aspects of the Knebworth Fair theme.

As part of the general extravagance we were asked to use a design company called Hipgnosis, run by Storm Thorgerson and Aubrey Powell to provide all the artwork that was to be used for the event. We had worked with them the previous year and found them to be in another world when it came to prices. However, (and I would never have said this to Storm's face, because the price would have immediately gone up even further) I thought their work was clever and imaginative. Whilst it was Peter Rudge who came up with the concept of a circular poster to avoid all the usual billing problems, it was Hipgnosis who made it work. The first time I saw it I loathed it and very nearly didn't agree to have it printed. However, over the years I have come to realise what a brilliant and original piece of work it is. It completely caught the spirit of the Knebworth Fair that we were trying so hard to project.

Bill Harkin, after the great job he did with the Floyd, was given the task of designing the stage. It was to be an awesome structure measuring over three hundred and fifty feet from side to side, including the P.A. towers. The original idea was that Mick Jagger, using a radio mic, would roller skate from side to side. However, when it was pointed out to him that there would be a drop of at least fifteen feet if he made a mistake and no safety rail he, rather sensibly changed his mind. The biggest difficulty Bill faced was forming the lips and tongue in such a way that they would remain out of sight while the other bands were on stage and could be activated as soon as the Stones were ready to perform. Bill got round this by using huge air pumps to blow up the bags that helped form the key features. I believe he had a lot of trouble getting everything to work properly, but the whole effect worked spectacularly well on the evening of the show.

Now started a seemingly endless round of meetings. The first was with the police. To avoid the previous year's total mayhem on the A1 that caused a government minister to be severely delayed by the jams around Knebworth, they considered it essential that a full contra flow system was implemented. The cost, if I remember correctly, was around £6,000 - a considerable sum in 1976. However, in the interest of good public relations, we agreed. To save time and improve communications between the various parties involved in the event, we regularly held meetings in the Barn Restaurant at Knebworth, which was located near the part of the park that we used as the arena. The meetings were usually attended by up to eighteen or twenty people and comprised representatives from the local council, the police, emergency services including Release and occasionally we would invite representatives from companies that were providing specialist services, such as security, car parking, catering etc. Although at times it seemed a cumbersome way to do things, it worked, as every organisation that was involved in providing essential services felt fully involved. I was sometimes invited to meetings organised by the county council. On one particular occasion, when a meeting had been arranged with representatives of British Rail, I was surprised to find amongst the council officers and policemen, a vicar, who, it seemed, had taken upon himself responsibility for the spiritual welfare of the kids attending the festival. Halfway through the meeting, the vicar appeared to collapse, his head falling onto the table. Worried looks were exchanged. Should we call an ambulance? A couple of minutes later, he appeared to be back to normal. It was only then that we realised that he had been praying. Just before the meeting drew to a close we had been discussing the problems of getting the kids back to Stevenage Station after the show and more importantly how we could get them across the roads in the dark. The answer, it seemed, was coaches and lots of them. Suddenly, the vicar made his only observation.

'It's all very well,' he said, 'getting them to Stevenage Station but what happens when they get to Kings Cross in the early hours of the morning. Would it not be possible for the organisers to arrange taxis at their expense to take them all home?'

For once, booking a support programme wasn't really difficult. In fact, 10cc approached us. Lynyrd Skynyrd were also easy as they were managed by Peter Rudge, who must have had quite a difficult job reconciling their demands with those of the Stones. Hot Tuna, one of my favourite live bands, were part of the Jefferson Airplane family with whom we still had a close relationship. The rest, I seem to remember, jumped at the chance to play with the 'greatest rock 'n' roll band' in the land'.

The additional attractions were also pretty easy to find, once we discovered that there were several specialist agencies that could supply any number of clowns and jugglers, though where the giant millipede came from, I've no idea.

# CHAPTER 48

Once we got on site, in preparation for the event, the fun started. The first thing that happened was 10cc, feeling a little upstaged by the Stones extravagant structure, decided to hang an enormous nose complete with a Zapata style droopy moustache over the representation of Jagger's lips. How they thought they could get away with it, I'm not really sure, as they had brought a sixty foot crane on site to help hang it - hardly the sort of thing you could overlook. They seemed really put out when we asked them to take it down, arguing that it was their way of paying tribute to the Stones. In their opinion, they said, it was a great improvement on the original concept.

On the Thursday before the Festival, the Stones came along for a sound check. While we were all hanging around waiting for some problem or other to be sorted, a large limo arrived and Michael Lindsay Hogg, who was directing the film of the concert, stepped out. I happened to be standing next to Mick, who, along with the other Stones, was undoubtedly footing the bill for this extravagance, when the director made his entrance.

'Fuck me,' Mick exclaimed looking at the limo. 'The cheeky bugger - I drove up in my mini'.

Conditions for the sound check were perfect. It was a lovely warm evening with scarcely a breath of wind and with no more than a dozen or so people sitting in front of the stage, a total contrast, I thought, to the hundred thousand people we were expecting on Saturday. As the sound check pro-gressed and the volume was increased, I started to worry that the several hundred kids who had already started to arrive on the campsite would invade us. This could have been a major problem as we only had a minimum number of stewards on site. Luckily, none of them, despite the loud music, realised that the Stones were on stage. The sound was good and the band continued playing well after they needed to, I think just for the sheer joy of it - totally laid back and really cooking. All of a sudden and totally unexpectedly several dozen-girl guides invaded us. I was vaguely aware that there was a guide camp on the far side of the park and presumed they had heard the music and had come rushing over to see what was going on. How, I wondered, were we going to handle the inevitable requests for autographs? I just couldn't believe it when some old crone wearing a guide uniform started yelling hysterically at the band. According to Chryssie Lyton Cobbold in her book 'Knebworth Rock Festivals', this woman had already burst into a meeting David was holding at the house, demanding that the dreadful noise was stopped immediately, as her girls could not enjoy their campfire singsong. David, rather mistakenly I think, had told her to take the matter up with Mick Jagger and this is what she was doing with a highly aggressive show of middle class resolve. It was an

I wasn't the only one feeling the heat

astonishing display of bad manners that brought little credit to the guiding movement. Somewhat to my surprise and before I even had time to get involved, the band started to leave the stage. I was certain that Mick or Keith would tell her exactly where she could put her guides. However, they seemed to find her naive outburst amusing. I am certain they wouldn't have been so tolerant if the sound hadn't been so good.

Despite the carefully worded paragraph included on both our handbills and tickets stating 'there will only be a very small amount of camping space available and this will not be available until 1pm on Friday 20th August' people once again started flooding in on Thursday. So many people had arrived by Friday morning that I kept popping up to the campsite to see if the site could accommodate the ever-growing influx. During one of my visits I was standing just outside the main gates, chatting to the police, who were also rather anxiously monitoring the situation, when a large and very battered van pulled up next to us. Almost before it stopped, the doors flew open and what seemed like several dozen children emerged. They were all totally naked and without exception covered in festering sores - the tepee people had arrived.

'Can we help you?' one of the policemen politely asked an adult member of the group.

'Sure. We're looking for Arabella Spencer Churchill,' he announced, 'We're running the field kitchen.'

I knew Arabella was around somewhere as she was helping out with one of the festival welfare organisations. I was also pretty sure that she wouldn't want to get drawn into any debate with the public health officers over the suitability of the tepee people to provide food for public consumption.

'Sorry. I don't know where she is,' I said, thinking to myself how the hell am I going to get out of this one?

It was left to one of the police inspectors to come to the rescue. He explained that no one was being allowed into the park and as they could see for themselves there was no room for a food kitchen on the rapidly filling campsite. However, he did know of an ideal place some five or six miles away where they could wait until matters were resolved. To my surprise and great relief the van was turned round and driven off in the general direction of the alternative campsite. Arabella is Winston Churchill's granddaughter and a great friend of Bill Harkin, which is how we had come to know her. They were both to some degree or other involved with the Glastonbury Festival. Bill, of course, had designed the original Pyramid stage, whilst Arabella had been concerned with the general organisation of the event.

If Friday morning and afternoon had been busy, then Friday evening was just ridiculous. By midnight the campsite was just about jam packed full.

There was no alternative but to try and rent additional space, as we had the previous year. Making a rather late call to Farmer Young, we were invited round to his house which was situated a short distance from the park, for what he described as a little chat. This was really ominous. The previous year we had arranged everything on the telephone, so I wondered just what sort of figure he had in mind this time. I soon found out. It wasn't as bad as I had been expecting. However, it was still bad enough. I discovered later that these little deals enabled him and his family to take an annual holiday in the Caribbean.

I never managed to get any sleep on Friday. I was up all night checking that everything was running smoothly on the campsite, that the local roads weren't clogging up and, most importantly, making sure that our security was tight and the stewards were doing their job. Around 3am things started to quieten down and I decided to go to The Roebuck for a quick wash and brush up. I had only been there a few minutes when I heard, loud and clear, the strains of the Dam Busters March

'Good God,' I said to Wendy,' I can't believe the military are out this late.' Then the phone rang. It was Barry Turner.

'You had better come back,' he said, 'Peter Rudge is going ape shit and he won't turn the PA off until he sees you.'

I immediately went rushing back, tearing down Lime Avenue and into the backstage area. Taking the steps two at a time, I bounded onto the stage to be greeted by a noticeably less aggressive Peter Rudge.

'Oh there you are,' he said 'I just wondered where you'd got to.'

Peter could be a pain in the arse sometimes. However, I did like his graffiti, painted no doubt while he was waiting for me. All around the backstage compound he had sprayed slogans on the corrugated iron fence. Things like 'Welcome to Knobworth,' 'Wendy rules OK' and, just in case you missed that one, 'Freddy doesn't rule OK.' But his finest achievement, which I think sums up rock'n'roll so completely, was when he attempted to paint the legend 'There must be a better way' on the bottom step of the stairs leading up to the stage. The artist started off promisingly enough, with a bold statement made before he realised that he couldn't fit everything in. The next three words became progressively smaller and closer together as he tried to correct his mistake, before finally admitting defeat and leaving the last word out completely.

As soon as it was daylight, the enormous crowd crammed into the extended campsite, started to get restless. We had anticipated this and to make sure we weren't caught out, had arranged for a number of our staff to sleep in caravans in the park. This way we could make sure the ticket offices and gates were fully manned before we were forced, by sheer pressure of

Artwork courtesy of Peter Rudge

numbers, to open the main gates into the park. At first it all seemed a little unreal. You could see this huge crowd of at least ten or fifteen thousand people charging towards you. Because of the distance involved, for the first couple of minutes they didn't seem to be getting any closer. Then, suddenly, they were on you. To slow everyone down and bring some order to the general chaos, we had stewards positioned a hundred yards or so from the arena fence, directing people to the various entrances placed along the Lime Avenue boundary. This stopped a potentially dangerous build up of people, all trying to get in through the closest entrance.

After the first extremely hectic thirty to forty minutes, things started to settle down. It was always the fanatics, who had to have a place right in front of the stage, that made life difficult.

Around 9am the peripheral acts started to straggle in, the clowns arriving all together in one large coach. A more sinister looking bunch of individuals was hard to imagine, I thought, when I first saw them. However, they all entered into the spirit of the event and helped entertain people during those boring moments when the bands changed over. In addition to the clowns, we had engaged some rather unusual speciality acts, including Lindbergh, a man who dived from a tall platform into what looked to me like a large bucket of flaming water, Blondini and his exploding coffin, an escapologist and an act that was billed rather dramatically as the 'Battle of the Dinosaurs'. We had also booked a number of aircraft to provide an aerial circus throughout the day, with such exotic items as the Red Devils parachute team, a Tiger Moth dogfight and aerobatics, provided by a Pitts Special

Try as I might, I could never find anyone to run the stage at Knebworth as efficiently as I would like. Each year I always promised myself that I would spend more time on stage, making sure that the supporting acts, at least, would get on and off on time. Of course, it was impossible. Whenever I left the office there immediately seemed to be a dozen people looking for me with queries any one of our staff could usually have dealt with. The worst offenders were usually the road crews, whose egos it seemed would only be assuaged if they spoke directly to me.

The police had once again insisted they control the flow of traffic within the park and this year they were applying the one-way traffic system they had instigated with more vigour than ever. One of Wendy's jobs was to collect the cash from the ticket booths and, of course, make sure they were well supplied with tickets. The ticket offices just outside of the arena were not a problem as Wendy could walk there from our offices. However, the two situated over three quarters of a mile away, just outside the main gates, could only be reached by car. The trouble was that the police had designated both roads in the park as one way in and were not allowing any vehicles out. This was not a real problem for Wendy, as she could drive on the grass most of the way. However, to reach the actual box offices she had to pass through one of the two main entrances against the traffic and here she met her nemesis in a woman police officer built like a small tank who would not let her through. When she tried to explain what she was there for, the policewoman, quite rightly I think, demanded to see her pass. Now Wendy had never worn a pass in her life and wasn't going to start now. In fact, I feel sure she had already lost the one we had given her probably along with her bag, keys etc. In the end in response to the entreaties of one of the stewards who was with Wendy, she let her through. Exactly the same thing happened when she returned; only this time the policewoman was more bloody-minded than ever. This unnecessary game went on all morning with neither side giving an inch. I dread to think what the outcome would have been if she had discovered that Wendy did not possess a driving licence, let alone taken a driving test. However, luckily for her the policewoman was not aware of these transgressions. Matters were only finally resolved when Don Murfitt tactfully explained to the policewoman who Wendy was and why it was necessary for her to visit the ticket offices so often.

Almost on time, the Don Harrison Band kicked off the festival. I was expecting them to do well with two ex-members of Credence Clearwater in the band. However, they only received a lukewarm reception, probably because people were still arriving in large numbers and hadn't yet settled down to the business in hand. Hot Tuna started off well enough, but succumbed to the bad habit many West Coast American bands have of playing for far to long. Anyone who has seen a Grateful Dead concert will know what I mean. Todd Rundgren's Utopia at last started to get everyone in the mood. Todd's imaginative and melodic songs married to a heavy rock beat, plus his energetic performance, earned him a well-deserved encore. It was left to Lynyrd Skynyrd to really get the crowd on their feet with some good old Southern Boogie. It looked to me as if the band were really enjoying themselves, especially during their extended version of Free Bird when singer Ronnie Van Zant and the band's three lead guitarists came down from the stage on to the thrust that was to serve as the tongue during The Stones performance, the guitarists taking it in turns to play long searing choruses. The BBC filmed this particular number and it didn't surprise me one bit when some years later it turned out to be the most requested performance by viewers of the Old Grey Whistle Test.

After the exceptionally hot weather we had been enjoying throughout the summer, there was great risk of fire in the park, especially on the campsite and the neighbouring car parks, both of which adjoined a wooded part of the estate. In the circumstances, we had been asked to make sure that the normal campfires were curtailed. Instead, one large communal one would be allowed, under the supervision of our staff. The local Fire Brigade had given the firm that handled our car parking specific instructions regarding the distance they should leave between rows of cars to enable their fire engines to gain access should it be necessary. Luckily, the firm had followed their advice because in the middle of the afternoon a car caught fire. Within minutes it was burning fiercely, threatening to engulf the cars either side. In fact, it was such a blaze that it appeared a whole row of cars could be destroyed. The marshals were soon on the spot. However, the trouble was that all the cars were locked and, with the limited manpower available, it was almost impossible to drag them out of the way. Help came from an unexpected quarter. A rather shifty looking young guy, who had been seen earlier hanging around the cars, volunteered to open the two vehicles immediately adjacent to the one that was burning. Expecting some sort of wait, the marshals couldn't believe it when he had them open in a matter of seconds. In fact, while they were still moving these cars, he had opened the rest of the line. As one of the boys later remarked, it was a privilege to meet a real professional.

The sound had been really good all afternoon. That is, until it was time for 10cc to take the stage. Already behind schedule, the band seemed to take an inordinately long time setting up. Just as they were ready to start playing, a deep, throbbing buzz was noticed on the P.A. Of course, this delayed things even further while an investigation into the noise was carried out. This went on for so long that I was finally sent for. Looking at the band standing ready to play, I felt they looked too relaxed, rather as if they knew what was going on. In view of the nose and moustache incident, I felt it was another attempt by 10cc to upstage the Stones by making sure that they had the best spot of the day, which as far as I am concerned is around 8pm, just as the sun is starting to set and the poor put upon audience haven't yet lost the feeling in their backsides. Seeing the band laughing and chatting in a casual and uncaring manner, I lost my temper.

Turning to Harvey Lisberg, their manager, I said, ' If they are not playing in two minutes, tell them to go home.'

'Will you still pay us?' he asked.

'Now that's an interesting point...' Before I could finish my sentence, the buzz had miraculously disappeared and 10cc were playing.

They didn't get away with their little stunt, if stunt it was, without paying a price, as the sound for their first number was appalling. The guys on the mixing desk had totally changed the pre-marked controls in a vain attempt to find out what was causing the noise and they had to totally remix the sound while the band was playing. I think they did a fantastic job as, by the second

All the Fun of the Fair

number, everything was back to normal.

It was just as well, after all this hassle, that the band played as well as they did. In fact, they were going down so well they seemed reluctant to come off and at one point, because we were running so late, it looked as if we might have to pull the plug on them. Fortunately, they finished just before such drastic action was required. I think it must have been the last major show that 10cc played before Kevin Godley and Lol Cream left to pursue their own interests. It was a gig, I'm sure, that none of them would forget.

While the Stones' roadies were getting everything ready, Bill Harkin, very calm and professional, was busy transforming the stage into a giant Rolling Stones' logo. Backstage was a different matter. I had just told Mick that the local fire officer had finally decided that there were to be no fireworks. Mick was livid and I could see his point, as the fireworks were to be the climax of the show. However, the long, hot summer that we had been enjoying meant that the woods adjoining the stage area were timber dry and could easily be set alight by a stray rocket.

As time slipped by, I was getting more and more anxious. The curfew set by the council was midnight and it was now 11pm, with no sign of the band, other than Mick, who was poncing around, carrying out his warm-up exercises. We were by now more than three hours behind schedule and the audience were getting decidedly restless. In fact, quite a few had already called it a day and were heading home. It didn't help that, just as I was placating the Assistant Chief Constable of the Hertfordshire Police and two of his senior colleagues, explaining the reasons why we were so behind schedule, Peter Rudge came rushing up to me.

He yelled at the top of his voice, 'Get everybody out of the backstage area,' adding, 'and I do mean everybody' and looked pointedly at my companions, who fortunately found it all very amusing. I suppose that over the years a policeman learns to develop a thick skin.

While I was waiting, Charlie Watts came over to me. Pointing towards the crowd he said, 'And what is my personal percentage likely to be?'

'How the hell do I know what arrangement you have with the band?' I said,' 'I think you should ask Peter that question.'

I already had a pretty good idea that with the huge fee we were paying the Stones, and the way the expenses had burgeoned, we were not going to show much of a profit.

Finally, and with no great sense of urgency, the band climbed the stairs onto the stage. No one made a move to plug in a guitar. It appeared that the pantomime was going to continue for a while yet.

Mick beckoned me over, 'I want the stage cleared,' he said, 'I don't care who it is. Get them all off.'

'Oh great,' I thought, looking around at all the celebrity liggers trying hard to find somewhere from where they could watch the show. I suddenly noticed Paul and Linda McCartney.

'Surely not Paul?' I asked.

'No, of course not,' he replied. 'Just find him somewhere to sit that's out of the way and do it quickly.'

After the lengthy build-up, I think everyone felt that the opening number 'Satisfaction' was something of an anticlimax, including the Stones themselves. However, encouraged by Mick, they persevered and by the third or fourth number had won the audience over. They continued to delight everyone by playing several of their seldom-heard songs like 'Around and Around.' Wendy and I watched from the wings for a while before walking round to the back of the arena. The stage really worked and Mick really worked the stage, running, skipping, jumping, first on the tongue and then, using a radio mic, taking a walk along one of the narrow wings until he was a hundred or so feet away from the band, picked out by a solitary spotlight. One of our entertainers, dressed as a monkey, threw a banana to him, which he pretended to eat. The crowd loved it. Standing right at the back of the arena, I could appreciate the importance of projection screens. We had two extremely large ones set up so that anyone who couldn't see exactly what was happening on stage only had to turn round and see everything in lurid detail.

We stayed on in the arena to watch the rest of the show. As the last number was announced, the London Philharmonic Choir, of whom Sally Arnold was a member, appeared for the grand finale. Their rendition of Jerusalem was very stirring. However, it lacked the impact that a colossal firework display would have added, so it was with a whimper rather than a bang that the Stones left the stage. At two and a half hours, it was the longest performance in the band's history. Finishing so late also meant we had broken the conditions imposed by the council licence, something I had been particularly keen to avoid at all costs.

Whilst the Stones went up to the house for a party, we got on with the job of winding down the festival. The traffic jams were not nearly as bad as they had been the previous year, possibly because people had got tired of all the endless waiting and had left before the end. By 6am most people had left. However, there was still a sizeable number left on the campsite, sleeping off the excesses of the day. In the harsh light of day, the litter problem was worse than ever but bearing in mind the huge numbers attending the festival, there was surprisingly little damage to the estate.

Once again we waited anxiously for the reviews. This time, no doubt because of the notoriety of the Rolling Stones, some of the Sunday papers

Well, It was a hot weekend!

had picked up on the festival, carrying photographs of the crowds and short, fairly unbiased reports of the concert. However, it was the by-lines that bothered me. With all the delays and problems with equipment we had experienced, we were worried that the festival would get a real drubbing. In fact when the music paper reviews came out, they were all pretty objective.

It was the one in the Melody Maker that caused us real concern. Written by Geoff Brown, the second paragraph said, 'They drew a vast crowd variously estimated at between 170,000 and 250,000 to an exhausting drawn-out event, and showed once again that they still have power and relevance.'

What an irresponsible thing to I write, I thought. Everybody knows that if it's written in the paper, then it must be true. That is, if they want to believe it and the Stones certainly did. I wonder if this man Geoff Brown ever gave any thought to his statement and the problems it was likely to cause. His estimate contained a give or take margin of 80,000 people, which equated to every man, woman and child living in a city the size of St Albans or Lincoln and all these people, plus 170,000 more, were supposed to be accommodated on a tiny 32 acres within a 250 acre park. It made me wonder where he obtained this information and just how qualified was the person or persons who supplied him with these figures. The truth is that, when the final figures were received from our various ticket offices and added to the number of tickets we had sold on site, it came out in round figures to 103,000. If you add to this the 1,000 or so comps given to the record companies and various other people, plus our 500 / 600 staff and finally allow for a very generous 2/3,000 gatecrashers, you come to a maximum of 108,000. I know some people have suggested we had more gatecrashers than I have allowed for, but our security certainly wasn't that bad. I definitely wouldn't allow any part of the arena fences to be dismantled if there was the possibility of more than a couple of dozen people freely walking in. As I expected, a couple of days after the concert, I received a call from the Stones' office.

'We want all the tickets you collected at the gates,' said a voice, 'so we can count them.'

'Good luck,' I thought as the tickets had been torn in half at the gates and the pieces dropped in a bin. However, if that was what they wanted, that was what they would get. In due course, around 50 large plastic bags of tickets were sent over to their office. It wasn't long before I was invited to a meeting with Peter Rudge to discuss the matter. When Wendy and I arrived, we were surprised to see that in addition to Peter and Sally Arnold there was Brian Croft, the sound engineer, and two or three other people whose names I have forgotten. Of the tickets, there was no sign. Seated around a large wooden table, I was subjected to a barrage of questions, which I tried to

Mick Jagger with film crew in close attendance

answer as truthfully as possible. It seemed that the ticket count had been inconclusive.

Suddenly Brian Croft interrupted me.

'I think I should let you know, Freddy, that Keith Richards has some very heavy friends, some of whom have been known to carry knives,' he said a propos nothing.

Well, at least I now knew why he was at the meeting.

Reaching into my jacket pocket, I drew out my gardening knife and sticking it into the table said, 'Do you mean like this?'

The effect was really quite gratifying. Several sharp intakes of breath could be heard, chairs were hurriedly moved back and Peter, bless him, ran to the loo and locked himself in. It was all a futile waste of time. I had not cheated the band. The original agreement I had with Peter allowed us to make a quite generous figure before splitting any remaining profits 80 - 20 in favour of the Stones. We had not made anything like the amount Peter and I had agreed. In fact, due to the extravagance of the production, we had barely made a quarter of the permitted figure. For all the work and worry and financial risk it was a derisory sum and into the bargain it looked quite possible that we would not get a licence for next year. If I had known before-hand the likely outcome, I would have most certainly remained with Queen. I am damn sure that John Reid would not have treated me this way. What I didn't realise at that time, and which was to be our undoing sometime in the future, was just how friendly Peter Grant was with the Stones. It appears that at about this time he had a wish to manage both Led Zeppelin and the Rolling Stones, the ultimate power trip, and it must have been the highly exaggerated and totally untrue story he heard about this event that coloured his dealings with us in 1979.

Towards the end of the year, I met Charlie Watts again. Wendy and I were waiting with Herb and Suzanne Cohen for a table in the Dumpling Inn, one of our favourite Chinese restaurants, when who should be leaving but Charlie and his wife.

When he reached me he stopped and with mock surprise said, 'I didn't expect to see you in London. I thought that you would be in the Caribbean spending some of the money you stole from us.'

His boorish behaviour left me in no doubt that my surmise about the Stones and Peter Grant was correct. With hindsight, it is easy to see why Charlie was so uptight. Since writing the original hardback book 'There Must Be A Better Way', I have seen a copy of a Stones royalty statement from March 1971 that shows that Charlie, along with the estate of the late Brian Jones and Ian Stuart all received $251 with Bill Wyman receiving $662. Mick and Keith were paid just a little more - Mick getting $805,581 and Keith

The Rolling Stones crowd

The stage revealed in all it's tawdry splendour

$805,629. Seeing this, I suddenly realised why Charlie was so bitter and accusative. As a non-writing member of the band, live gigs were obviously an important part of his income. At last I could understand, if not sympathise with, his chippy attitude. Whatever his reasons, I am sure he made a damn sight more out of the event than I did.

Ironically, a Stones' fan recently told me that a contract issued in 1962 between The Rolling Stones and a promoter for an appearance fee of £15 at The Woodstock Hotel, North Cheam had been sold by Christies a couple of years ago at one of their pop memorabilia sales. Greatly intrigued, as Steve always claimed he must have been the only person to have paid The Stones £15 for an appearance and still lost money, I researched the story and when I finally tracked the article down to a local Surrey paper, I was delighted to read that the promoter was indeed Wendy's father. So, it seems that our family is probably responsible for paying the Stones, in this country anyway, the highest and lowest fees.

# CHAPTER 49

Later that year, looking around for bands to tour, I was surprised to receive a call from Malcolm McLaren, the legendary manager of The Sex Pistols.

'How would you like to arrange a tour for us?'

'Great!' I replied.

I really liked high-energy bands and, as something of an anarchist myself, the punk philosophy didn't bother me, though I wasn't too sure about all that gobbing. I could always buy a So'wester and some oilskins, I thought.

'Good,' he said, 'I'll bring the boys round to meet you.'

When they arrived, it was a total anticlimax. I had never been to a Sex Pistols' gig, but through television and the music paper, I had a good idea of what they were about. I was very disappointed. I had hoped, at the very least for some loose mouth sneering, but they were quiet as lambs. Malcolm, I thought, must really have had a go at them. I think it was because we enjoyed a fairly high profile, mainly because of Knebworth and the fact that we had a good relationship with the various venues, allied to our slight and thoroughly undeserved establishment image, that made Malcolm want to use us. As soon as we tried to book the first venue, we realised it was going to be even more difficult than we had at first thought. Surprisingly, most of the venues would accept the band. However, it was their demands for huge escrow deposits and separate insurance to cover potential damage that was the stumbling block. Dropping the whole question of insurance back on Malcolm was no solution since he didn't want to know, so in the end we gave up. There were just too many hassles and all this was before we'd even started to deal with the potential antics from band and fans alike. Fortunately, it was not a total waste of our time. When we withdrew from the tour, the Melody Maker carried the story on its front page and although I didn't originally intend it that way, it did look as though we had turned the tables on Malcolm McLaren and ripped him off for the resulting publicity.

During the seventies, I was always popping into Warner Brothers to liaise with them concerning bands we were touring or using at one of our festivals. During one visit, I was a little surprised when one of the numerous pretty girls, who I knew by sight, if not by name, came over and started chatting. Unfortunately, she wasn't trying to pick me up. Instead, she wanted to see if I would be interested in promoting a few dates with a band that her brother, Michael Browning, managed, called AC/DC. She explained that they were big in Australia and were trying to crack the UK. They had already laid the groundwork, she went on, having played a number of smaller venues, including a successful residency at the Marquee Club and were now ready to move up to bigger things. Unfortunately, I wasn't terribly impressed, even though I had heard of them. I thought it was early days and they still had some more work to do before they could fill the larger venues. I must say that I forgot all about them until a few weeks later I received a phone call from someone at Warners reminding me of the conversation I'd with Coral Browning and telling me that Warners, or to be more accurate, Atlantic Records, were now right behind the band and would I reconsider my decision? After my conversation with Coral, I had in fact carried out a little more research on AC/DC and this time I agreed.

At my first meeting with the band's manager, I must admit I was expecting a stereotypical Australian, all 'g'day' and 'right sport,' especially in view of the band's image. But Michael Browning turned out to be the very opposite of what I had imagined - quiet, shrewd and very charming. We were talking about an autumn tour and to get an idea of what AC/DC were all about, Michael suggested I should see them at the Reading Festival.

Sitting in front of the stage, in what I suppose was the guest area, it started to rain - not a lot, just a steady drizzle, but enough to give me a new respect for the people who attended our events and who sat there come hell or high water waiting to see their heroes. It wouldn't hurt Charlie Watts, I thought, to sit in front of a stage for a few hours, even without the rain, to see and feel for himself just what his audience had put up with at Knebworth.

I thought AC/DC were really good and I enjoyed their performance immensely. Unfortunately, it was an opinion not altogether shared by the audience, who were surprisingly subdued.

The tour was finally set to start at the end of October and consisted of 16 dates, of which we were responsible for nine, with the balance made up of University gigs and was called after their latest album 'Dirty deeds done cheap.' Wendy, who on a bad day has been known to sound rather like the Queen, was given the job of providing the voiceover for the radio ads, which were to be used to help publicise the tour. The advertisement featured a loutish sounding kid extolling the virtues of AC/DC, to which Wendy made the observation in a suitably glass accent 'It's dirty, it's disgusting, it's obscene.' It was a terrible ad. However, it did its job, as, once broadcast, ticket sales were pretty healthy.

I liked the band as soon as I met them, especially the late Bon Scott - friendly, outgoing and thoroughly unpretentious. This, I thought, was going to be a nice, easy and relaxed tour and as far as the band as individuals were concerned, it was. It was only when they got on stage that the trouble started. Angus, appearing as always in short trousers, had this habit of dropping his pants whenever the mood took him. Frankly, I couldn't see what all the fuss was about. However, the hall management saw it differently and in Liverpool and Glasgow, Angus narrowly escaped being arrested. I was told that the vice squad followed the band from town to town, which is quite believable when you consider how paranoid the authorities in this country can be. However, I must say that I never came across them myself.

The only time on the entire tour that I was at all concerned was at the Odeon, Hammersmith. We had a capacity crowd of 3,500 boisterous, somewhat overexcited kids and no Bon Scott. I suppose Angus was the person everyone had come to see, but Bon was also extremely popular. It also remained to be seen if the band would even consider going on without him. Fortunately, I didn't have to find out because a couple of minutes before show time, Bon came bursting through the stage door.

'I'm really sorry I'm late,' he said, 'but there was a hold- up on the tube.'

What a great idea, I thought. The next time an American 'star' demands a limo, I'll explain that it's not necessary as London has a highly efficient underground rail system.

## Tedoar Limited

4 Chester Street, London, S.W.1

Telephone: 01-235 5518

AC/DC AGREE TO INDEMNIFY TEDOAR LTD. AGAINST THE COST OF REPAIRING ANY DAMAGE HOWSOEVER CAUSED TO THE CONCERT HALLS WHERE THEY ARE APPEARING, FOR TEDOAR LTD. DURING THEIR OCT/NOV '76 TOUR. AC/DC ALSO AGREE TO INDEMNIFY TEDOAR LTD. AGAINST ANY CLAIMS FOR PERSONAL INJURY TO ANYONE WHETHER STAFF,PERFORMER OR MEMBER OF THE GENERAL PUBLIC,RESULTING FROM THE CONCERTS.TEDOAR LTD. RETAIN THE RIGHT TO WITHOLD THE COST OF REPAIR FROM AC/DC'S NIGHTLY FEE, IF ANY DAMAGE IS CAUSED TO THE CONCERT HALLS DURING THEIR CONCERTS.

SIGNED...................... SIGNED......................

(for and on behalf of Tedoar Ltd.) (for and on behalf of AC/DC)

The AC/DC disclaimer

# CHAPTER 50

As soon as the New Year arrived, following our usual procedure, we sent offers to everyone we felt would be a suitable Knebworth headliner - Bowie, Dylan, McCartney, Crosby Stills Nash and Young and, rather desperately, the Beach Boys, plus of course our standing offer to Led Zeppelin. This time no one, it appeared, was vaguely interested. Whether it was negative feedback from the Stones concert, I am not certain. I did, in fact, have lunch with Brian Brolley, Paul McCartney's business manager, on several occasions. However, nothing ever came of it. Try as we might, and we really did try, we could not come up with a band that would guarantee a big enough crowd to justify the enormous expenses involved in setting up a Knebworth concert. By mid-April I was becoming resigned to the fact that this year, at least, there would be no festival. I don't think David and Chryssie Lytton Cobbold thought I had tried hard enough, but it wasn't them taking the financial risk. They decided that to prevent this sort of thing happening again, I would have to pay a non-returnable deposit to secure the park for the following year.

1977 was the year that the Arabs with suitcases bulging with money came to town. If we were going to have the summer off, why not, we reasoned, let our house to make some extra cash. Approaching one of the specialist agents, we were told that the visitors were looking for large houses in the best part of London to accommodate their large families and staff. Our house wasn't large by central London standards. However, we were lucky as our next-door neighbour had the same idea as ourselves and between us we could offer something like ten bedrooms, six bathrooms and seven reception rooms. This arrangement obviously had its attractions because our agent quickly found a tenant, supposedly a member of the Saudi royal family, who took it for eight weeks. The men all moved into our neighbour's house and the women into ours. There were a lot of horror stories going around at this time about how the Arabs treated the properties they rented. Fortunately, when we moved back, the house was just as we had left it, thanks in no small part to our loyal daily who had agreed to stay on during the let. Looking back, I wish we could have also rented out our house for the summer months the previous year because it would have saved us the hard work, worry and general unpleasantness of the Stones gig and would have actually been more profitable.

14-2-78.

TEDOAR LTD. HEREBY AGREE TO PAY LYTTON ENTERPRISES LTD. THE
SUM OF £2,500 TO BE HELD AS A DEPOSIT AGAINST ONE OR MORE
CONCERTS HELD AT KNEBWORTH PARK DURING THE SUMMER OF 1978.
THIS DEPOSIT ENTITLES TEDOAR LTD. TO THE SOLE RIGHTS TO
PROMOTE ANY POP CONCERT PROMOTED AT KNEBWORTH PARK THIS
SUMMER AND WILL BE FORFEITED IF THXXCONCERTXCANNOT TEDOAR LTD
DECIDE NOT TO RUN A CONCERT, BUT WILL NOT BE FORFEITED IF THE
CONCERT CANNOT TAKE PLACE FOR REASONS BEYOND THE CONTROL OF
TEDOAR LTD. I.E. INJUNCTIONS, REFUSAL OF LOCAL LICENSE,UNLESS
THE LICENSE REQUEST DIFFERS IN PRINCIPLE FROM PREVIOUS YEARS
AND BECOMES UNREASONABLE.

..............................SIGNED LYTTON ENTERPRISES LTD.

.........................SIGNED TEDOAR LTD.


The option agreement for 1978

# CHAPTER 51

With the dawn of 1978, we again started our seemingly never-ending quest to find a headliner for Knebworth. This year I felt it was more important than ever to find a suitable bill-topper, or at the very least, a strong, composite programme. If we failed once again to produce a festival, I was pretty sure that the Lytton Cobbolds would look for someone who could. Miraculously, the problem was solved for us. For the first time since we had begun promoting at Knebworth, a manager of a potential headliner approached us. Early in the New Year, I received a phone call from Tony Smith, the manager of Genesis, who explained that the band were quite keen to play an outdoor festival and they felt Knebworth would be an ideal place. Funnily enough, we had considered approaching Genesis the year before, but felt that, at that time, they were not quite big enough. I was still not totally convinced. However, after a quick phone call to Hugh Fielder, news editor of Sounds Magazine and a big-time fan of Genesis, who gave me a quick and accurate breakdown of the crowds they had been drawing and the number of albums they had sold, I was won over. What really clinched it though, was the fact that Tony was prepared to gamble with us and participate in the event on a percentage basis. I had known Tony by reputation for a number of years. He initially worked with his father, John, a very successful promoter in the fifties and sixties, and later had taken over the management of Genesis from Tony Stratton Smith the founder of Charisma Records, along with around £200,000 of debts. This had been back in 1973 and by dint of hard work and shrewd decisions; Tony had helped to build the band into one of the most popular live acts in the country, as I was just about to find out.

In the meantime, we had four dates with Frank Zappa at the Odeon Hammersmith to take care of. By this time Frank had fallen out with Herb Cohen and had acquired a new manager, a lawyer named Bennet Glotzer. He was highly experienced, having looked after acts such as Janis Joplin, Blood Sweat and Tears and Dr John, working closely with Dylan's one-time manager Albert Grossman. Bennet, who loved to party, was accompanied on this trip by his girlfriend Holly, a pretty, young thing about half his age. The first time Wendy and I went out to dinner with them, Holly, towards the end of the meal, visited the ladies cloakroom and was gone for so long that we all started to get worried that something had happened to her. Bennet went looking for her and came back a few minutes later.

'She's passed out on the loo,' he said.' What should we do?'

There was only one thing we could do - tell the staff. In the end they had to take the door off to reach her. Thank God, I thought, we're only doing the English dates. Frank, as usual, stayed at The Royal Garden Hotel in

Kensington and we suggested that the band were booked into The Portobello Hotel, as everyone there was very laid back and familiar with groups and their little habits. Like most Americans, the band felt safer in a hotel chain with which they were familiar and insisted we booked them into The Holiday Inn in George Street. We knew they didn't like rock 'n' roll musicians, since they had in the past refused to take our bookings for groups. Therefore, when Wendy rang to book the rooms, instead of saying they were for an American group, she said they were for a group of Americans. Worded this way, she had no problems in booking the rooms. However, when the band checked in, the receptionists were not exactly amused with the way they had been duped. However, they honoured the booking. I am sure things would have been fine if one of the party hadn't let off a fire extinguisher in a corridor and alienated the hotel detective, who promptly called the police, claiming that the band were in possession of drugs. In fact, the police, when they arrived mob-handed and searched everyone's rooms, could only find a miniscule amount of cannabis and traces of cocaine in, I believe, Tommy Mars' room. Waking him up, they promptly hauled him off to the local police station still in his pyjamas and without even allowing him time to put on his shoes. We managed to arrange bail the next day but everyone in the band was badly shaken. After their five sold out shows at the Odeon Hammersmith, the whole party seemed to be relieved to be heading for Europe.

A few days later, Bennet called, 'Can you come out to Paris and help sort out Tommy's bust? While you're at it, can you check out who would be best guy to represent him?'

When we got to Paris, I told them that with the small amount involved, it wasn't going to be a hanging offence. I explained that if they really wanted the best, then it was probably Sir David Napley. However, I wasn't sure he would take on the case.

'Go back to London,' said Bennett,' and see if he'll do it.'

Sir David turned out to be, as you would expect, extremely astute, and subjected me to a barrage of questions. In the end he accepted the case. When I called Bennet with the good news, he told me that, after all my hard work, they had decided that Tommy would plead guilty and throw himself on the mercy of the court. It was probably the right decision because when he finally appeared before a magistrate, he just received a slap on the wrist and a nominal fine.

In view of the speed at which the first five shows had sold out, we had arranged two additional shows to coincide with the end of the European dates. Halfway through the first of these, I was standing at the side of the stage enjoying the music, when I saw Frank look up into the stage roof and suddenly freeze. Following his gaze, I saw two men perched precariously on the rigging about forty or fifty feet above the bands heads, attempting to climb down. Ever since his assault at The Rainbow, Frank had taken the precaution of bringing his extremely large black bodyguard, John Smothers, on every tour. John, at that moment, was on the other side of the stage, directing the hall stewards who were patrolling the area in front of the stage. Rushing over to where he was standing, I quickly explained the position to him. Leaving several stewards to look after Frank, John, a couple of security staff and I, along with the hall manager, who had miraculously appeared, shot outside and round to the back of the Odeon. Looking up, we saw near the top of the building a loft door, with a flight of stairs leading up to it where the intruders had obviously entered the theatre. John and one of the stewards climbed up to the door and, after a few minutes, persuaded the pair who were still clinging perilously to the rigging to climb back out. When they reached the ground the two miscreants turned out to be nothing more threatening than a couple of kids who wanted to gatecrash the show. Nevertheless, it was a thoughtless and bloody stupid thing to do and could have very easily ended in tragedy.

After the show, Frank sent for me.

'I don't know what it is about England but I've had enough. I know it wasn't your fault,' he said, 'but what would it cost to cancel the last show?'

'I would have to work it out' I said.

' Well do it and let me know.'

A few minutes later I was back with the figures, Frank looked at them quickly.

'Do it' he said.

Well, I thought, whatever else it is, you can never call a Zappa tour boring

# CHAPTER 52

The date that was decided on for the Genesis Festival was the 24$^{th}$ June, which happened to be midsummer's day, so, rather unoriginally; I titled the event 'A Midsummer Night's Dream'. It was left to Tony to come up with the bright idea of inserting flyers, incorporating an advance ticket order form, in the album that was being released a couple of months before the Festival. Entitled 'And Then There Were Three' it was Genesis' first album after the departure of guitarist Steve Hacket. It sold remarkably well and the return from the ticket vouchers really surprised us all.

People were always approaching us, hoping to work on the festivals. Normally when we interviewed them it would turn out, reading between the lines, that they were hoping to score some free drugs or groupie it up with some of the bands. Normally they would phone or call round to our office. Occasionally, they would write, usually trite, rather rambling missives that went on far too long and failed to hold my interest. Therefore, when we received a letter from someone called Steve Jackson, which was literate, funny and succinct, I decide that I really had to see him. When he came along to the interview, I was very flattered to find that Steve, through our promotions at Knebworth, had a very high and totally misplaced view of our business acumen and thought that he could learn something by working for us over the summer. He came over as a very bright, responsible, young man and I jumped at the opportunity to take him on. He instantly repaid us by working out a new system for dealing with postal ticket sales that was more secure and efficient. As we got to know him better, we found out that he had recently started his own business selling games with a partner named Ian Livingstone. While we were chatting one day, he mentioned that just before he started work with us, he had visited a games convention in Chicago, where he had come across a game called Dungeons and Dragons, for which he was trying to obtain the UK rights. I tried to tell him the game sounded long-winded and boring as hell, but what did I know. He and Ian, based on the interest shown in this game, founded a company they called Games Workshop and went on to build a business with over 200 employees before eventually selling up for a great deal of money.

1978 was a vintage year for staff as another young man we took on was Adrian Reynard, who helped us out as a van driver. He was in the process of establishing a company, Reynard Motorsport Ltd, that has since become the biggest manufacturer of racing cars in the world, winning championships in virtually every category in both England and the USA. He is also visiting professor of engineering at Cranfield University - some van driver!

Although Genesis were riding high in the popularity stakes, in view of Knebworth's enormous size, we all thought that it was a good idea to have a strong support programme. First choice, because of our long-standing relationship, was Jefferson Airplane, or as they now styled themselves, Jefferson Starship. They were still immensely popular and the fact that they hadn't been seen in England since 1970, when they played for us at the Bath Blues Festival, was also a distinct plus. They were not terribly happy with the idea of Genesis closing the show. However, providing they received equal top billing on all the publicity material, they agreed to appear. If this situation had arisen in America, where they were already legends, there is no doubt they would have refused the offer point blank. To make the trip financially more viable, we agreed to find them another festival date in Europe and ended up arranging for them to headline the Lorelei Festival near Hamburg. The rest of the Knebworth programme was made up with Band X, Phil Collins' pet project and managed by Tony Smith, The Atlanta Rhythm Section, Devo and Tom Petty and the Heartbreakers, with Nicky Horne acting as compere. We had actually booked Jeff Beck to appear third on the bill, as an advertisement we placed in Sounds shows, but in the end he couldn't get a band together and pulled out, so we replaced him at fairly short notice with Tom Petty.

To help with the detailed planning of the stage set-up, Tony thought it would be a good idea if we saw the band in action and as Knebworth was to be their only UK date, he suggested that we fly out to Zurich to see them

Brand X

perform. We watched the show from the mixing desk in the middle of a packed hall. The three remaining members of Genesis had been joined by guitarist Darryl Stuermer and drummer Chester Thompson and sounded really integrated, as if they had played together for years. The lighting was really spectacular. However, it was Phil Collins who made the greatest impression on me. A slight, wiry figure, he moved about the stage simply bursting with pent-up nervous energy, jumping, weaving and punching the air with the sheer joy of performing.

It was a useful trip as we had plenty to discuss with Bill Harkin on our return. A particular area of concern was the stage roof. The problem was to find lightweight metal beams long enough to provide a sufficiently wide stage and strong enough to bear the weight of the lighting rig, which in Genesis' case, was aggravated by the need to cope with the 200 or so jumbo jet landing lights they were using in their show at that time.

The Starship was due to play the Lorelei Festival the week before Knebworth. Ordinarily, I would have been in Germany with them to sort out any problems. However, with Knebworth and it's attendant hassles so close, I had no option but to stay in England. It was a bad mistake. I have read many stories in the intervening years about what happened, but the story I was told at the time was that Grace, a couple of hours before they were due to go on stage, told the rest of the band that she was too ill to perform. An argument developed which ended when Paul Kantner, her former boyfriend of many years, punched her young husband, the band's lighting director, Skip Johnson. Finally accepting that Grace, for whatever reason, was not going to perform, the band with typical laid-back, west coast, hippy cool, asked the local promoter to tell the audience that they would take a rain check and try to reschedule the date. A big mistake and one that I am sure I could have prevented if I had been there.

To be fair to the Starship, a couple of them went with the promoter to speak to the crowd. They would probably have got away with their offer of a rescheduled date in America, but not in Germany. If they had been prepared to play a shortened set without Grace, I am sure the audience would have been sympathetic. But the bald statement that Grace was unwell wasn't enough to appease those in the crowd, who in some instances had travelled considerable distances to see this legendary band. Disappointment soon turned to anger. The band, it seemed, must be punished for what many saw as arrogant behaviour and with typical Teutonic efficiency, the mob started to dismantle and destroy the Starship's equipment.

The first thing I knew about the events at the Lorelei was when Brian Croft rang from Germany to put me in the picture. By all accounts it was a well-organised riot. The other bands on the festival were spared - nothing belonging to them was touched. However, anything and everything belonging to the Starship was systematically and very conscientiously taken apart and destroyed. Brian, who with his crew was looking after the Starship's equipment, as well as providing a large number of items on hire, tried to save as much of the equipment as he possibly could. He had a simple technique. As the rioters carried amplifiers or speakers etc away from the stage area to throw them onto the bonfire that had been started, Brian and his boys would be waiting for them and gesturing for the rioters to follow, led them to their lorry discretely hidden in the woods, where they tried to explain that the gear did not belong to the Starship. If they could not make themselves understood, they simply snatched the item and locked it away. This way they managed to save some of their own equipment but, unfortunately, not very much of the Starship's.

Brian couldn't give me any indication of the band's intentions other than to say they were still deeply shocked by the audience reaction. That's it, I thought, they certainly wouldn't want to play Knebworth after everything that's happened. As soon as I could, I spoke to Bill Thompson, who, somewhat to my surprise, was quite upbeat.

'I have spoken to the band,' he explained. 'And they still want to play Knebworth. Of course, you'll have to rent extra equipment as we have just about lost everything.'

Again, I wished that I'd made the time to be in Germany with them because the very next day the band, using borrowed equipment, appeared on a German TV programme. This time Grace, somewhat drunk, made a rambling, incoherent speech about the troubles they had experienced at the Lorelei Festival and started to reproach the audience for starting World War Two and, according to one report, continued by trying to stick her fingers up a fan's nose. This, as far as the band was concerned, was the final straw and Grace returned home immediately after the show. Despite this further upset, or perhaps because of it, the band remained determined to appear at Knebworth.

A great shot of Craig Chaquito, legendary Jefferson Starship Guitarist

# CHAPTER 53

Meanwhile, with less than a week to go, things were running smoothly for once. I had been worried that the stage, another mega structure measuring around two hundred and twenty five feet from end to end, would be finished in time. I needn't have worried as Showex, the firm we used to construct our stages, had once again pulled out all the stops and had everything ready for when the Genesis crew moved in. It wasn't until Friday, the day that Genesis were due to sound check that disaster struck. Early in the morning it started to rain. In fact, it was really more of a full-scale monsoon and the stage roof, which probably wasn't designed to withstand this sort of deluge, started to leak badly on one side. Unfortunately, it was the side where a lot of delicate equipment was set up, including several mixing desks. Bill Harkin had rolls of polythene on site for just this sort of emergency, but of course wrapping this around mixing desks wasn't the answer, as you had to be able to operate them. Try as he might, he just couldn't stop the water coming in. To make matters worse the BBC were on site setting up their cameras to film the Genesis sound check, plus other more general aspects of the festival, all very embarrassing. In the end we decided that I had better give the Showex manager a call at his office in London. When I got through, I explained our predicament and asked him to come up to Knebworth to help sort out the problem. He was less than thrilled and refused point blank, explaining that he was extremely busy and just did not have time to drive all the way out especially as it was his anniversary and he was taking his wife out to dinner that evening.

At that moment Tony Smith walked into the office. Putting my hand over the phone's mouthpiece I said to him, 'Shout at me.'

'Do what?' he said, looking at me blankly.

I briefly explained and the penny dropped. We then put on a performance of the angry band manager and the browbeaten promoter, which if it wasn't good enough to get us into RADA, would certainly have got us through the first round of a TV talent contest. I am sure Tammy, Showex's manager, didn't believe a word of it. However, bowing to the inevitable, he agreed to drive up straight away. When he arrived, he came up a simple solution to our problem. He had his men use scaffolding to build what was, in effect, a small room at the side of the stage, clad with tarpaulins. It was totally waterproof and provided the perfect answer. Ironically, as often seemed to happen at our Knebworth Festivals, the day of the concert, which was forecast to be wet and windy, turned out to be sunny and dry.

As usual on the Friday evening, I was up all night keeping an eye on things. This year there was no Peter Rudge to disturb our neighbour's sleep.

Instead, it was left to Jo Lyons to provide the entertainment.

For the previous three concerts we had been allowed to make our own catering arrangements. However, in early 1978, David Lytton Cobbold had reached an agreement with Town and Country, the outdoor catering division of J. Lyons and Co, for them to provide all the catering on the estate including all events in the park. Unfortunately, David had omitted to tell us and the first we knew was when we received a letter from Town and Country asking us what type of food we would like them to provide for the festival. When we contacted them to see what was going on, we found that as far as they were concerned, we no longer had any interest, financial or otherwise, in the catering. This came as a tremendous blow, as this money sometimes made all the difference between a nominal and a reasonable profit. However, in the end, we did receive a percentage of the profits from the catering, which I feel was probably given to us out of David's own pocket, just to keep the peace.

For those of you too young to remember, the Lyons Corner Houses and Tea Shops were a catering company that at one time had over 250 branches throughout the country, staffed by young and not so young woman dressed in smart black and white uniforms. They were the very epitome of middle class respectability, so you can imagine my surprise when I discovered a slightly different side to them. At 3am, driving along Old Knebworth Lane, a minor road that led to the private entrance of Knebworth House, I saw a large coach halfway across the lane, with it's right front wheel in a ditch. Thinking there had been an accident I jumped out of my car to see if I could help. It was only then that I noticed seven or eight heavies armed with baseball bats standing all around the coach, stopping the occupants from getting out. It was at that point that I noticed all the heavies were wearing Town and Country jackets.

'What the hell is going on?' I asked one of them, whom, I suddenly realised, I had already met at the Barn Restaurant during one of our interminable meetings.

'Nothing much,' he said cheerfully. 'We're just stopping some pirates and their gear getting into the park.'

Now there's a company, I thought, that's really moving with the times. What a pity Lyons Catering went out of business a couple of years later!

Opening up wasn't so difficult this time. The people attending the concert were rather older than in previous years, some even bringing young babies with them. I was initially rather surprised that is until I realised that it was nine years since we had organised our first festival on the Recreation Ground in Bath. Age, I thought, and the responsibilities it brings, was no reason to lose your love for music, or indeed your enjoyment of a certain lifestyle.

Jesus, receiving a little help from his friends

Again, breaking with precedent, we actual started the concert half an hour early, with an unadvertised appearance by Roy Harper, who for some reason had been added to the programme at the very last minute.

Brand X were the first of the scheduled bands to play, putting in a good solid performance, but struggling, as every opening act does, with people still arriving, trudging around trying to find the ideal vantage point, looking for friends, checking out the facilities and a dozen other fidgety things people do at festivals before settling down with eager anticipation to watch their favourite band, which for some strange reason is never the opening act.

This year it was The Atlanta Rhythm Section who provided my regular helping of good old southern boogie. I thought they played really well and tried hard to get through to the crowd, their singer, Ronnie Hammond, using every trick in the book. However, that early in the day, they found it pretty hard going. At least their energy and enthusiasm was finally rewarded with an encore.

The only really black spot of the day, apart from the occasional shower and a rather strong breeze that tended to distort the sound early on in the day, was the treatment Devo received from a section of the crowd. I was really quite pleased with the programme I had put together; a good selection of musical styles that were nevertheless compatible. Of course, I had not allowed for the closed minds of some members of the audience. Perhaps if Devo had not worn their rather bizarre outfits looking like civil defence suits, with orange skateboard helmets and knee and elbow protectors, they would have been taken a little more seriously. Instead of giving them a chance, the more reactionary members of the audience gave them a hard time, hurling missiles and abuse in roughly equal proportions. It was a sickening display, which proved nothing and only succeeded in putting one unfortunate guy in hospital with a head wound that required sixteen stitches caused by a wine bottle that failed to reach the stage.

After this, things could only get better. Tom Petty really hit the spot. This was what everyone was waiting for - a proper American rock 'n' roll band, complete with guitar pyrotechnics, and they certainly were not disappointed. Tom and the Heartbreakers played a simply blinding set which included several encores before leaving the stage with the crowd howling for more.

Just before the Starship came on, I had been keeping a careful eye on the sky. It looked as if our luck was about to run out. However, just as the band took the stage, the sun broke through and it stayed dry for the rest of the evening. It was the first time that the band had played without Grace, either as the Jefferson Airplane or Starship and I think they were very worried about how they would be received. Normally the vocals would be shared between Grace and Marty Balin. However, with Grace back in the States,

Genesis in action

Marty had to rely on Paul Kantner to supply the harmonies. After a tentative start, they soon settled down and began playing some of their old favourites including 'Have you seen the Saucers' and 'Volunteers', which really began to warm up the audience. Still, I think it was the brilliant playing of Craig Chaquito, their young virtuoso guitarist, who was ultimately responsible for lifting and inspiring the band to give a terrific performance. At the end of their set they received an ovation that more than justified their decision to play without Grace.

Up to now, the programme had rather amazingly been running to time. Genesis were originally scheduled to appear at around 9pm. However, as it was still quite light at this time, they decided to wait an extra hour or so for it to grow sufficiently dark for their lighting effects to be seen to the best advantage. Ever the opportunist, Roy Harper for once proved to be an asset when he came on stage during this long delay to entertain a surprisingly responsive audience.

Unlike the Stones concert where the interminable delays tended to arouse bad tempered resentment, the much shorter wait for Genesis only seemed to enhance the audience's sense of eager anticipation. So when Bob Harris from the Old Grey Whistle Test mounted the stage to announce the band, the mood for the whole performance was already set. They were not to be disappointed. Genesis played extremely well, covering all aspects of their musical oeuvre with large helpings from the current album 'Then There Were Three'. They played so well, in fact, that John Gill who was covering the event for 'Sounds', remarked in his review that Knebworth was a 'triumphant assertion of their mammoth reputation'. High praise indeed.

It wasn't just the fact that they played well. The presentation was also truly stunning and complimented the music perfectly. In addition to the mega array of stage lights, they had even incorporated lasers into their show, spectacularly shooting beams out over the heads of the crowd. 'Prog Rock' at its very best, a genre on which I was not particularly keen, until I started working with Genesis. At the end of their performance the enormous crowd gave them what I think must have been the best reception of any band that we promoted at Knebworth. It was so loud and went on for so long that I was seriously worried about getting complaints from our 'neighbours'.

As every one was leaving, we had the worst incident that we had experienced so far at one of our festivals. A Land Rover, towing a broken-down vehicle, drove over what the driver thought was an empty polythene bag, only to find that it contained two youngsters who, too tired to walk back to the camp site, had fallen asleep in a busy part of the park. We were all worried sick, as it appeared at first that they were seriously injured. However, when an ambulance took them to hospital, it was discovered they were just badly bruised. It was no one's fault. However, something would have to be done, we thought, to stop the same happening at future festivals.

Nonetheless, as far as the council and police were concerned, the whole event had generally gone smoothly and we all felt that there probably wouldn't be too much of a problem obtaining a licence next year. There was one moment, however, towards the end of the festival when it appeared that the whole of our admin team were losing it, and, with efficiency at low ebb Wendy resolved to do something about it. Popping along to Release, she enquired whether they could provide anything to keep everyone awake, knowing there were still a number of hours to go.

'Of course,' they said, 'that's what we're here for - all your drug problems!' and promptly gave her a handful of Blue Meenies.

I don't know about efficiency, but morale certainly improved and indirectly, I suppose, efficiency did as well. At 5am the next morning, Bev, one of our great assistants, was still scrubbing the floor of the admin office. I bet the hire company never had one of their mobile offices returned in such mint condition, well not from us anyway.

The reviews, when they came out, were generally pretty good, with most of the music journalists reacting favourably to Genesis' performance. However, it was noticeable that they all seemed to feel, to a greater or lesser extent, that the day of the giant rock festivals and, as they termed it, the dinosaur rock bands, were coming to an end. 'The times they were a changing' once again and this time it was the new wave bands that were, in their opinion, about to take centre stage.

The week after the festival, we received an invoice from Brian Croft's company for the equipment that we had hired on behalf of the Starship and had allegedly been lost at the Lorelei Festival. I cannot remember the exact amount, but it was bloody ginormous, something like £15,000 to £20,000, which today would equate to around £150,000 plus. They had insisted that we sign a contract but hadn't bothered to check it when we sent it back. When they got round to looking at it after the riots in Germany, they found that we had taken out the clauses they had inserted that made Wendy and myself personally responsible for any loss or damage to the equipment. We had also removed virtually every clause or condition that we considered unreasonable, leaving them with an almost clean sheet of heavily tippexed paper. Their only option was to make an insurance claim, which is what, in our opinion, they should have done in the first place.

In one end ...

.... and out the other

# CHAPTER 54

It was while we were busy clearing up the park that I started to think about a second Festival later that summer. Looking at the giant stage standing ready to be dismantled, I wondered how much it would cost to keep the basic structure in place until the beginning of September. Phoning Showex I was surprised to find that the weekly rent was quite reasonable. I had often thought of running a smaller event at Knebworth, especially in 1977, but the high cost of a stage had always been a problem. You can scale everything else down i.e. perimeter fencing, loos, even security. However, I always felt, rightly or wrongly, that it was important to have a decent sized, well-constructed stage to act as the main focal point. It was this cost that had deterred me from running anything other than mammoth events. This seemed like an ideal opportunity to see if I could run a much smaller concert and still make a profit. The next move, because the Genesis gig had borne the initial cost, was to see if Tony Smith would have any objections to me using the stage for another event. Luckily, being a nice bloke, he didn't. David Lytton Cobbold was also quite happy to try out my idea and as usual was very realistic when it came to discussing the rent. The only problem we had this time was with the police. They just would not believe me when I told them that this was to be a much smaller event than the last one with Genesis, and we were only aiming to attract an audience of between 30,000 to 40,000. Once they knew who was appearing, they were even more convinced that I was trying to mislead them. Their estimates of our attendance were always wildly optimistic. I was somewhat taken aback when one of the officers that I dealt with stated that they were firmly of the opinion that this programme would attract an attendance of between 75/80,000 and they would be basing their charges on these estimates. Good grief, I thought, after working on four shows they already think they know more about promoting than I do!

'If you're that confident,' I said, 'why don't you come in as 50/50 partners?'

I wasn't totally surprised when they rather hastily turned down my offer.

We chose September 9th as the date for the festival because it would give us plenty of time to book a programme and advertise the event. What's more, we thought, at that time of the year we might be lucky enough to enjoy an Indian summer. At the end of the week following the festival Bill Thompson called us from France. With remarkably good timing, they always seemed to be on holiday just when we needed to unwind after a festival.

'Judy and I are having a great time.' he said, 'Why don't you come and join us for a few days?'

We could do with a short break, I thought, especially if we were going to organise another Knebworth.

'OK' I replied and arranged to meet up with them in at the Chateau d'Artigny in the Loire Valley.

The Château was truly spectacular, having belonged at one time to the Coty perfume family, who lavished a fortune on it. Using a French guide to the Chateaux of France, we goggled and ate our way across France. Bill and Judy were excellent company and although we extended our holiday by a couple of days the time went all too quickly. It was expensive, but just the break we needed to set us up for another festival.

Now we were no longer promoting club nights, it struck me again that it was not so easy for me to keep in touch with all the changes that were beginning to take place in the music scene. Nevertheless, for our small concert I could feel it was important for us to try something different and use a diverse mix of bands including one or two from the so-called new wave.

I didn't want to jeopardise my relationship with David Lytton Cobbold or the local authorities by holding a full-scale punk festival so I tried to tread a middle path. My first choice as headliner was Frank Zappa. Although he no longer played with the Mothers of Invention, probably because of contractual reasons after his break up with Herb Cohen, he still enjoyed a fanatical following. With his caustic wit and scatological sense of humour, I thought he would be ideal. As we had worked with him many times over the years he was quite easy to approach, although I didn't find Bennet Glotzer, his new manager, quite as straightforward to deal with as I had Herb Cohen.

The Tubes seemed a logical choice; equally as bizarre and anarchistic as Zappa and being very visual, they would be ideal to close the show, if I could get Frank to agree. Peter Gabriel was also very idiosyncratic and would fit in very well. I chose The Boomtown Rats mainly because they were extremely popular and had in their leader, Bob Geldof, a very charismatic front man.

Adding Dave Edmund's and Nick Lowe's Rockpile and Wilko Johnson's Solid Senders to the programme was, if I remember correctly, partly political. Dave Edmunds latest album, Pray for Rain, had just been released on Swansong Records and I was probably sucking up to Peter Grant in one of my regular attempts to change his mind about allowing Led Zeppelin to play at Knebworth. Whatever the reasons, they were still two bands that I was delighted to have on the programme although I have to admit that I nearly changed my mind about Nick Lowe playing the Festival when his long-time associate, Jake Riviera, founder of Stiff Records, came to see me on his behalf. I had already had a run in with Jake at the Odeon Hammersmith, during one of the Zappa shows earlier in the year, and we nearly came to blows when he tried to hijack my office for his own use. What the hell he was

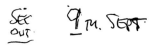

# TRINIFOLD LIMITED

Telephone: 01-439 8411

Telex: 896691 TLXIR G

ARTIST MANAGEMENT

112/114 WARDOUR STREET
LONDON W1V 3LD

12th June, 1978.

Mr. F. Bannister,
Teodar Ltd.,
4 Chester Street,
London,
S.W.1.

Dear Freddy,

Please sit down and take a few deep breaths before you begin to read this letter, I am worried about your blood pressure.

The next question is purely tentative. If THE WHO <u>were</u> to accept your offer to appear at Knebworth what would be the latest possible date you would consider ?

If, (and I stress <u>if</u>,) we were to do the show, we would want total control over the design of the poster advertising it.

Have tried to reach you on the telphone but yours was constantly engaged.

Best wishes,

BILL CURBISHLEY

THIS LETTER DOES NOT CONSTITUTE A CONTRACT !

A great letter, but as usual with The Who nothing came of it doing there I have no idea. He was no different when he arrived at our house, lippy, with an enormous chip on his shoulder and obviously spoiling for another fight. Suddenly, for absolutely no reason other than, I suppose, to establish his street cred, he started ranting about people like me ripping off the people and trotted out all the hackneyed Maoist clichés. At this point I noticed that he was wearing a really expensive leather jacket, designer sunglasses and what looked like Gucci loafers. Without saying a single word, I lifted my right foot showing him the large hole in the sole of my shoe. Jake, probably for the first time in his life, was lost for words.

I called the festival 'Not Another Boring Old Knebworth' because it so obviously wasn't. Also, in part, to counter the criticism that the Knebworth Festivals and other large-scale events, such as the recent appearance by Bob Dylan at Blackbush Airfield, had been receiving from some of the music journalists.

Setting up the event was, of course, a lot easier this time. With everything scaled down, we had plenty of time to get everything ready and for once we managed to avoid the last minute panics that we had experienced regularly at previous events. We still had our usual problems with the egos of the sound engineers, riggers, lighting technicians etc but with the pressure off, even these difficult and, in some instances, unpleasant people, were not such a problem to deal with.

Despite my protestations, I was still having trouble with the police. I had gone to the previously unknown lengths of offering to show them a box office-by-box office breakdown of our ticket sales, which had resulted in a slight scaling down of their operation. However, they still insisted on treating the event as a major threat to the safety and security of every one living in the area. They simply could not believe, after the crowds we had generated over the last four years, that it was the headliners rather than the event itself that drew the masses. This is why we ended up with such an enormous number of policemen sitting around in the park with nothing to do except chat or play cricket.

Opening up was a doddle. As usual we had the gates manned early. However, this time there was no mad rush from the campsite, just a nice steady flow building up to a peak at around midday.

First to take the stage were Wilko Johnson and the Solid Senders, who justified their inclusion on the programme and their name by playing a solid set that was very well received.

The weather was not quite as sunny and warm as I had been hoping but at least it was dry, if rather blustery. The wind, initially at least, tended to affect the sound and perhaps, because of this, Rockpile seemed to have real problems getting across to the audience. In the end, although they played

Peter Gabriel

exceptionally well, they did not receive the acclaim they unquestionably deserved.

The Boomtown Rats, who were next on, certainly did, although the band, when they started to play, sounded just a little tired and listless - not surprising, I suppose, as they had flown in from Europe that morning and were flying out again immediately after the concert. They soon started to show their worth, encouraged by a charismatic Bob Geldof, who by using every trick he knew, really worked the crowd, finally getting them on to their feet with a selection of Rat hits.

It was left to Peter Gabriel to introduce some well-needed controversy into the event. Climbing up a ladder from the press enclosure, with a large toy panda strapped to his back, he started to sing a chorus of, Me and My Teddy Bear. Two or three songs later, he shinned back down the ladder into the crowd before appearing with a radio mic at the start of the walkway that led out to the sound desk and proceeded to walk into the crowd singing, 'Waiting for the Big One'. The effect carried rather more impact than I am sure he intended. People stood up to get a better look, blocking the view of those further back. Cans were chucked in a vain attempt to get people to sit down. It was only when Peter climbed back onto the stage that things quietened down a little. Until, that is, he devoted a punk version of 'Whiter Shade of Pale' to an impression of Bob Geldof, complete with Bob's over the top mannerisms. In fact, it was so far over the top that a section of the crowd again started to throw cans, this time at him. He soon got the crowd back on his side with a fine version of 'The Lamb Lies Down on Broadway', and even ventured once again into the crowd before finishing his set to a standing ovation.

I must admit that Zappa's performance disappointed me a little, not musically I hasten to add because, as the biggest fan of Frank's music, I've never heard him or his band play badly. However, I was hoping that he would show some of the attitude and humour that made him such an icon in the mid to late sixties. Instead, he was content to leave outrage to the Tubes and concentrate on his music. Even then he took something of a back seat, singing a lot less than on the recent shows we had promoted. It seemed he wasn't really prepared to enter into the spirit of the festival, which, as most of the crowd had come to see him, was rather strange. In a performance lasting just over an hour, he only played two of his old favourites, which must have disappointed a lot of Zappa freaks.

Unfortunately, The Tubes' performance coincided with one of my busy periods when I was out and about in the park, supervising the removal of fencing, making sure the lights were fuelled and turned on and still in the right position, and most importantly, that our staff were in place to direct cars to the correct exit so I missed what I was told was an energetic and spectacular performance. I thought that it was a very nice gesture that, for their encores, they played 'Baba O'Reilly' and 'The Kids Are All Right' as a tribute to Keith Moon, who had sadly died earlier in the week. Unbeknown to me, they had been joined on stage for the tribute by Todd Roddgren, who obviously liked the place, as he would eventually end up playing four of the seven festivals we promoted at Knebworth.

## CHAPTER 55

We barely had time to recover from the second festival before we had to start preparing for the Bette Midler concerts. The European segment of Bette's world tour was organised by Arnie Worsoe of I.C.O. based in Copenhagen, with whom we regularly worked quite closely on tours that either he or I instigated. The competition to promote the London dates was particularly fierce and I was very grateful to Arnie for sticking by us, especially as it appeared that even Bette's record company, Atlantic Records, thought the dates should be given to one of their more favoured promoters. Aaron Russo, Bette's manager, had decided on a week at the London Palladium and for obvious reasons, I suppose, a date in Brighton. We were lucky. The Palladium, which was normally booked solid, was available for the dates we required. I spoke to Louis Benjamin, at that time a director of Stoll Moss, the owners of the theatre, who seemed to know all about Bette and mentioned several times that owing to the venue's unique reputation and its royal connections, obscene language was not allowed and he indicated that a clause to this effect would be incorporated into the contract. We had booked the main party into the Lowndes Hotel and Bette and Aaron, along with his assistant, into the Hyde Park Hotel, just a few hundred yards away. Meeting the party at Heathrow was a little daunting - there were so many of them. Apart from Bette and her three backing singers, The Harlots, there was of course Aaron and his assistant, also a tour manager, a musical director, a scriptwriter, a wardrobe mistress, several dressers and two or three roadies.

As soon as they had checked into their hotels, Aaron suggested that we sit down with his assistant and go through the contract point by point - an overwhelming job, as the contract consisted of about forty tightly packed pages. Why this formality was left until they were actually in the country rather than taken care of before they left the United States I'm not sure. However, I was happy to leave it to Wendy, who spent over four hours renegotiating various points before signing it!

During rehearsals, Wendy and I were cornered by Bette's scriptwriter who insisted on trying out on us various new gags he had written especially for London. His jokes were hilarious but they would have been funnier still if he hadn't insisted on reading them out in a totally deadpan manner, as if he was reading from the obituary column of The Times. He was particularly anxious that all his local references were correct and we were kept busy suggesting the local equivalent of The Bronx or the East Sixties.

Opening night was quite glitzy, not our normal sort of thing at all. We had rented a couple of giant searchlights, which had been placed either side of the entrance. The audience was cool, trendy and distinctly lucky, as tickets for the whole week had sold out almost immediately they went on sale. A number of people had gone as far as to wear evening dresses and dinner jackets. Even I had made an effort to make myself smarter by buying a new Marks and Spencer woolly to replace the one with holes in the elbows that I habitually wore.

Watching Bette from the wings, I thought she was fantastic. Her stage presence was overpowering and she could even sing! This, I thought, is going to be a great week. Her chat between numbers was hilarious, although, after twenty or thirty minutes, I noticed a certain coarseness start to creep in. After the third or it could have been the fourth 'fuck', Bette turned towards where I was standing.

'Well that's it Fred,' she said. 'They're not going to let either of us back into this place again.'

Christ, I thought. After all the lectures I've received from the venue management, she's right. I'm not sure that they are going to let us back in tomorrow night. Just to make doubly sure, Bette started making Princess Anne horse jokes.

Sure enough, bright and early the next day, Louis Benjamin was on the phone.

'Could you please ask her to tone down her language?' he pleaded,' She's a great girl. Does she really need to indulge in all this obscenity?'

Well, at least were not being thrown out. Obviously a week of sold out shows counts for something. Assuring him that I would do my best, I hung up.

The next evening I watched some more of the show. This time it was the Harlots that caught my attention - three girls, each with her own very distinctive personality, who besides acting as backup singers played an integral part in the show acting as foils to Bette during her many sketches. Their energy, like Bette's, was simply overwhelming. It was only recently that I discovered that Katey Sagal, one of the Harlots, went on to play the outrageous Peggy Bundy in the TV sitcom Married with Children. At least this explained why I felt I was watching a Bette Midler clone every time I saw the programme.

A couple of evenings later, Bette once again pushed the tolerance of the Palladium management to the limit. Half way through the show, during one of her many monologues, she spotted a large banner being held up in the dress circle. Shielding her eyes against the glare she slowly read out the words 'Show us your tits Bette'.

'Oh,' she said with huge delight, 'Do you mean like this?' and promptly pulled her dress down to her waist, immediately dispelling any notion the audience may have had that she would wear anything as mundane as a bra.

Astonishingly enough, I didn't hear a word of complaint from Louise Benjamin. However, when I arrived at the Palladium the following evening, one of the Harlots told me that Aaron Russo, whom, in my total naivety, I hadn't realised was also Bette's boyfriend, had been so angry with her over the incident that he had allegedly hit her. A story that Russo subsequently denied.

At the end of the London shows, Atlantic Records threw a celebration party at the Waldorf Hotel in the Aldwych. I thought it was an excellent choice, with its extravagant art nouveau interior and its long association with leading members of the theatrical profession, including actresses such as Lily Langtry and Gertrude Lawrence. Judging by the number of liggers present, the party was really the one to be seen at that autumn. Music industry parties have never been my scene, so I tend to keep a low profile. I was told by Wendy that the place was packed with the rich and famous, but the only ones I personally recognised were the late Lee Remick (very pretty), Jack Nicholson, who sat at a table all evening with his arm around his girl friend, who appeared to be around fifteen years old and Alan Bates. I regret to say that I only knew who he was because someone introduced us. Still, everyone, including Bette, appeared to enjoy themselves and the national press were impressed which I suppose was the main thing.

After all this, Brighton seemed something of an anticlimax. Chip Monk, a charming laid back American, who was in charge of lighting on the tour, provided the only distraction when he misjudged the time the rather elaborate lighting rig would take to set up and was still working on a truss 30 feet in the air in the middle of the auditorium when the manager decided he could no longer hold the door, and despite my pleadings, let the audience in. This little lapse was not at all typical of Chip, who was well known for the work he did at the 1969 Woodstock Festival and was normally a byword for efficiency. Swinging like a trapeze artist, only without the benefit of a safety net, he gave the audience something to watch until the show began.

The next day Wendy and I drove over to The Hyde Park Hotel to say goodbye to Bette and Aaron. They seemed very happy with the way things had gone and I must say that Aaron had proved to be one of easiest of the American managers to deal with. What I cannot understand is why, after her successful London shows, and make no mistake they really were a personal triumph for Bette, with both ecstatic reviews in the press and wildly enthusiastic audiences, she has hasn't returned in over twenty three years. Could she, I wonder, be waiting for me to make her an offer?

# CHAPTER 56

There were only a limited number of super groups that could be relied upon to draw a really large crowd and now that Dylan had chosen to play Blackbush Airfield, a flat, boring, featureless piece of ground that I knew quite well, having flown in several times when I was training for my private pilots licence, there was one less.

There was always the possibility of The Eagles, I thought, as I had already had several telephone conversations with their manger Irv'Azoff. He had expressed interest but he had never sounded really positive.

I had also been talking to Steve O'Rourke about the possibility of another appearance of the Floyd. I always got on well with Steve, probably because he was very easy going, but mainly because we shared a similar taste in collectible cars. Just how similar I found out when, during a lunch we had arranged to discuss Knebworth, I excitedly told him about my new purchase - a Ferrari 250GT SWB.

'Not the one owned by Ralph Millais,?' he asked.

'That's the one,' I replied.

'You bugger,' he said, 'I was after that!'

Steve was really keen to see the car and I arranged to take it to his house the following weekend. While Steve and I were out with the Ferrari, Wendy was left in the house with Steve's wife and several friends, one of whom Wendy got on with very well and chatted to most of the time we were out. Driving home, I casually asked her how she had got on with Nick Mason, the Floyd's drummer.

'Very well,' she said and then after a short pause added, 'Is that who it was? I thought he was a Ferrari salesman.'

'Actually,' I explained, 'he just buys and collects them.'

In the end, I reasoned, 1979 just had to be the turn of Led Zeppelin. What, I wondered, would grab Peter's attention. Possibly something we hadn't tried before. Perhaps two consecutive Saturdays? What the hell, it was worth a try. Peter was by now pretty used to my letters, which I must say were always acknowledged, either by a short note usually explaining that the boys had other commitments, or occasionally a phone call. This time, in addition to my suggestion of two dates, I doubled my previous financial offer.

'I hope we know what we're doing,' I said to Wendy, as I posted the letter.

I didn't have to wait long for some sort of reaction. A couple of days later I received a phone call from Peter.

'Well, your timing's right for once ' he said,' The boys were thinking of playing an outdoor festival this summer. You had better come down to

Horselunges and talk about it.'

When we arrived, we were surprised to see that since our last visit, a giant security camera and floodlights had been installed above the entrance to the bridge that led over the moat. Already, it seemed, Peter's paranoia was showing itself. Ray Washburn, Peter's general factotum, met us. Peter, it seemed, was still in the middle of a meeting, and we were shown into the music room and were left to listen to early mixes of Zep's new album 'In Through The Outdoor'.

'What do you think?' Peter asked when he was finally through with his meeting.

'Fantastic,' I replied, although in truth I would really have needed a couple more listens to come up with an honest assessment.

When we finally got down to the nitty gritty, Peter explained that this time the Zeppelin were seriously interested in playing Knebworth. They liked the idea of two dates, but he thought our offer was still too low. The figure he named gave me palpitations, but with a higher ticket price was, I thought, manageable. The really nasty surprise was that they wanted us to fly a giant Showco sound system in from America. We had, of course, allowed a figure for sound and lights. However, we had hadn't budgeted for a system this size or for the additional airfreight costs. We eventually agreed to their demands, but strictly on the understanding that we would only go ahead with the second show if it looked like being a sell-out. Peter agreed, saying that Led Zeppelin wouldn't want to play to a half empty venue anyway. It was at this point that it was agreed we would initially only advertise one show.

Half way through the meeting, Peter received a phone call from his daughter Helen, who attended a drama school, and from the conciliatory noises he made, was obviously quite distraught. It turned out that she hadn't been given a leading part in a school production and wanted Peter to call the school principal to find out why and to ask the woman to intervene on her behalf. It was obvious from what Peter said that he did not want to get involved and found the whole situation embarrassing. Strange, I thought, if it had been a similar problem in the music industry, he wouldn't have given it a second thought. He would have just steamed right in. He was obviously not comfortable dealing with people he was not in a position to bully to get his own way.

Once we had reached an agreement, we shook hands on it. In all my dealings with Peter we never had a written contract, something he prided himself on. This time, I think it would have been better for me if everything had been committed to paper.

Driving home, Wendy and I were both rather subdued. We were delighted that at last Zeppelin were going to play Knebworth. However, we very worried about our commitment. I was also slightly uneasy about the changes in Peter's manner. He was now, it seemed to me, just a little too used to getting his own way. The warning signs were undoubtedly there if I'd had the wit to see them. I had taken my Ferrari down to a test day at the Goodwood Racetrack in West Sussex. While I was having fun on the track, Wendy kept in touch with our office using the local phone box. Around lunchtime, during one of her routine calls, she was told that Peter wanted to speak to me. When I called him, he seemed annoyed that I wasn't in the office.

'I don't know what you are doing down there,' he said, 'when there's so much to be done.'

As the show was still nearly three months away, I thought he was over-reacting somewhat.

'Why don't you come over in the D type?' I said, trying hard to change his mood.

Ignoring my invitation completely, he muttered, 'I just hope you know what you have let yourself in for,' and hung up.

It was about this time that Bill Harkin asked us if we would drive down to Glastonbury and advise them on security. I didn't realise at the time, but Bill Harkin and Arabella Churchill were the main instigators of the 1979 Glastonbury Fayre, which was backed by Michael Eavis, who it seems, actually put the deeds of his farm up as security for the festival. When we arrived, Bill introduced Wendy and me to Michael Eavis, who showed us around the farm. I must say I was extremely impressed with the site and everyone's idealistic attitude and when we got back to the farmhouse both of us tried to give as much practical advice as we could. When we had finished, Bill and I went into an adjoining room to admire the baseball bat that Arabella's son, Winston Churchill's great grandson, had recently acquired, leaving Jean Eavis, Arabella and Wendy chatting in the kitchen. After a quick inspection, and just as I was preparing to rejoin the others, I heard a loud thud followed by a sharp intake of breath and a stifled groan. Quickly turning round, I saw Bill on the floor eyes crossed holding his balls. The young man, it seemed, had been giving a practical demonstration of the baseball bat's potential. Of such stuff, I thought, were leaders of this country made.

To avoid the sort of problems we had experienced with the music papers in 1974, we had agreed with Peter that we would give the story to Bob Harris to announce on the Old Grey Whistle Test. The week after the story broke, we placed full-page advertisements in the Melody Maker, NME and Sounds, giving details of where tickets could be obtained and also gave the news editors information regarding the event.

As a publicity gimmick, we had arranged for a number of box offices to open on Sunday 2nd June. This was well before seven-day trading was taken for granted and we hoped, by encouraging the Led Zeppelin fanatics to start queuing on the Saturday night, we would be able to get pictures of enormous crowds on the television news, and in this way encourage similar scenes when the rest of the box offices opened on Monday morning. When we arrived at the London box office in New Oxford Street, just before the doors opened, we were disappointed. True, there was a large queue and Moira Bellas, Warner Brothers' press officer, who had brought along several pho-tographers, was delighted, but Wendy and I knew otherwise. The queues were not as long as we had hoped for, nor was there the unfettered enthusi-asm that you would have expected for a monster band that had not been seen in the UK for nearly four years. Phoning around the other ticket offices confirmed our fears. It was going to be a long hard job selling out both shows.

Meanwhile I had received a written quotation from Showco, which just knocked me sideways. Sound $55,000 per show, lights $30,000 per show, special effects lasers $20,000, cross-hire of sound $15,000, air fare for 20 crew $14,000, hotels for 20 crew $14,000, and the real killer, return air freight $80,000. This little lot came to a total of $313,000. However, just to show where they were coming from, it was rounded up to a nice even figure of $325,000, at that time approximately £175,000.

I think even Peter, hardened as he was to rock 'n' roll rip-off prices, found these figures difficult to accept, especially as I made it quite clear that unless a compromise was found, it would be impossible to go ahead with the concerts. Later that month, at Peter's insistence, Jack Calmes flew in to London to discuss the problem. He and Peter arrived at our house in Chester Street around 4pm in Peter's brand new Mercedes Benz 450 SEL 6.9 saloon, a present from Bad Company, the other supergroup he managed. It was at that time the fastest saloon car in the world and Peter was thrilled with it, inviting me out into the street for a closer look. Jack Calmes was not quite what I had been expecting from the savage quotation we had received from his company. I don't know if he was originally from Dallas, where Showco was based. However, he displayed a great deal of southern charm and despite his company's outrageous estimates, I instantly took to him. When Peter was in the mood, the small talk could go on for some hours and it was probably around 10 pm before we got down to discussing the quotation. Our first breakthrough was when Jack Calmes admitted that the figures were loaded to compensate for any shows the company might miss in the States. The second was when he conceded that he wasn't interested in making money out of the lights. This was an important admission, as Brian Croft's Company, T.F.A, had only quoted $11,000 to supply the same amount of equipment and of course, as it was already in the country, it also helped to reduce the freight costs. By now it was close to 4am and Peter was keeping himself going with long lines of cocaine plus the occasional Mogadon to maintain the balance. Wendy and I stuck to coffee, a rather more prosaic and decidedly cheaper stimulant. The negotiations continued all the next day, with Jack Calmes trying his best to help break the impasse by suggesting that it should be possible to save half of the freight costs if the equipment was sent back to the States by sea, but would only be possible if there were no major dates shortly after Knebworth. Eventually, piece-by-piece, we managed to bring the costs down to around £100,000, still a colossal sum but rather more acceptable than the figure we had started with. Twenty-six hours after he had arrived, Peter went home. God knows how much cocaine he got through during the course of the meeting, but Wendy and I were both of the opinion that the cost, if set towards the freight charges, would have reduced them quite significantly! The next morning Peter phoned. Wendy took the call.

'I rang you when I got home only there was no reply. You must have gone to bed,' he said.

'No we hadn't,' Wendy replied. 'Actually we went out to dinner with Herb and Suzanne Cohen'.

'Blimey,' Peter said for once a little taken aback, 'I went straight to bed.'

Rather unexpectedly a few days later I received a phone call from Irv Azzoff.

'The Eagles are quite keen to play Knebworth. Just send over the money you offered and if we like the look of it, we will do the show,' he explained in all seriousness.

I always made it a rule never to be rude to managers, well influential ones anyway, but there have to exceptions and this was one of those times.

Apart from the problems with Showco, we were having trouble booking a supporting programme. No one, it seemed, wanted to play with Led Zeppelin. It was at this point, rather belatedly, that I began to realise just what a reputation the band enjoyed for their egotistical behaviour, especially in America. What's more, of course, no one was prepared to play in front of an audience who for over four years had been deprived of an opportunity to see their heroes and who would be counting every minute until they came on stage. Practically every band we approached turned us down, including J.J. Cale, Little Feat, Roxy Music and more significantly Ian Drury and the Blockheads. Ian, at this time, was very popular and his presence on the bill would certainly have helped ticket sales. I was also of the opinion that his very individual style of music would ideally compliment Zeppelin's heavier sounds. I made several offers through his manager, Pete Jenner, with no luck, and in desperation finally offered him an eye-watering £100,000 for the two shows. However, Ian was adamant and would not budge.

No: 8664

# Showex

A DIVISION OF
SCAFFOLDING (GREAT BRITAIN) LIMITED

## INTERNATIONAL SHOW AND EXHIBITION SERVICES
WILLOW LANE MITCHAM SURREY CR4 4TQ     Telephone: 01-648 4408 & 4560

Tedoar Ltd.
4 Chester Street
LONDON   SW1

Ref:   TJMcH/JB

Date:   12th July 1979

Attention: F. Bannister, Esq

Dear Sirs,        <u>RE: Knebworth House</u>

 We thank you for your enquiry in connection with the above and have pleasure in submitting our quotation.

 Should you have any further points to raise we would be glad to give the matter our immediate attention and look forward to being favoured with your order.

Yours faithfully,

T.J. McHUGH
SHOWEX
GENERAL MANAGER

---

No. __1__   PRICE  £35,349 (Thirty-five thousand, three hundred and forty-nine   PLUS V.A.T.
SHOW                                                    pounds)

FOR AN OCCUPATION PERIOD OF 4th Aug. '79 *irrespective of completion in less than this time.*

SPECIFICATION:

To:  Supply, erect and finally clear SHOWEX materials to form the following:-

1) Temporary stage as per our drawing no. A/S 1359/1A/2/A.  Built to your specification, paragraph B.

 Front to be clad in ¾" plywood unpainted.  The ¾" plywood will be butt jointed.  The joints will, therefore, be open because of the radius. If matching joints is required then a price adjustment will be necessary.

 Stage to be decked with new plywood.  Equipment Bay and P.A. wings are to be decked with second-hand ply.

 Rear of P.A. wings are to be draped with waterproof material.  Rear and sides exposed.

 The Equipment Bay clad as per your paragraph D.  Access staircase and ramp as per your specification.

 NOTE
 You have asked for your ramp to run to ground.  Should this not finish at vehicle height?

 P.A. wings dimensions not as your specification but as our drawing.

With extras it came to considerably more

In the end I chose Chas and Dave to open, partly because we had just toured them and knew them well that and partly because I thought, with their warm East End personalities, they might just be able to get the crowd into the right frame of mind. Peter Grant suggested Fairport Convention. I was surprised to find they were still in existence, as I thought they had disbanded several years earlier. Unfortunately, due to a previous booking, they could only appear on the first date. The Marshall Tucker Band were at one time booked to appear but eventually pulled out. Instead, I managed to book the New Commander Cody Band. I was really delighted when South Side Johnny and the Amboy Dukes agreed to appear, their energetic Springsteen influenced music was, I thought, just what was needed to keep every one in the right mood. Todd Rundgren was an easy choice. He was an excellent performer, very popular and a great fan of Knebworth. Not a vintage support programme, but in view of the difficulties I had been experiencing, it could have been worse.

In an attempt to stimulate interest we announced that the first show was sold out and that a second show was scheduled for 11$^{th}$ August. By the first week in July we had sold around 115,000 tickets. Far short of the 150,000 or so I felt we needed to have sold by this time to make the second show vaguely viable. Of these, we allocated 100,000 for the first show and sent tickets for the second show to the remaining 15,000 unlucky postal applicants, with a letter guaranteeing that we would refund their money if they could not attend this show. Instead of stimulating sales, we had to face the fact that a huge number of the 15,000 we had held back for the second show were being returned for a refund. What we hadn't allowed for was that this was the peak time for holidays.

Things looked very bleak. Tickets were just not selling and finally, in desperation, I called Peter and told him we would have to cancel the second show.

'Hang on a day or so,' he said, 'I'll talk it over with the band.'

When he came back, he told me the boys really wanted to do the extra date and in his words 'would see us OK'. From what he said, I presumed he meant that they would renegotiate their fee for the August 11th date. He also told me not to advertise the event as he was trying to get a big attraction to bolster the second show. The days passed, and in desperation I spoke to him again. This time I found out that the big attraction he had previously spoken of was The New Barbarians, a band put together by Ronnie Wood and containing, amongst other superstar musicians, Keith Richards. Two out of five of the Stones can't be bad I thought. I wonder if Mick will come along. As soon as Peter gave me the word, we distributed the story to the music press and placed full-page advertisements in the music papers, following it up by fly-posting huge 10ft banners all around London and the larger cities. Given the delay whilst we waited for the Barbarians to decide whether or not to play at Knebworth, we finally ended up with just three weeks to publicise the additional concert.

Four or five weeks before the festival, Richard Cole had rung to tell me that Led Zeppelin wished to go to Knebworth to look at the park and also the house. Jimmy Page, in particular, was very interested in the memorabilia of Bulmer Lytton, one of David Lytton Cobbold's forebears. Bulmer Lytton, apart from being a distinguished novelist, having written The Last Days of Pompeii, was also well known for his interest in the occult and it was this aspect of his life that Jimmy found particularly engrossing. My presence was required, I was told, so that I could introduce them to the Lytton Cobbolds and generally show them where the stage and other facilities would be situated.

Richard was always making appointments for the visit and, because one or other of the band couldn't make it, for one reason or the other, had to cancel them. On one occasion I had driven all the way up to Knebworth before I was told the band weren't coming. This happened so frequently that I tended to disregard these arrangements. It wasn't until I received a phone call from the Swansong office saying that band was looking for me in the park that I suddenly remembered I was supposed to be meeting them that day at Knebworth. Driving as fast as I dare, I arrived at the estate in record time. The first person I saw when I arrived was Richard, who it appeared had lost the boys. Since Richard didn't know the park as well as I did, I volunteered to help him find them. Jumping into his Range Rover, we set off. Just past the estate church, in the eastern end of the park, I spotted a small cluster of people. Pointing them out to Richard, he turned in their direction and accelerated hard. As we got closer, we were both rather amused to see all four members of Zeppelin standing in line having their photograph taken by Storm Thorgerson, from Hipgnosis. Next to him, posturing for all she was worth, was a naked young woman obviously placed there by Storm to make the band less conscious of the camera. As soon as she noticed us she ran to where she had left a raincoat and quickly pulled it on. Such modesty seemed strangely at odds with her earlier behaviour. Rumour has it that amongst the many photos taken that day is an interesting one of Jimmy Page minus his trousers, but regrettably I have never been able to confirm this. One thing I do know is that after the session, when the photographs were processed, it was decided that the sky was not sufficiently blue and Storm, or it could have been his partner Po, was sent out to Texas to take photos of proper blue skies that were later superimposed onto the Knebworth shots. After all this trouble and expense it was good to see that the photographs were eventually used in number of different ways, including a rather nice Knebworth Festival poster.

According to Steve Gett of the Melody Maker, it rained heavily on the eve of the concert. If it did, it must have been overnight, because I remember clearly that it was quite dry with excellent visibility when, in the late afternoon, the helicopter bringing Jimmy Page to the sound check landed in the arena, on a flat piece of ground just in front of the stage. There were no problems during the run through, the sound proving to be really excellent.

Afterwards, the band went up to Knebworth House for a drink. Peter was at his arrogant best, sneering at everything in the house, which in addition to the truly outstanding 17th century Banqueting Hall, with its fine carved timber, also contains some truly impressive, high Victorian decorations in the State Drawing Room. I don't think David Lytton Cobbold was any too impressed when Grant told him that his own house, Horselunges Manor, was a grade one listed building and that Knebworth House, as far as he knew, was only grade two.

Despite the fact that this time all our adverts, flyers and even our tickets stated that camping would only be allowed from midday Friday this year, people started to arrive as early as Tuesday. By Friday we had run out of camping space. Instead of the quiet, well-behaved twenty and thirty some-things from the Genesis concert, the campsite was wall-to-wall blue denim and studs. The fans were frantic to get into the arena, even if they had to sit there for two solid days and twice they tore down the fences that we had erected between the campsite and the park. In the end, the senior police officer on duty placed a line of Land Rovers on the park side of the fence, backed up by policemen with dogs from around 10pm on the Friday until we opened the gates. It was sheer, bloody, murder and the police, for once, really justified their presence, their cool professionalism really earning my respect. Luckily, by 3am we had enough staff on site to open up. However, before we could there was a moment of panic when Barry couldn't find the keys to the padlocks securing the entrance gates into the arena. I thought my police liaison officer was going to have kittens. Even I felt like taking an immediate holiday to somewhere warm and sunny and as far from the site as possible. Then reason returned and I sent Barry off for the bolt croppers he always kept on site for just such an emergency. Meanwhile Wendy was also suffering from lost key syndrome, this time to the ticket offices. Her saviour was a young man, who like the guy who helped us by unlocking cars in 1976, seemed to have a way with locks and had all four ticket offices open within a minute or so.

It was always rather strange seeing what appeared to be avenging hoards descending on us from across the park, suddenly changing into regular, relatively well-behaved festivalgoers once they entered the arena. I hoped they were well prepared as they were going to have a very long wait before Led Zeppelin were due on stage and our catering units weren't due to open until 10am. In fact, the catering this year was a marked improvement on our previous festivals and was surprisingly international, with such enticing delicacies as French crepes, Indian pita bread sandwiches, German sausage, Japanese tempura as well as normal festival favourites like hot dogs and hamburgers. I always tried to keep the price of food to a reasonable level by writing mutually agreed prices into the contracts we had with our caterers. However, it was not always possible to stop pirates gatecrashing the arena and, of course, I had no control over their prices and no percentage of their profits. We tried very hard to crack down on these unauthorised caterers, but it sometimes seemed that as soon as we had expelled one unit, another took it's place.

As usual, after the initial mad rush there was quite a slow period before the crowds really started to pour in and it was a big relief when, around 8am, a convoy of coaches arrived bringing with them the rest of our 400 Stewards. Half an hour later everything was in place and we were ready to face the day. Nicky Horne had the unenviable job of entertaining the crowd before the bands started to play. I thought it was very brave of him to come back after facing a two hour deluge of cans and bottles during the 10cc debacle in 1976. Perhaps, being small, he thought he was more difficult to hit. Whatever the reason, he always did a great job. However, I'm sure he was relieved when virtually on time the Commander Cody Band took the stage to open the festival.

Around mid morning, Richard Cole came into my office looking rather embarrassed.

'What's the matter?' I said, thinking he had come to score drugs.

'No it's not that,' he said, 'Peter wants you to sign this.'

I looked at the form. It was a waiver for the film rights. The band were having their performance filmed and Peter wanted me to sign away any rights I had as the promoter of the event for the princely sum of a shilling (5 new pence).

'Get lost,' I said, 'No fucking way.'

Richard persisted, 'With the mood Peter's in these days you really don't need the aggravation'.

The argument dragged on and in the end I signed. Richard then handed me the shilling and left. In fact, Grant's meanness was his undoing. If he had given me £250, the agreement would have been quite legal. However, the only way someone signs their rights away for 5 pence is under duress, as I was, and this, I was told sometime afterwards, totally invalidates the contract.

Shortly after Richard left I had another visitor. This time it was Phil Carson, head of Atlantic Records' UK office. After the normal formalities, he

1979 and I'm obviously feeling the pressure

a pensive Todd Rundgren

revealed what subsequently appeared to be the true reason for his visit.

'What a crowd,' he said, 'There must be at least a couple of hundred thousand people out there.'

I had already asked Grant to check the gates - a request he turned down as being unnecessary. With the benefit of hindsight, I think I should have challenged Carson's observation there and then and insisted that Peter Grant ran an immediate audit of our tickets or at the very least appointed someone from his considerable entourage to do it for him.

As soon as Chas and Dave came on it was obvious that it was big mistake to include them on the festival. They were just fine in the intimacy of a small theatre but on the giant stage, trying to project novelty songs to a hundred thousand rock hungry kids, it was a different matter. They tried hard, playing well, receiving good-natured encouragement from some of the audience. However, I think everyone was relieved when they left the stage.

South Side Johnny and the Amboy Dukes were a different matter. Tight and aggressive, they succeeded in rousing the audience to the point where people actually started to get on their feet and dance. I was worried that Todd Rundgren and Utopia, coming on just before Led Zeppelin, would find it rather hard going. However, Todd managed to make their set a personal triumph. I thought he was pushing his luck somewhat when he started slagging off the music press; perhaps he just didn't care if he got a bad review. Alternatively, I thought, perhaps he was secure in the knowledge that the crowd loved him. He really seemed to understand just what the kids wanted and at the end of his set had every one up and yelling for more.

By now it was getting cold and dark but no one seemed to care. This was what everyone was here for and the band they had waited so long to see was now only minutes away. When they finally appeared, the cheers could probably be heard in the next county. Four years is a long time in rock and roll and after such a long absence every one was anxious to see if Zeppelin could still cut it. They soon had their answer. Opening with 'The Song Remains The Same' it was clear to everyone that it should have been retitled the 'Band Remains The Same'. Initially they appeared a little nervous and Jimmy, I thought, seemed just a little rusty. However, as the show pro-gressed, they started to loosen up and it soon became apparent they were still a force to be reckoned with.

Like a royal edict, Wendy and I were summoned by Peter Grant to be on stage for Zeppelins' performance. Looking around, I noticed that seats had been set out in the wings for Peter's guests who included Ahmet Ertigon, a very important figure in the music business, who, along with his brother Nesuhi, had founded Atlantic Records. We stayed for two or three numbers before leaving. Although it was great to experience the power and charisma

Jimmy Page

Robert Plant

of the band close up, I was much happier watching from the arena with the fans, where I could get a real feel for how the band was going down and also get a better idea of how good the special effects were. I was particularly impressed with the huge projection screen placed at the back of the stage. It was so large it ensured that wherever you were sitting in the arena you were virtually drawn into Zep's performance. I also liked the spectacular giant pyramid of lasers that at one point surrounded Jimmy Page.

It was a great show and there was no doubt that the band was really enjoying itself. They played for more than three hours and finished with a fantastic version of Stairway to Heaven, during which the audience them-selves became part of the show by holding aloft anything that would burn including cigarette lighters, matches, rolled up newspapers, even flags - an amazing sight. After this, they played three well-deserved encores before calling it a day. By now it was 1am and we were once again in breach of the licence, which stipulated that the music must stop at midnight.

A bone of contention amongst the local people, when a licence was granted for two consecutive Saturdays, was that 'all those dreadful rockers' would hang around the area all week. Of course, as usual they were wrong. True, a few did stay on but not many and the vast majority of those were roped in to help Captain Olley and his team clean the site. Six days is not very long to clear the debris of 100,000 people and although everyone worked really hard, the site was by no means perfectly clean by the following Saturday.

On Tuesday the shit hit the fan. Wendy received a phone call from Joan Hudson, Led Zeppelin's accountant. She wanted to collect Led Zeppelin's fee for the second show. Having no idea who Joan Hudson was, as Peter had never mentioned her, Wendy explained that we hadn't sold enough tickets to cover the cheque and we were waiting to speak to Peter. Ignoring this Joan Hudson said in her prissy way, 'I understand you claim that the second show isn't selling, but of course you did have 250,000 last Saturday at the first show, so of course there will be plenty over to pay the band in full for the second show. '

'I assure you,' said Wendy, 'There were no more than 104,000 people there.'

When Wendy came off the phone and told me what had happened I was shocked. I had been waiting for Peter to call me to discuss the fee for the second show. Trust Peter to get someone else to do his dirty work, I thought, the words 'the boys will see you're OK' ringing hollowly in my ears. As we discussed the implication of this phone call we realised that this was probably Peter's way of avoiding the need to reduce the fee.

I should have realised how Peter had changed when after the first show he had wanted Warners' to sack Moira Bellas because she had gone home feeling unwell shortly before Led Zeppelin had finished their show. Given the amount of work she had put in, both in the period leading up to the shows and on the day itself, this was totally unreasonable. Moira was one of the most capable and conscientious women I came across whilst promoting and she proved this by later becoming managing director of Warner Bros UK, a position she held for many years, unlike many of the male record company MD's I had dealt with, who came and went with monotonous regularity.

Almost immediately after Joan Hudson's telephone call we received a call from Peter summoning us to a meeting at Horselunges Manor. Phil Carson was already there when we arrived. Peter had this great act. Rather like a character in a Tarantino film, he would initially be all charm and inconsequential niceties before suddenly coming on with the sting.

'So how are we going to resolve this matter of your having had over a quarter of a million people at Knebworth last weekend, and yet you don't have enough money to pay the group in full for the second show?' he asked.

When I tried to explain the implausibility of his statement, he was not interested. Every answer we gave, he brushed aside. What he was suggesting was that we had grossed well over a million pounds more than we were declaring. If he had really wanted to find out the truth, simple questions like 'who printed the tickets?', 'how many did he print?' and 'can we speak to him?' would have been a start but this was never mentioned. He just got ever more angry and incoherent.

'Why would I lie?' I said, 'If we had actually grossed that amount we could have paid you and there would have been a thumping great profit left for us to split and more importantly there would have been no dispute.'

At one point when Wendy, close to tears, tried to explain something to him, this 20 stone bully lunged at her, waving his fist a foot away from her face.

'Don't get smart with me,' he snarled.

That was it. There was no point in trying to reason with him so we left. He did have the good grace to apologise to Wendy when he walked with us out to our car. However, it was too late. He had totally changed from the Peter we knew and trusted in the sixties and early seventies. I should have realised this earlier, of course, as I had already started to notice the difference when he pulled the band out of the first Knebworth concert in 1974. I suddenly, if a little belatedly, remembered what Tony Smith said to me when I told him Zeppelin was playing Knebworth.

'That's great,' he said. 'But do you really need all that aggro?'

On the Wednesday we had a visit from an American calling himself Herb Atkins. He was wearing an over-smart, cheap, dark suit, dark shirt and dark glasses. Every thing about his appearance was intended to suggest he was CIA or the Mafia. However, I think he was probably just a private detective. Still, it was clear that he had been sent to intimidate me. He arrived in an equally sinister dark Volvo, fitted with tinted glass and was accompanied by a rather seedy looking Englishman in his fifties who was introduced to me as a former Metropolitan Police Superintendent. They claimed to have photographs of the first Knebworth Concert that had been analysed by NASA, which they said were so detailed you could read the time on watches that members of the audience were wearing. Unfortunately, it turned out these photos were still with NASA and the shots they showed me were identical in quality to photographs friends of the Cobbold's had taken of the concert from their helicopter and proved absolutely nothing.

'How the hell can you fit a quarter of a million people into an arena only 36 acres in size?' I yelled. 'They would have to be piled three or four deep at the front of the stage and fill the arena to every corner and I still doubt if they would all fit in.'

Despite many requests we were never shown these ultra high-resolution photos or copies of any correspondence from NASA. It was only while researching for this book that I came across the report that Mr Pruette, the Licensing Officer made after the Rolling Stones Festival. If only I had

Led Zeppelin aerial view August 4th

bothered to read it at the time, I could have probably saved myself a great deal of aggravation.

'The number of persons attending the concert has been a matter of some controversy.

During debriefing discussions with the police they have stated that for reasons of resources etc., in their view attendance at any future concert should not be any greater than the numbers attending this year. It is a point of view with which I agree, although I can advance no cogent reasons for doing so.

Attendances at the concert were fixed by the media before the concert took place at various figures between 200,000 — 250,000. To give them their due, they stuck to it after the event. "One acre can reasonably be expected to take about 3,000 people"(Department of Environment Report on Pop Festivals). To accommodate 250,000 persons therefore, would require a concert site of more than 83 acres. The actual size of the concert site was 36.4 acres.

The police (basing their calculations on the numbers of cars parked and the number of persons that arrived by train) estimate that the number of persons attending this year's concert was more than 100,000 and in excess of the number attending the 1975 concert.

In a letter of the 2 September 1976 (circulated to members in the Agenda for the Committee meeting on the 16 September) Mr. F. Bannister, the promoter, writes. 'Regarding numbers attending the concert, I should 1ike to state quite categorically that, contrary to the reports carried in both the national and local press we did not, in fact, exceed the permitted number for which we were licensed.'

The site, if entirely occupied, would have accommodated approximately 109,300 persons on the basis of 3,000 persons per acre, the Department of the environment figure. My own estimation, however, is 4,000 persons per acre, which equals a maximum capacity of 145,000. It should be borne in mind however that parts of the site were occupied by medical tents, caterers, entertainers, lavatories, lighting towers and trees. At a very conservative estimate, the area thus occupied would equal 4.5 acres, leaving an effective area of 32 acres. The whole of this area, however, was not densely occupied. Aerial photographs show about three quarters of the site to be densely occupied, a quarter lightly or sparsely occupied. The figures that emerge are as follows (assuming that the lightly occupied areas are accommodating 1,000 persons per acre')

| Department of Environment estimate of 3,000 persons per acre. | Licensing Officer's estimate of 4,000 persons per acre. |
|---|---|
| 24 Acres densely occupied = 72,000<br><br>8 Acres lightly occupied = 8,000<br><br><br>Total    80,000 | 24 Acres densely occupied = 96,000<br><br>8 Acres lightly occupied = 8,000<br><br><br>Total    104,000 |

Which is the exact number I told the Stones we had for their concert. These figures and the argument that accompany them also, of course, apply to the Led Zeppelin Festival as this event was held in exactly the same arena.

Whilst I feel that Mr Pruette's premise was correct, he appears to have overlooked the fact that the 36.4 acres he quoted as the arena size also contained the stage and back stage area covering a further 3-4 acres which would have reduced the ultimate capacity of the arena still further.

# CHAPTER 57

On Thursday evening, Peter Grant, along with Herb Atkins arrived at our house for yet another meeting. This time a great bull of a man, who was introduced as their driver, accompanied them. Expecting trouble, we had our lawyer in the kitchen and a minder in our bedroom on the floor above the sitting room, where the meeting was being held. In over 20 years of promoting, this was something that we had never required before. We allowed Peter Grant's driver to wait in our office on the ground floor. It was fortunate we had a six-storey house at that time and were able to keep everyone apart.

After a great deal of discussion, Grant told us that, although he still didn't believe the figures we had given him he was prepared to reduce Led Zeppelins fee for the second show, to enable us to pay the rest of the bands. He then went on to warn us that they were going to take over the running of the festival and would be putting their people on the gates. Joan Hudson would check all the cash, they would also pay the bands and on day expenses out of the proceeds and keep everything else.

I was furious but swallowing my temper said, 'That's fine, at least you'll know the truth' and I added 'What a pity you didn't check the doors when I asked you last weekend.'

As Peter left, like something out of the film the Godfather, he kissed Wendy 'goodbye' something he had never done before.

Ironically, the minder we had employed stole a camera and £200 cash from our bedroom in which he was hiding.

There was a very different atmosphere on the campsite the day before the last show. Instead of the frantic scenes of the previous week, it was quite calm and orderly. It was the same on the morning of the concert. No frantic 3am dash for the stage, just a nice, orderly, stream of people, waiting patiently to enter the arena at 8am.

Peter had arranged for cashiers from some of the local banks to work in the ticket offices. When they arrived, no one seemed to know what to do. Someone asked Wendy if she could help.

'Don't ask me,' she snapped, 'ask Joan Hudson.'

Rather typically, some of Peter's heavies had taken over one of the estate offices in which to count the cash. They didn't bother to ask David Lytton Cobbold's permission first, but had simply thrown out the estate staff. David was understandably furious.

The previous week I had been appalled to find that Town and Country Catering had done a deal with Billy Blundell for the ice cream concession for the two concerts. Billy, a tough Londoner whose family had a fleet of vans selling ice cream in central London, would not have been my first choice because of his reputation as a person difficult to deal with. In fact, I experienced this for myself when he came storming up to me followed by Don Murfitt, my head of security, to complain about the positioning of his vans in the arena. He was not happy with the areas he had been allocated and had moved the vans to areas he considered more suitable. Unfortunately, he'd blocked off a view of the stage for a large number of the audience in the process. Don had quite rightly asked him to move the vans and he had refused. The argument escalated until I was finally dragged in. It wasn't so much a face-to-face confrontation as a nose-to-nose and things got very heated. I realised we had lost the psychological advantage when I noticed that Billy Blundell's 18ct gold chain bracelet was over twice as big as Don's. However, I wasn't going to give in to his determined bullying. He eventually realised that I meant what I said and in the end he moved his vans.

You can imagine how I felt after this confrontation, when early on the morning of the second show, two of our staff showed me a programme that they claimed was being sold by members of Billy Blundell's staff between Stevenage Station and the Park. We had produced an excellent programme for the concert, which we were selling for 90p. It featured a colour picture of Zeppelin on the cover and also had lots of colour inside. The one they showed me was obviously a copy of ours, apart from the front cover, which had black lettering on a red background. Inside, the colour pages had had been dispensed with for reasons of economy, yet despite this it was still being sold for the same price. Now I had no proof that Blundell was behind this rip off and after our last run in, I was not particularly anxious to ask him. Instead, I arranged for a team of our lads with a large van to follow the route from the station to the park and snatch any of the bootlegged programmes they saw being offered for sale. The operation was a great success and the boys arrived back with around 24 large boxes full of programmes, which we hastily hid in one of the estate offices.

With no means of checking ticket sales, I could only estimate the size of the crowd from standing on the stage and looking out into the arena. I had hoped that adding the New Barbarians to the programme would boost tickets sales, especially on the day. However, by midday, when I again looked into the arena, there only seemed to be about a third the number of the previous week, a very depressing sight. By the end of the afternoon, to our utter amazement Joan Hudson, no doubt on Grant's instructions, handed the box offices back to us, along with all the cash they had taken that day, instructing us to make sure the security staff and bands were paid. Why they had this change of heart I have no idea. Perhaps it was all simply too much trouble? She confirmed that the total number of tickets they had sold, along with the pre-sold tickets came to no more than 40,000. This admission, rather than lightening the atmosphere, seemed to make it worse. Grant's heavies were everywhere. My accountant, Harvey Lawrence, thinking he could perhaps bring some sense to this fraught situation, decided to go and talk to Peter and his associates He was gone so long that I thought he had been taken hostage and sent a rescue party to bring him back. When they arrived at Grant's trailer they found Harvey quite safe, still patiently waiting to talk to someone.

According to the press, the New Barbarians were something of a disappointment. I suppose, compared to a full performance by the Stones, they were. Nevertheless, there was still a lot to enjoy. After a slow start, they really started to get it together and their interpretation of Dylan's Seven Days and Keith Richards Before They Make Me Run earned them a warm response from the audience, as did their encore Honky Tonk Woman.

As soon as Zeppelin came on we left, leaving Barry Turner to take charge of the event. He had worked with us on every one of the seven Knebworth Festivals we had promoted and knew exactly what to do. At that of the evening and with such a small crowd, there was a lot that could go wrong. Stopping briefly to ask directions from one of the policemen working on the event, we headed for the Travel Lodge Motel in Luton. We wanted somewhere where we could talk without any interruptions and this had seemed as good a place as any.

When we returned home the following evening we were alarmed to see lights on in what should have been a deserted house. Our nerves on edge, thinking it was Grant's heavies, we drove around the block to give us time to work out a plan of campaign. We couldn't decide whether to call the police or simply enter the house and face whoever was there. In the end we compromised and rang the house. It was a pretty pointless thing to do as I couldn't imagine anyone who had entered the premises illegally answering the phone. Much to our surprise, Herb Cohen's daughter, Lisa, answered the call. Suddenly, and with great embarrassment, we remembered that Lisa and a friend had come to stay the day we left for Knebworth and we had given her a key and the run of the house.

The whole of the following week was a nightmare. The press, sensing a good, juicy story simply hounded us. Although Peter never directly threatened us, Herb Atkins had made it fairly clear, with his talk of people from Miami, that there were American interests who could be something of a problem if we, to quote him, 'misbehaved ourselves.' We thought it would be a good idea to get away for a while so we rented a house in Petworth, West Sussex and with our young daughter, left for a week in the country. We kept in touch with our office, calling three or four times a day to see that every thing was OK. During one of these calls, I was told that Peter wanted me to phone him.

I called him from a phone box in Balls Cross, a tiny hamlet just outside of Petworth.

'I hear you still haven't paid one of the bands,' he said, without any preamble, 'You know I made sure there was enough money to take care of all of the bands.'

I felt like saying what's so bloody sacred about the fucking bands? How about sparing a thought for the unfortunate promoter that you have just screwed? But I didn't. Instead I explained that the reason one of the groups had not been paid was because Harvey had lost the draft and a new one was being issued in its place.

'Just make sure you sort it,' Peter growled. He then went on to remark, in a patronising manner, that it seemed a rather odd time to be taking a holiday and with this remark something inside me snapped.

Son of a bitch, I thought. With all the unpleasantness and threats of violence, he had the temerity to think I would actually go on holiday. All the pent up emotions of the past few months welled up and I started to tell him at the top of my voice exactly what I thought of him. I hadn't got half a dozen words out before there was a click and the line went dead. Ever the coward, he had hung up. It was to be the last time I ever spoke to Peter.

It wasn't, however, the last time I spoke to Herb Atkins. About a month later I received a phone call from Herb Atkins instructing me to meet him at The Dorchester in Park Lane and to come alone. If he wasn't ex CIA I thought, he obviously fantasised that he was. I certainly wasn't going alone. Instead I took Barry Turner, a very useful person if there was trouble. When we arrived, Herb was already there, sitting at a table in the lounge, drinking coffee. While I joined him Barry sat discretely at another table. It appeared Grant wanted me to absolve him and the band from any of the bad publicity the Festival was getting and wanted me to sign a letter to that effect. It wasn't the only reason he wanted me to sign, I am sure. After the trouble Peter, John Bonham and Richard Cole had been involved in at The Oakland Coliseum, California when they beat up one of the security guards, who they claimed had hit Peter's son, they had received suspended jail sentences and were put on probation. In view of this conviction, it wouldn't be that easy for them to obtain American work permits and if I made too much fuss about the way I had been so unjustly treated, it would probably aggravate an already delicate situation. I was not exactly thrilled with the request. However, after all the unpleasantness and worrying innuendo, I was scared for the safety of my family. I just wanted to put everything behind me and get on with my life, so I agreed to sign the statement.

Looking around, I was surprised to see that a heavily built man of about the same age as Barry had joined him at his table. On our way back to the office I asked Barry who he was.

'Oh that guy,' said Barry. 'He was Herb Atkins' minder - we were at school together.'

A couple of weeks later, Wendy received a call from the Melody Maker's advertising manager, someone she dealt with regularly and with whom she got on very well. He sounded worried.

'Are you aware of the full-page advertisement Peter Grant is placing?' he asked.

'What does it say?'

'It's a copy of a letter from Freddy to Peter Grant,' he said.' Do you want us to print it?

We had been expecting something like this but not on quite such an extravagant scale.

'Go ahead,' she said. 'If Grant feels the need to publish the letter in this way no one is going to believe it anyway,' and added 'no one who knows Freddy would believe that he would write such formal crap.'

It was during our meeting at the Dorchester that Atkins mentioned to me that his colleagues, whom he would never name, had looked into our financial position and had decided that we were quite insubstantial and weren't worth bothering with any further.

It seems, looking back, I only had myself to blame for the way things turned out. I had been warned that Peter had changed but I suppose I was arrogant enough to think that, because we had got on so well in the early days, that I could handle him. It had been obvious right from our first meeting that he had qualities that made him stand out from the rest. As we got to know him better and he became more successful, it became apparent that as well as his natural astuteness and innate charm, he had judgment and taste that belied his humble origins. I am sure that he would have been successful in almost anything he undertook, not just in the music business, but also as an international art or antique dealer. The furniture he collected was an excellent case in point. The two Tiffany armchairs he had acquired were not just fine examples of one of the best known of the 19th century American designers; they had actually come from Tiffany's own house. He also owned a fabulous and very important suite of fine Art Nouveau furniture produced by Louis Majorelle in his factory in the French town of Nancy. His good taste was not just confined to furniture, as he had a wide range of interests. His collection of cars was another indication of his depth of knowledge. Besides the Pierce Arrows and a D Type Jaguar, similar to the ones the factory raced so successfully at Le Mans and other circuits in the mid 1950's, he had also acquired probably one of the most famous record breaking Lagondas, the whereabouts of which, when he bought, it was only known to a handful of enthusiasts.

To  Mr. Peter Grant

There has been some misconceptions reported in the press
concerning the Led Zeppelin and Knebworth which, as
concert promoter, I would like to clarify.  First, before
anyone knew what the total ticket sales for the two
concerts would be, upon my request, the Led Zeppelin
voluntarily reduced their guarantee by a substantial amount
and were willing to accept an alternate arrangement in order
to help insure the best possible concert for the patrons and
payment to all concerned in the event there was insufficient
funds to pay everyone in full.  Mr. Peter Grant, Manager of
the Led Zeppelin, was particularly concerned that all acts
appearing at the concert be fully compensated.
Unfortunately, because of a huge increase in production and
staffing costs, increased V.A.T., among other reasons, this
very substantial guarantee reduction by the Led Zeppelin,
while very helpful, was unfortunately not sufficient.
Second, at all times the Led Zeppelin, their Manager and his
staff have been completely co-operative, the group's
performances at Knebworth truly outstanding and their
popularity, as evidenced by their number one album throughout
the world speaks for itself.
Finally, it would be a privilege and pleasure for me to
promote another Led Zeppelin concert in the future and hope
to have the opportunity of so doing.


                          Signed Frederick Bannister
                          Director, Tedoar Limited


The disclaimer that Peter Grant "insisted" I signed ...

Sept 20 1979

**There** have been some misconceptions reported in the press concerning Led Zeppelin and Knebworth, which as the concert promoter I would like to clarify.

Firstly, before anyone knew what the total ticket sales for the two concerts would be, at my request, Led Zeppelin voluntarily reduced their guarantee by a substantial amount and were willing to accept an alternative arrangement in order to help ensure the best possible concert for the patrons and payment to all concerned, in the event there was insufficient funds to pay everyone. Peter Grant, manager of Led Zeppelin, was particularly concerned that all acts' appearing at the concert be paid. Unfortunately, because of a large increase in production and staffing costs, increased V.A.T. amongst other reasons, this very substantial reduction by Zeppelin, while very helpful and very much appreciated was unfortunately not sufficient.

Secondly, at all times Led Zeppelin, the manager and his staff have been completely co-operative.

The group's performance at Knebworth, was in my opinion, really tremendous and their popularity, as shown by their album being No 1 throughout the world speaks for itself.

Finally it would be a privilege and pleasure for me to promote another Led Zeppelin concert in the future and hope to have the opportunity of so doing.

Signed Frederick Bannister
Director, Tedoar Ltd.

... and how it appeared in the music papers

Whilst we were never close friends, we knew each other well enough for Peter to phone me when his wife, Gloria, left him and spend over an hour on the phone discussing his problems, including how he was scared that she would attempt to come back for the two children and what steps he had taken to prevent her. All of these things, plus, of course, the fact that we had previously worked with him on the two Bath Festivals, appearances that Led Zeppelin themselves generously acknowledged were instrumental in helping to establish them as the biggest rock band in the country, led me to believe that we would have no trouble with Peter or the band. Obviously the four intervening years had changed everyone, Peter especially, who by this time I believe had begun to believe his own hype. Nor had I allowed for the effect that drugs had on his judgment. If I had been aware of all this, I would have given Zeppelin a miss and instead tried to have negotiated a deal with The Eagles. As it was, my final misjudgment was to over estimate the bands drawing power. Four years is a long time in the life of a band and not having been seen in the UK during this period is a serious test of the loyalty of their fans. They really should not have left it so long. The music business is very competitive and there were many bands that were anxious to fill the void they had left. I think the simple truth is that they were no longer at their peak of popularity and we were made the fall guys, with Peter seizing onto the highly exaggerated press reports of the numbers they claimed attended the events to maintain Led Zeppelin's reputation as the biggest act in the world.

I know I have mentioned it earlier in the book, when I dealt with the controversy over the numbers attending The Stones festival, but I think it bears repeating, because I really do wonder if music journalists know what problems they can cause with their poorly researched articles. For example, a journalist in his article for the NME dated $_{18}$th August 1979, covering the second festival, where even Peter Grant's staff admitted to us there were no more than 40,000 present, blithely wrote:

'Knebworth (part 2) came and went last Saturday and although there were mild 'memorable moments' one doubts whether the 150,000 to 300,000 people will cherish the event for eternity.'

If he had even half a mind, which I really doubt, surely he could see that his claims had absolutely no basis in reality. His upper estimate was 260,000 adrift - a figure that equates to approximately three times the number of people allowed into Wembley stadium for a cup final! Such irresponsible inaccuracy would probably have seen him sacked in any other profession.

The facts are that that we received 104,000 paid admissions for the first show and 40,000 for the second. If you allow comps and a few gatecrashers, you can probably round it up to 150,000 still a very impressive number to draw over two consecutive weekends. We did not cheat Led Zeppelin out of one penny, quite the contrary, as we not only lost money on the promotion but we lost our livelihood as well. We certainly would not have lasted over twenty years in a business as competitive as the music industry if we had not enjoyed a solid reputation, nor would we have ended up running large outdoor shows. I can honestly say over the whole of this period, we never cheated or failed to pay a band.

So why did we retire so abruptly? In a word, fear. By this time Peter Grant was in such a terrible state, both mentally and physically, we thought he was on the way out and would be delighted to take us with him. As it happened, he lived another 16 years and, I believe, became a born again Christian.

It was not just Grant, however, that influenced my decision. For some time I had been growing disillusioned with the greed and general unpleasantness of the contractors that provided equipment and services for the events, and also by the way the police and council, using moral blackmail, were driving up the cost of these events with their ever more unrealistic demands for money. Finally and perhaps more importantly, I could at last see from the way that the music scene was heading that the days of the commercial mega shows were basically coming to an end, at least for sometime to come.

Do I miss the music business? Of course. I miss the people, the humour, the camaraderie. Above all, I miss the great music, but come to think of it, doesn't every one?

## THE PAVILION - BATH

**Mon Feb 20th**

Please note change of programme instead of
Chuck Berry we now present

# The Jimi Hendrix Experience

(Hey Jo)

---

**Mon Feb 27th**

Look out It's

# Zoot Money

and his
**Big Roll Band**

---

**Mon Mar 6th**

America's most exciting new personality

# KEITH

(98·6)

---

7.30 — 10.30 p.m. | Adm 5/-

---

## THE PAVILION - BATH

| WHIT MONDAY 3rd JUNE | **SORRY NO SESSION** |

---

FROM LIVERPOOL
THE

**MONDAY 10th JUNE** 

# BEATLES

PLUS      PLUS
THE COLIN ANTHONY COMBO
and CHET AND THE TRIUMPHS

ADM 6/-

---

**MONDAY 17th JUNE**

# SHANE FENTON

AND THE
**FENTONES**

---

FROM AMERICA
THE GLAMOROUS

**MONDAY 24th JUNE** KETTY LESTER

(LOVE LETTERS IN THE SAND ETC)

---

7.30-10.30 p.m.      ADM. 4/-
(Except the Beatles Night)

---

TOP POP STARS EVERY MONDAY

# THE MALVERN WINTER GARDENS

## THE PAVILION — BATH

**Mon Oct 9th**

From America the exciting sounds of
THE

# Vanilla Fudge

(You keep me hanging on, etc)

Adm 5/6

**Mon Oct 16th**

"TOPS"

# The Move

Adm 5/6

**Mon Oct 23rd**

THE

# Pink Floyd

(See Emily Play)

Adm 5/6

**Mon Oct 30th**

THE

# Small Faces

We have been assured by the group that
this time they will definitely appear

Adm 6/-

| 7.30 — 10.30 | TWO GROUPS AT EVERY SESSION |

**TOP GROUPS EVERY MONDAY**

---

## MALVERN BIG BEAT SESSIONS
### WINTER GARDENS
**A BANNISTER · PROMOTION**

**Tues Nov 29th**

THE

# WHO

We regret the high admission price but a fab group
commands fab fees          7/6

**Tues Dec 6th**

Britians most dynamic vocalist

# Eric Burdon
and the
# New Animals

(Help me girl)

Adm 5/-

**Tues Dec 13th**

Malvern's first Happenings with

# The Creation

(Painter Man)

Adm 5/-

**Tues Dec 20th**

Fabulous Xmas Party Session
with

# The Cream

(Wrapping Paper)

**2 GREAT SUPPORTING GROUPS**

Adm 6/-

**2 GROUPS AT EVERY SESSION**

# THE PAVILION BATH  1963-1970

Listed below are the bands that played at The Pavilion, Bath for Bannister Promotions. It illustrates the changes and developments in the pop music scene throughout this period and whilst the list is fairly comprehensive it should not be considered definitive.

| | | | | |
|---|---|---|---|---|
| Mon | Jan | 21st | 1963 | JET HARRIS & THE JET BLACKS |
| (Opening night) | | | | |
| Mon | Jan | 28th | 1963 | EMILE FORD instead of MARTY WILDE |
| Mon | Feb | 4th | 1963 | SHANE FENTON |
| Mon | Feb | 11th | 1963 | JOHNY & THE HURRICANES |
| Mon | Feb | 18th | 1963 | MARTY WILDE |
| Mon | Feb | 25th | 1963 | JIMMY JUSTICE |
| Mon | Mar | 4th | 1963 | NO SESSION |
| Mon | March | 11th | 1963 | KENNY LYNCH |
| Mon | March | 18th | 1963 | THE JOHN BARRY SEVEN |
| Mon | March | 25th | 1963 | EMILE FORD |
| Mon | April | 1st | 1963 | Not known |
| Mon | April | 8th | 1963 | GENE VINCENT |
| Mon | April | 15th | 1963 | MIKE BERRY |
| Mon | April | 22nd | 1963 | THE VERNON GIRLS |
| Mon | April | 29th | 1963 | RUSS SAINTY |
| Mon | May | 6th | 1963 | SOUNDS INC |
| Mon | May | 13th | 1963 | JOHNNY KIDD & THE PIRATES |
| Mon | May | 20th | 1963 | JOHNY TILLOTSON |
| Mon | May | 27th | 1963 | JERRY LEE LEWIS + SUTCH +THE OUTLAWS |
| Mon | June | 3rd | 1963 | NO SESSION |
| Mon | June | 10th | 1963 | THE BEATLES |
| Mon | June | 17th | 1963 | SHANE FENTON & THE FENTONES |
| Mon | June | 24th | 1963 | KETTY LESTER |
| Mon | July | 1st | 1963 | BILLY J KRAMER & THE DAKOTAS |
| Mon | July | 8th | 1963 | JET HARRIS & TONY MEEHAN |
| Mon | July | 15th | 1963 | THE 'UK' EAGLES |
| Mon | July | 22nd | 1963 | SOUNDS INCORPORATED |
| Mon | July | 29th | 1963 | THE HOLLIES |
| Mon | Aug | 5th | 1963 | Not known |
| Mon | Aug | 12th | 1963 | THE SEARCHERS |
| Mon | Aug | 19th | 1963 | FREDDY AND THE DREAMERS |
| Mon | Aug | 26th | 1963 | SCREAMING LORD SUTCH & THE SAVAGES |
| Mon | Sept | 2nd | 1963 | GERRY & THE PACEMAKERS |
| Mon | Sept | 9th | 1963 | BRIAN POOLE & THE TREMELOES |
| Mon | Sept | 16th | 1963 | JOHN LEYTON |

| Mon | Sept | 23rd | 1963 | TOMMY BRUCE & THE BRUISERS |
|-----|------|------|------|-----------------------------|
| Mon | Sept | 30th | 1963 | GENE VINCENT & THE OUTLAWS |
| Mon | Oct | 7th | 1963 | THE SWINGING BLUE JEANS |
| Mon | Oct | 14th | 1963 | THE BIG THREE |
| Mon | Oct | 21st | 1963 | TOMMY ROE |
| Mon | Oct | 28th | 1963 | DEL SHANNON |
| Mon | Nov | 4th | 1963 | THE SPUTNICKS |
| Mon | Nov | 11th | 1963 | THE ROLLING STONES |
| Mon | Nov | 18th | 1963 | THE HOLLIES |
| Mon | Nov | 25th | 1963 | THE EAGLES |
| Mon | Dec | 2nd | 1963 | JOHNY KIDD & THE PIRATES |
| Mon | Dec | 9th | 1963 | NO SESSION |
| Mon | Dec | 16th | 1963 | THE BROOK BROS + THE MOJOS |
| Mon | Dec | 23rd | 1963 | XMAS PARTY SOUNDS INC |
| | | | | + Chet and the Triumphs |
| | | | | + Paul Vernon and the Raiders |
| Mon | Dec | 30th | 1963 | BERN ELLIOTT & THE FENMEN |

## 1964

| Mon | Jan | 6th | 1964 | THE SEARCHERS |
|-----|-----|-----|------|----------------|
| Mon | Jan | 13th | 1964 | PETER JAY & THE JAY WALKERS |
| Mon | Jan | 20th | 1964 | BRIAN POOLE & THE TREMELOES |
| Mon | Jan | 27th | 1964 | THE UNDERTAKERS |
| Mon | Feb | 3rd | 1964 | WAYNE FONTANA & THE MINDBENDERS |
| Mon | Feb | 10th | 1964 | THE MERSEYBEATS |
| Mon | Feb | 17th | 1964 | THE HOLLIES |
| Mon | Feb | 24th | 1964 | MARTY WILDE & THE WILDCATS |
| Mon | March | 2nd | 1964 | FREDDIE & THE DREAMERS |
| Mon | March | 9th | 1964 | THE UNDERTAKERS |
| Mon | March | 16th | 1964 | ADAM FAITH & THE ROULETTES |
| Mon | March | 23rd | 1964 | THE TORNADOES |
| Mon | March | 30th | 1964 | THE FOURMOST |
| Mon | April | 6th | 1964 | CILLA BLACK & SOUNDS INC |
| Mon | April | 13th | 1964 | SCREAMING LORD SUTCH & THE SAVAGES |
| Mon | April | 20th | 1964 | BIG DEE IRWIN & THE DIAMONDS |
| Mon | April | 27th | 1964 | JOHNY KIDD & THE PIRATES |
| Mon | May | 4th | 1964 | THE FOUR PENNIES |
| Mon | May | 11th | 1964 | LITTLE RICHARD |
| Mon | May | 18th | 1964 | THE BIG THREE |
| Mon | May | 25th | 1964 | MANFREDD MANN |
| Mon | June | 1st | 1964 | THE HOLLIES |
| Mon | June | 8th | 1964 | BIG BEAT BALL 5 local groups - Johny Carr & the Cadillacs, Pete Bud & the Rebels, The Raiders, Chet & the Triumphs and the Echoes |

| Mon | June | 15th | 1964 | THE UNDERTAKERS |
| Mon | June | 22nd | 1964 | MILLIE & THE EMBERS |
| Mon | June | 29th | 1964 | THE ANIMALS |
| Mon | July | 6th | 1964 | TOMMY QUICKLY + REMO 4 |
| Mon | July | 13th | 1964 | THE SEARCHERS |
| Mon | July | 20th | 1964 | THE DENNISONS |
| Mon | July | 27th | 1964 | THE MERSEYBEATS |
| Mon | Aug | 3rd | 1964 | NO SESSION  (Bank Holiday) |
| Mon | Aug | 10th | 1964 | THE MOJOS |
| Mon | Aug | 17th | 1964 | THE NASHVILLE TEENS |
| Mon | Aug | 24th | 1964 | GENE VINCENT & THE SHOUTS |
| Mon | Aug | 31st | 1964 | THE YARDBIRDS |
| Mon | Sept | 7th | 1964 | NO SESSION |
| Mon | Sept | 14th | 1964 | THE PRETTY THINGS |
| Mon | Sept | 21st | 1964 | DAVE BERRY & THE CRUISERS |
| Mon | Sept | 28th | 1964 | JOHNY KIDD & THE PIRATES |
| Mon | Oct | 5th | 1964 | THE ZOMBIES |
| Mon | Oct | 12th | 1964 | THE NATURALS |
| Mon | Oct | 19th | 1964 | HERMANS HERMITS |
| Mon | Oct | 26th | 1964 | SWINGING BLUE JEANS |
| Mon | Nov | 2nd | 1964 | CLIFF BENNETT & THE REBEL ROUSERS |
| Mon | Nov | 9th | 1964 | THE DOWNLINERS SECT |
|  |  |  |  | + THE TOGGERY FIVE |
| Mon | Nov | 16th | 1964 | THE HOLLIES |
| Mon | Nov | 23rd | 1964 | TONY JACKSON & THE VIBRATIONS |
| Mon | Nov | 30th | 1964 | THE POETS |
| Mon | Dec | 7th | 1964 | BIG BEAT BALL 8 Groups including |
|  |  |  |  | Redcaps, Peters Faces, Cops & Robbers |
|  |  |  |  | and The Herd etc |
| Mon | Dec | 14th | 1964 | WAYNE FONTANA |
| Mon | Dec | 21st | 1964 | THE FOUR PENNIES |
| Mon | Dec | 28th | 1964 | ROCKIN' BERRIES |

**1965**

| Mon | Jan | 4th | 1965 | THE KINKS |
| Mon | Jan | 11th | 1965 | THE ANIMALS |
| Mon | Jan | 18th | 1965 | THE YARDBIRDS |
| Mon | Jan | 25th | 1965 | THE PRETTY THINGS |
| Mon | Feb | 1st | 1965 | DAVE BERRY & THE CRUISERS |
| Mon | Feb | 8th | 1965 | WAYNE FONTANA & THE MINDBENDERS |
| Mon | Feb | 15th | 1965 | THEM |
| Mon | Feb | 22nd | 1965 | MANFRED MANN |
| Mon | March | 1st | 1965 | THE ZOMBIES |
| Mon | March | 8th | 1965 | JOE BROWN & THE BRUVVERS |

| Mon | March | 15th | 1965 | THE MOODY BLUES |
|-----|-------|------|------|-----------------|
| Mon | March | 22nd | 1965 | PJ PROBY |
| Mon | March | 29th | 1965 | THE NASHVILLE TEENS |
| Mon | April | 5th | 1995 | THE MOJOS |
| Mon | April | 12th | 1965 | HERMANS HERMITS |
| Mon | April | 19th | 1965 | TOM JONES & THE SQUIRES |
| Mon | April | 26th | 1965 | DAVE BERRY & THE CRUISERS |
| Mon | May | 3rd | 1965 | UNIT FOUR PLUS TWO |
| Mon | May | 10th | 1965 | THE HONEYCOMBS |
| Mon | May | 17th | 1965 | THE WHO |
| Mon | May | 24th | 1965 | THEM |
| Mon | May | 31st | 1965 | THE ROCKIN BERRIES |
| Mon | June | 7th | 1965 | NO SESSION  (Whit Monday) |
| Mon | June | 14th | 1965 | THE WALKER BROS |
| Mon | June | 21st | 1965 | DONOVAN |
| Mon | June | 28th | 1965 | THE HOLLIES |
| Mon | July | 5th | 1965 | THE YARDBIRDS |
| Mon | July | 12th | 1965 | GOLDIE AND THE GINGERBREADS |
| Mon | July | 19th | 1965 | MOODY BLUES |
| Mon | July | 26th | 1965 | UNIT FOUR PLUS TWO |
| Mon | Aug | 2nd | 1965 | THE MERSEYBEATS |
| Mon | Aug | 9th | 1965 | THE ANIMALS |
| Mon | Aug | 16th | 1965 | THE BYRDS |
| Mon | Aug | 23rd | 1965 | THE WALKER BROS |
| Mon | Aug | 30th | 1965 | MANFRED MANN |
| Mon | Sept | 6th | 1965 | WAYNE FONTANA |
| Mon | Sept | 13th | 1965 | NO SESSION |
| Mon | Sept | 20th | 1965 | NO SESSION |
| Mon | Sept | 27th | 1965 | THE KINKS |
| Mon | Oct | 4th | 1965 | THE FORTUNES |
| Mon | Oct | 11th | 1965 | THE SMALL FACES |
| Mon | Oct | 18th | 1965 | ROCKIN' BERRIES |
| Mon | Oct | 25th | 1965 | THE WALKER BROS. |
| Mon | Nov | 1st | 1965 | THE YARDBIRDS |
| Mon | Nov | 8th | 1965 | THE FOUR PENNIES |
| Mon | Nov | 15th | 1965 | THE WHO |
| Mon | Nov | 22nd | 1965 | THE ZOMBIES |
| Mon | Nov | 29th | 1965 | WAYNE FONTANA |
| Mon | Dec | 6th | 1965 | THE PRETTY THINGS |
| Mon | Dec | 13th | 1965 | UNIT FOUR PLUS TWO |
| Mon | Dec | 20th | 1965 | THE SPENCER DAVIS GROUP |

(CANCELLED HALL FLOODED)

| Mon | Dec | 27th | 1965 | HEDGEHOPPERS ANONYMOUS |
|-----|-----|------|------|------------------------|

**1966**

| Mon | Jan | 3rd | 1966 | THE SMALL FACES |
|---|---|---|---|---|
| Mon | Jan | 10th | 1966 | THE NASHVILLE TEENS |
| Mon | Jan | 17th | 1966 | THE HOLLIES |
| Mon | Jan | 24th | 1966 | THE MERSEY BEATS |
| Mon | Jan | 31st | 1966 | DAVE DEE, DOZY, BEAKY, MICK AND TICH |
| Mon | Feb | 7th | 1966 | SPENCER DAVIS GROUP |
| Mon | Feb | 14th | 1966 | THE KINKS |
| Mon | Feb | 21st | 1966 | CHRISPIAN ST PETERS |
| Mon | Feb | 28th | 1966 | ST LOUIS UNION |
| Mon | March | 7th | 1966 | MANFRED MANN |
| Mon | March | 14th | 1966 | YARDBIRDS |
| Mon | March | 21st | 1966 | THE MINDBENDERS |
| Mon | March | 28th | 1966 | PINKERTONS ASSORTED COLOURS |
| Mon | April | 4th | 1966 | LOU CHRISTIE |
| Mon | April | 11th | 1966 | ALAN PRICE SET |
| Mon | April | 18th | 1966 | Big beat ball The Crying Shames+3 local groups |
| Mon | April | 25th | 1966 | THE WHO |
| Mon | May | 2nd | 1966 | GRAHAM BONNEY |
| Mon | May | 9th | 1966 | NEIL CHRISTIAN & THE CRUSADERS |
| Mon | May | 16th | 1966 | THE SMALL FACES |
| Mon | May | 23rd | 1966 | PAUL & BARRY RYAN |
| Mon | May | 30th | 1966 | THE MOODY BLUES |
| Mon | June | 6th | 1966 | THE TROGGS |
| Mon | June | 13th | 1966 | WAYNE FONTANA |
| Mon | June | 20th | 1966 | NO SESSION |
| Mon | June | 27th | 1966 | THE MINDBENDERS |
| Mon | July | 4th | 1966 | THE KINKS |
| Mon | July | 11th | 1966 | DAVE DEE, DOZY BEAKY MICK & TICH |
| Mon | July | 18th | 1966 | THE MERSEYS |
| Mon | July | 25th | 1966 | THE YARDBIRDS |
| Mon | Aug | 1st | 1966 | CRISPIAN ST PETERS |
| Mon | Aug | 8th | 1966 | THE SMALL FACES |
| Mon | Aug | 15th | 1966 | THE PRETTY THINGS |
| Mon | Aug | 22nd | 1966 | THE NASHVILLE TEENS |
| Mon | Aug | 29th | 1966 | NO SESSION |
| Mon | Sept | 5th | 1966 | THE TROGGS |
| Mon | Sept | 12th | 1966 | THE SEARCHERS |
| Mon | Sept | 19th | 1966 | CLIFF BENNET & THE REBEL ROUSERS |
| Mon | Sept | 26th | 1966 | LOS BRAVOS |
| | | | | (Pulled out replacement unknown) |
| Mon | Oct | 3rd | 1966 | MANFRED MANN |
| Mon | Oct | 10th | 1966 | THE WHO |
| Mon | Oct | 17th | 1966 | IKE & TINA TURNER |

| | | | | |
|---|---|---|---|---|
| Mon | Oct | 24th | 1966 | THE SPENCER DAVIS GROUP |
| Mon | Oct | 31st | 1966 | THE ALAN PRICE SET |
| Mon | Nov | 7th | 1966 | ST LOUIS UNION |
| Mon | Nov | 14th | 1966 | THE MERSEYS |
| Mon | Nov | 21st | 1966 | CREAM |
| Mon | Nov | 28th | 1966 | ERIC BURDON |
| Mon | Dec | 5th | 1966 | BOBBY HEBB |
| Mon | Dec | 12th | 1966 | THE CREATION |
| Mon | Dec | 19th | 1966 | THE EASY BEATS |
| Mon | Dec | 26th | 1966 | NO SESSION |

**1967**

| | | | | |
|---|---|---|---|---|
| Mon | Jan | 2nd | 1967 | THE MOODY BLUES |
| Mon | Jan | 9th | 1967 | NO SESSION |
| Mon | Jan | 16th | 1967 | WAYNE FONTANA |
| Mon | Jan | 23rd | 1967 | THE ZOMBIES |
| Mon | Jan | 30th | 1967 | THE KINKS |
| Mon | Feb | 6th | 1967 | THE MOVE |
| Mon | Feb | 13th | 1967 | CAT STEVENS |
| Mon | Feb | 20th | 1967 | THE JIMI HENDRIX EXPERIENCE |
| Mon | Feb | 27th | 1967 | ZOOT MONEY |
| Mon | March | 6th | 1967 | HERBIE GOINS |
| Mon | March | 13th | 1967 | THE EASY BEATS |
| Mon | March | 20th | 1967 | THE ALAN BOWN SET |
| | | | | (THE WHO CANCELLED) |
| Mon | March | 27th | 1967 | THE TROGGS |
| Mon | April | 3rd | 1967 | THE LOOT |
| Mon | April | 10th | 1967 | PINK FLOYD |
| Mon | April | 17th | 1967 | JEFF BECK |
| Mon | April | 24th | 1967 | THE WHO |
| | | | | Our flyer advertising The Who states 'Bannister Promotions are please to announce that their legal representatives have negotiated a definite appearance of The Who.' |
| Mon | May | 1st | 1967 | WHISTLING JACK SMITH |
| Mon | May | 8th | 1967 | THE PURPLE GANG |
| Mon | May | 15th | 1967 | THE MOVE |
| Mon | May | 22nd | 1967 | THE ALAN BOWN SET |
| Mon | May | 29th | 1967 | NO SESSION |
| Mon | June | 5th | 1967 | THE YARDBIRDS |
| Mon | June | 12th | 1967 | CAT STEVENS |
| Mon | June | 19th | 1967 | DAVE DEE, DOZY BEAKY, MICK AND TICH |
| Mon | June | 26th | 1967 | SIMON DUPRE & THE BIG SOUND |
| Mon | July | 3rd | 1967 | GENO WASHINGTON & HIS RAM JAM BAND |

| Mon | July | 10th | 1967 | JOHN WALKER |
|-----|------|------|------|-------------|
| Mon | July | 17th | 1967 | THE KINKS |
| Mon | July | 24th | 1967 | THE MOVE |
| Mon | July | 31st | 1967 | THE JEFF BECK SOUND |
| Mon | Aug | 7th | 1967 | THE HERD |
| Mon | Aug | 14th | 1967 | JIMMY JAMES & THE VAGABONDS |
| Mon | Aug | 21st | 1967 | THE BEE GEES |
| Mon | Aug | 28th | 1967 | Not known |
| Mon | Sept | 4th | 1967 | AMEN CORNER |
| Mon | Sept | 11th | 1967 | THE ALAN BOWN SET |
| Mon | Sept | 18th | 1967 | HERBIE GOINS |
| Mon | Sept | 25th | 1967 | THE SMALL FACES |

Did not turn up Booked The Jug & Bottle Band
from Swansea at short notice

| Mon | Oct | 2nd | 1967 | SIMON DUPRE & THE BIG SOUND |
|-----|-----|-----|------|------------------------------|
| Mon | Oct | 9th | 1967 | KEITH WEST & TOMORROW |

booked instead of THE VANILLA FUDGE

| Mon | Oct | 16th | 1967 | THE MOVE |
|-----|-----|------|------|----------|

(some doubt possibly The Pink Floyd)

| Mon | Oct | 23rd | 1967 | CRAZY WORLD OF ARTHUR BROWN |
|-----|-----|------|------|------------------------------|
| Mon | Oct | 30th | 1967 | THE SMALL FACES |

Our flyer states 'We have been assured by the
group that this time they will definitely appear.

| Mon | Nov | 6th | 1967 | THE FOUNDATIONS |
|-----|-----|-----|------|-----------------|
| Mon | Nov | 13th | 1967 | THE MOVE |
| Mon | Nov | 20th | 1967 | THE TEMPTATIONS |
| Mon | Nov | 27th | 1967 | JIMMY JAMES & THE VAGABONDS |
| Mon | Dec | 4th | 1967 | THE ELECTRIC PRUNES |
| Mon | Dec | 11th | 1967 | AMEN CORNER |
| Mon | Dec | 18th | 1967 | THE WHO |
| Mon | Dec | 25th | 1967 | XMAS DAY |

## 1968

| Mon | Jan | 1st | 1968 | THE EYES OF BLUE NEW YEARS' PARTY |
|-----|-----|-----|------|------------------------------------|

+ 4 GROUPS

| Mon | Jan | 8th | 1968 | THE HERD |
|-----|-----|-----|------|----------|
| Mon | Jan | 15th | 1968 | THE KINKS |
| Mon | Jan | 22nd | 1968 | ALAN BOWN |
| Mon | Jan | 29th | 1968 | TRAFFIC |
| Mon | Feb | 5th | 1968 | SIMON DUPRE & THE BIG SOUND |
| Mon | Feb | 12th | 1968 | THE SPECTRUM |
| Mon | Feb | 19th | 1968 | AMEN CORNER |
| Mon | Feb | 26th | 1968 | THE LOVE AFFAIR |
| Mon | March | 4th | 1968 | THE PLASTIC PENNY |

| | | | | |
|---|---|---|---|---|
| Mon | March | 11th | 1968 | THE TROGGS |
| Mon | March | 18th | 1968 | STATUS QUO |
| Mon | March | 25th | 1968 | THE MOVE |
| Mon | April | 1st | 1968 | THE TREMELOES |
| Mon | April | 8th | 1968 | THE JEFF BECK SOUND |
| Mon | April | 15th | 1968 | NO SESSION |
| Mon | April | 22nd | 1968 | THE EASY BEATS |
| Mon | April | 29th | 1968 | JIMMY JAMES & THE VAGABONDS |
| Mon | May | 6th | 1968 | GENO WASHINGTON & HIS RAM JAM BAND |
| Mon | May | 13th | 1968 | THE ALAN BOWN SET |
| Mon | May | 20th | 1968 | THE HERD |
| Mon | May | 27th | 1968 | THE EASYBEATS |
| Mon | June | 3rd | 1968 | NO SESSION |
| Mon | June | 10th | 1968 | JOHN FRED'S PLAYBOY BAND |
| Mon | June | 17th | 1968 | DAVE DEE, DOZY BEAKY, MITCH AND TICH |
| Mon | June | 24th | 1968 | HERBIE GOINS |
| Mon | July | 1st | 1968 | NO SESSION |
| Mon | July | 8th | 1968 | THE LOVE AFFAIR |
| Mon | July | 15th | 1968 | AMEN CORNER |
| | | | | (Possibly cancelled because of floods) |
| Mon | July | 22nd | 1968 | THE EQUALS |
| Mon | July | 29th | 1968 | MARMALADE |
| Mon | Aug | 5th | 1968 | CUPIDS INSPIRATION |
| Mon | Aug | 12th | 1968 | AMEN CORNER |
| Mon | Aug | 19th | 1968 | JOHN MAYALL'S BLUES BREAKERS |
| Mon | Aug | 26th | 1968 | THE CRAZY WORLD OF ARTHUR BROWN |
| Mon | Sept | 2nd | 1968 | AYNSLEY DUNBAR'S RETALIATION |
| Mon | Sept | 9th | 1968 | CANNED HEAT |
| Mon | Sept | 16th | 1968 | FLEETWOOD MAC |
| Mon | Sept | 23rd | 1968 | JIMMY JAMES & THE VAGABONDS |
| Mon | Sept | 30th | 1968 | CHICKEN SHACK |
| Mon | Oct | 7th | 1968 | EDWIN STARR |
| Mon | Oct | 14th | 1968 | THE MOVE |
| Mon | Oct | 21st | 1968 | THE NICE |
| Mon | Oct | 28th | 1968 | THE SAVOY BLUES BAND |
| Mon | Nov | 4th | 1968 | CHICKEN SHACK |
| Mon | Nov | 11th | 1968 | AYNSLEY DUNBAR'S RETALIATION |
| Mon | Nov | 18th | 1968 | THE SHOWSTOPPERS |
| Mon | Nov | 25th | 1968 | MUDDY WALTER'S BLUES BAND |
| Mon | Dec | 2nd | 1968 | JOHNY JOHNSON & THE BANDWAGON |
| Mon | Dec | 9th | 1968 | THE WHO |
| Mon | Dec | 16th | 1968 | LED ZEPPELIN |
| Mon | Dec | 23rd | 1968 | JOHN MAYALL'S BLUES BREAKERS |
| Tues | Dec | 31st | 1968 | TEN YEARS AFTER (New Years Eve Party) |

**1969**

| | | | | |
|---|---|---|---|---|
| Mon | Jan | 6th | 1969 | JETHRO TULL |
| Mon | Jan | 13th | 1969 | AYNSLEY DUNBAR'S RETALIATION |
| Mon | Jan | 20th | 1969 | LOVE SCULPTURE |
| Mon | Jan | 27th | 1969 | JEFF BECK'S BLUES BAND |
| Mon | Feb | 3rd | 1969 | MOBY GRAPE |
| Mon | Feb | 10th | 1969 | AMEN CORNER |
| Mon | Feb | 17th | 1969 | JOHN LEE HOOKER |
| Mon | Feb | 24th | 1969 | THE LOCOMOTIVE |
| Mon | March | 3rd | 1969 | THE NICE |
| Mon | March | 10th | 1969 | THE CRAZY WORLD OF ARTHUR BROWN |
| Mon | March | 17th | 1969 | THE MOVE |
| Mon | March | 24th | 1969 | TASTE |
| Mon | March | 31st | 1969 | TOP GEAR WITH JOHN PEEL, BRIDGET ST JOHN, PRINCIPAL EDWARDS MAGIC THEATRE |
| Mon | April | 7th | 1969 | Not known |
| Mon | April | 14th | 1969 | Not known |
| Mon | April | 21st | 1969 | CHICKEN SHACK |
| Mon | April | 28th | 1969 | DESMOND DECKER |
| Mon | May | 5th | 1969 | MIKE ABRAHAM'S BLODWYN PIG - believed cancelled |
| Mon | May | 12th | 1969 | TYRANOSAURUS REX |
| Mon | May | 19th | 1969 | SPOOKY TOOTH |
| Mon | May | 26th | 1969 | NO SESSION |
| Mon | June | 2nd | 1969 | FLEETWOD MAC |
| Mon | June | 9th | 1969 | THE ALAN BOWN SET |
| Mon | June | 16th | 1969 | MICK ABRAHAM'S BLODWYN PIG |
| Mon | June | 23th | 1969 | FAMILY |
| Mon | June | 30th | 1969 | CLOSED AFTER 1ST BATH FESTIVAL |
| Mon | July | 7th | 1969 | CLOSED |
| Mon | July | 14th | 1969 | CLOSED |
| Mon | July | 21st | 1969 | THUNDERCLAP NEWMAN |
| Mon | July | 28th | 1969 | Bonzo Dog were to have played but on our flyer we have put, 'We regret that for reasons best known to themselves Bonzo Dog have decided against playing at The Pavilion - so there will be NO SESSION' |
| Mon | Aug | 4th | 1969 | THE WHO |
| Mon | Aug | 11th | 1969 | FAT MATTRESS |
| Mon | Aug | 18th | 1969 | CHICKEN SHACK |
| Mon | Aug | 25th | 1969 | THE EDGAR BROUGHTON BAND |
| Mon | Sept | 1st | 1969 | LIVERPOOL SCENE |
| Mon | Sept | 8th | 1969 | THE NICE |

| Mon | Sept | 15th | 1969 | KING CRIMSON |
|-----|------|------|------|--------------|
| Mon | Sept | 22nd | 1969 | ECLECTION |
| Mon | Sept | 29th | 1969 | TASTE - believed cancelled |
| Mon | Oct | 6th | 1969 | ATOMIC ROOSTER |
| Mon | Oct | 13th | 1969 | Not known |
| Mon | Oct | 20th | 1969 | Not known |
| Mon | Oct | 27th | 1969 | TASTE |
| Mon | Nov | 3rd | 1969 | THE GRAHAM BOND ORGANISATION |
| Mon | Nov | 10th | 1969 | DEEP PURPLE |
| Mon | Nov | 17th | 1969 | KEITH RELF'S RENAISSANCE |
| Mon | Nov | 24th | 1969 | KEEF HARTLEY'S BLUES BAND |
| Mon | Dec | 1st | 1969 | According to the Western Daily Press we cancelled these three dates because of poor attendances and the fact we could not find decent groups |
| Mon | Dec | 8th | 1969 | Not Known |
| Mon | Dec | 5th | 1969 | Not known |
| Mon | Dec | 22nd | 1969 | XMAS RAVE possibly The John Peel Show |
| Mon | Dec | 29th | 1969 | JON HISEMAN'S COLISEUM Believed to be the last regular gig |

PROBABLY CLOSED FOR GOOD BEFORE THE JUNE 1970 FESTIVAL

| Sat | March | 13th | 1971 | LED ZEPPELIN |
|-----|-------|------|------|--------------|
| Thur | July | 8th | 1971 | THE WHO |

I am greatly indebted to Roger Parkhouse and Kelvin Scudamore for much of this information.

BATH FESTIVAL OF BLUES : SAT 28 JUNE
RECREATION GROUND (PAULTNEY ST. ENTRANCE)
FLEETWOOD MAC
JOHN MAYALL
TEN YEARS AFTER
LED ZEPPELIN
NICE
CHICKEN SHACK
JON HISEMAN'S
COLOSSEUM
MICK ABRAHAM'S
BLODWIN PIG
KEEF HARTLEY
GROUP THERAPY
LIVERPOOL SCENE : TASTE
CHAMPION JACK DUPREE
SAVOY BROWN : CLOUDS
PRINCIPAL EDWARDS MAGIC THEATRE
BABYLON : DEEP BLUES BAND
JUST BEFORE DAWN & D.J.
JOHN PEEL.
12 NOON - 11PM : TICKETS MAY BE PURCHASED IN ADVANCE FROM :-
BATH FESTIVAL BOX OFFICE. ABBEY CHAMBERS, ABBEY CHURCHYARD BATH. PRICED AS FOLLOWS
IN ADVANCE - ALL DAY 18/6. EVE ONLY 14/6 : ON THE DAY - ALL DAY 22/6 : EVE ONLY 16
REPRINTED 1998

**NB.** These lists are difficult to obtain and do not cover every band that performed at these festivals. No guarantee is made to their accuracy or to the personnel of the bands involved

## THE 1969 Bath Festival

### Colosseum

John Hiseman - drums
Dave Greenslade - keyboards
Dick Heckstall Smith - sax
Tony Reeves - bass
James Litherland - guitar

### Chicken Shack.

Stan Webb - lead and vocals
Christine Perfect (later McVie) - vocals, piano
Andy Sylvester - bass
Dave Bidwell - drums

Roy Harper did an unscheduled slot performing
*I Hate the Whiteman and Hell's Angels.*

### Blodwyn Pig

Mick Abrahams - guitar, vocals
Jack Lancaster - flute, violin
Andy Pyle - electric bass
Ron Berg - drums

### Taste

Rory Gallagher - vocals, harp, guitar
Richie McCracken - bass
John Wilson - drums

### John Mayall's Blues Breakers

John Mayall - keyboard, vocals, guitar, harmonica
Duster Bennett - guitar, vocals
Jon Mark - guitar
Johnny Almond - sax
Steve Thompson - bass

## Fleetwood Mac

Peter Green - guitar, vocals
John McVie - bass
Mick Fleetwood - drums
Jeremy Spencer - guitar, vocals
Danny Kirwan - guitar, vocals

## The Nice

Brian Davison - drums
Lee Jackson - bass, vocals
Keith Emerson - keyboards

## Ten Years After

Alvin Lee - guitar, vocals
Leo Lyons - bass
Ric Lee - drums
Chick Churchill - keyboards

## Led Zeppelin

Robert Plant - vocals
Jimmy Page - guitar
John Paul Jones - bass
John Bonham - drums

# BATH FESTIVAL OF
# BLUES & PROGRESSIVE MUSIC '70

## BATH & WEST SHOWGROUND. SHEPTON MALLET

**SATURDAY 27th. JUNE**

CANNED HEAT
JOHN MAYALL
STEPPENWOLF
PINK FLOYD
JOHNNY WINTER
IT'S A BEAUTIFUL DAY
FAIRPORT CONVENTION
COLOSSEUM
KEEF HARTLEY BAND
MAYNARD FERGUSON BIG BAND
CONTINUITY BY JOHN PEEL AND MIKE RAVEN

**SUNDAY 28th. JUNE**
LED ZEPPELIN
JEFFERSON AIRPLANE
FRANK ZAPPA AND
THE MOTHERS OF INVENTION
MOODY BLUES
BYRDS
FLOCK
SANTANA
DR. JOHN THE NIGHT TRIPPER
COUNTRY JOE
HOT TUNA

**TICKETS**

WEEKEND IN ADVANCE ..... 50/-
WEEKEND ON DAY ..... 55/-
SUNDAY ONLY IN ADVANCE ..... 35/-
SUNDAY ONLY ON DAY ..... 40/-
TICKETS AND ADDITIONAL
INFORMATION AVAILABLE
BY POST FROM
BATH FESTIVAL BOX OFFICE
LINLEY HOUSE
1 PIERREPONT STREET,
BATH (S.A.E.)

# THE 1970 Bath Festival

## Donovan.

*Setlist*:
Waiting To Be Born
First There Is a Mountain
Hey Gip (Dig The Slowness)
Wherever You Want Me
Sunshine Super Man
I'll Sing A Song For You
Mellow Yellow
Catch The Wind
Hurdy Gurdy Man
There Was An Old Lady
Riki-Tiki-Tavi
Season Of The Witch

## Hot Tuna

Jorma Kaukonen - lead guitar, vocals
Jack Casady - bass
Marty Balin - vocals
Joey Covington - drums
Paul Ziegler - rhythm

*Setlist*:
Baby What You Want Me To Do
Come Back Baby
The Old Man
Up Or Down
Star Track  Emergency
You Wear Your Dresses Too Short

## The Byrds

Roger Mcguinn - guitar, vocals
Clarence White - guitar, vocals
Skip Batten - bass, vocals
Gene Parson - drums, banjo, guitar, vocals

*Setlist*:
Its All Right Ma
Ballad Of Easy Rider
Willin'
Soldiers Joy

Goin' Back
Baby What Do You Want Me To Do
Drug Store Truck Drivin' Man
You Don't Miss Your Water
Jesus Is Just Alright
Turn! Turn! Turn!
Mr. Tambourine Man
Eight Miles High
Oh Mary
Black Mountain Rag
Just a Season
Amazing Grace
So You Want to Be a Rock 'n' Roll Star
You Ain't Goin Nowhere
Old Blue
Wasn't Born To Follow
Glory Glory
Take A Whiff On Me

## Colosseum

John Hiseman - drums
Dick Heckstall Smith - saxes
Louis Cennamo - bass
Dave Greenslade - keys
Dave Clemson - guitar, vocals

## Country Joe.

*Setlist*:
Here I Go Again
Silver and Gold
(Not so Sweet) Martha Lorraine
For no reason (Change My Style)
Balancing on the Edge Of Time
Ring Of Fire
Roll On Columbia
Flying High / Freedom
Maria (You know the reason)
Fish Cheer Fixing To die Rag
Fish Cheer
John Duprez
Fish Cheer

## It's a Beautiful Day

David LaFlamme - violin, vocals
Fred Webb - keys
Hal Wagenet - guitar
Mitchell Holman - bass
Val Fuentes - drums
Pattie Santos - vocals.Don & Dewey

*Setlist*:
White Bird
Hoedown
It Comes Right Down To You
Soapstone Mountain
Time Is
Open Up Your Mind
Bulgaria

## Jefferson Airplane

Grace Slick - vocals
Paul Kantner - vocal, guitar
Marty Balin - vocal
Jorma Kaukonen - lead guitar, vocal
Jack Cassidy - bass
Joe Covington - drums

*Setlist*:
Volunteers
Somebody to Love
The Other Side of This Life
Won't You Try/Saturday Afternoon
3/5th Of A Mile In 10 Seconds
Rock Me Baby
The Ballad of You and Me and Pooneil

## John Mayall Band

John Mayall - mouth harp, guitar, vocal
Peter Green - guitar
Ric Grech - bass
Aynsley Dunbar - drums
Rod Mayall - keys

*Setlist*:
It Might as Well Be Raining,

I Might Catch Up With You
No Place to Go
Crazy Woman
My Pretty Girl
What's Wrong Now

## Pink Floyd

Roger Waters - bass, vocals
Dave Gilmore - lead, vocals
Nick Mason - drums
Rick Wright - keys, vocals
Plus a brass and choir section for Atom Heart Mother

*Setlist*:
Green is the Colour
Careful With That Axe, Eugene
A Saucerful of Secrets
Set the Controls for the Heart of the Sun
Atom Heart Mother

## Santana

Carlos Santana - lead guitar, vocals
David Brown - bass
Greg Rolie - keyboards
Jose Areas - conga drums, trumpet and timbales
Mike Shrieve - drums
Mike Carrabello - congas

*Setlist*:
Se A Cabo
Black Magic Woman/Gypsy Quen
Jin Go La Ba
Oye Como Va
Incident a Neshabar
Toussaint L'Overture/Evil Ways
Persuasion
Soul Sacrifice
Encore: Gumbo

## Steppenwolf

John Kay - rhythm guitar, vocals
Goldie McJohn - organ
Jerry Edmonton - drums

Larry Byron - lead guitar
George Biondo - bass

*Setlist*:
Sookie Sookie
Hoochie Koochie Man
Tighten Up Your Wig
Monster
Screaming Night Hog
From Here To There Eventually
Corrina Corrina
Hey Lawdy Mama
The Pusher
Born To Be Wild
Magic Carpet Ride

## Johnny Winter Band

Johnny Winter - lead guitar, vocals
Tommy Shannon - bass
John Turner - drums
Edgar Winter - organ, amplified sax/drums, vocals

*Setlist*:
Guess I'll Go Away
R&R Hoochie Koo
Mama Talk To Your Daughter
Prodigal Son
Rollin' & Tumblin'
Black Cat Bone
Have You Ever Been Mistreated ?
Good Morning Little School girl
Johnny B. Goode
Mean Town Blues

## Frank Zappa And The Mothers of Invention

Frank Zappa - vocal, guitar
Mark Volman - tambourine, vocal
Howard Kaylan - vocal
Aynsley Dunbar - drums
Jeff Simmons - bass
Ian Underwood - sax, keyboards
George Duke - keys

*Setlist*:
Wonderful Wino
Concentration Moon
Mom & Dad
The Air
Dog Breath
Mother People
You Didn't Try To Call Me
Call Any Vegetable
The Return Of The Hunch Back Duke
A medley consisting of Little House I used To Live In, Holiday In Berlin and Cruisin' For Burgers. There may be fragments of others - possibly Igor's Boogie. During this rave-up the audience are asked to join in the chorus, *c'mon sing, just like in the movies*!
King Kong

## Fairport Convention

Richard Thompson - guitar, vocal
Dave Swarbrick - violin /vocal
Dave Pegg - bass
Simon Nicol - guitar, vocal
Dave Mattacks - drums

*Setlist*
Walk Awhile
Dirty Linen
Staines Moriss
Lark in the Morning
Medley of Jigs /reels
Now Be Thankful
Matty Groves
Banks of the Sweet Primroses
Fatback Caper
Sloth
Tam Lin
Sir Patrick Spens

## Keef Hartley Band

Keef Hartley - drums
Gary Thain - bass
Miller Anderson - guitar
David Caswell - trumpet
Lyall Jenkins - tenor sax

*expanded line-up*
Barbara Thomson - baritone
Ray Warleigh - alto
Derek Wadsworth - trombone
Mike Davis -trumpet
Bud Parks - trumpet

## The Maynard Ferguson Big Band

Maynard Ferguson - trumpet
Pete Jackson - piano
Randy Jones - drums
Morton Drover - ead trumpet
Alan Downey - lead trumpet
Albert Wood - trombone
Billy Graham - trombone
Johnny Huckeridge - backing trumpet
Nigel Carte - backing trumpet
Rob Watson - baritone sax

## Canned Heat

Bob 'The Bear' Hite - vocals
Al 'Blind Owl' Wilson - guitar, vocals, harmonica
Adolpho"Fito "De la Parra - drums
Henry Vestine - lead guitar
Tony de la Barreda - bass

*Setlist*:
Roll Me Over Baby
Reefer Blues.
Somethings Gotta Go
Country Blues jam
(with Al and Fito whilst Henry fixes a string )
Human Condition
Future Blues
Slow Blues by Al
So Sad ( World in a tangle )
Lets work together
We Like to Boogie
Shake Rattle and Roll
Encore:You Never Miss Your Water (till the well runs dry)

## Led Zeppelin

Robert Plant - vocals
Jimmy Page - guitars
John Paul Jones - bass, keyboards
John Bonham - drums

*Setlist*:
Immigrant Song
Heartbreaker
Dazed and Confused
Bring It On Home
Since I've Been Loving You
Organ Solo>Thank You
The Boy Next Door ( Thats The Way).What Is and What Should Never Be.
Moby Dick, Rice Pudding Intro/How Many More Times (includes Down By the
River, The Hunter, Gotta Keep Moving, Boogie Woogie, Honey Bee, Sweet
Home Chicago, Need Your Love Tonight, that's Alright, Long Distance Call
Blues, Lemon Song, etc.)
Whole Lotta Love
Communication Breakdown
Rock Medley (includes Long Tall Sally, Johnny B. Goode, Rocky Road Blues,
Say Mama, That's Alright, etc

## Flock

Jerry Goodman - violin, guitar
Fred Glickstein - guitar, lead vocal
Ron Karpman - drums
Jerry Smith - bass
Rick Canoff - tenor sax
Tom Webb - tenor sax, harmonica
Frank Posa - trumpet

*Setlist*:
Big Bird.
Hornschmeyer's Island
Lighthouse
Crabfoot
Mermaid
Uranian Sircus
Store Bought Store Thought
Etc.

## Dr John

Nothing known

# TUPHOLME MANOR PARK Nr. LINCOLN

### FREDERICK BANNISTER PRESENTS

# A One Day Concert of Traditional and Contemporary Folk Music

## Saturday, July 24th

—————————— FEATURING ——————————

| | |
|---|---|
| James Taylor | The Byrds (ACOUSTIC SET) |
| Tom Paxton | Buffy Sainte Marie |
| Pentangle | Incredible String Band |
| Tim Hardin | Sandy Denny |
| Steeleye Span | Ralph McTell |

Sonny Terry  and  Brownie McGhee

Dion

Dave Swarbrick  and  Martin Carthy

From 12.00 (noon) until 11.00 p.m.

| | |
|---|---|
| All day ticket in advance £2.00 | Evening only (6.30 p.m.) ticket in advance £1.30 |
| All day ticket on day £2.30 | Evening only (6.30 p.m.) ticket on day £1.50 |

IF YOU HAVE ANY DIFFICULTY OBTAINING TICKETS FOR THIS EVENT OR REQUIRE ADDITIONAL INFORMATION, PLEASE WRITE TO:— FOLK CONCERT BOX OFFICE, HARLEQUIN RECORDS, 28 STRUTTON GROUND, S.W.1  Telephone 589 9749  (S.A.E. please).

## 1971 Lincoln Folk Festival

**Ralph McTell** - vocal, guitar
Streets of London etc

**Dion** - vocal, guitar
Abraham, Martin and John, Ruby baby etc

**Tim Hardin** - vocals
Lady came from Baltimore,
Black sheep boy,
Reason to believe etc

**Sonny Terry and Brownie McGhee** - Guitars, vocals, harmonica
Just rode in your town etc.

**Sandy Denny** - vocals

**Tom Paxton** - vocal, guitar

**The Byrds**
Roger Mcguinn - guitar, vocals
Clarence White - guitar, vocals
Skip Batten - Bass, vocals
Gene Parson - drums, banjo, guitar, vocals

Rock and roll star, Jesus is just all right, Chestnut Mare etc.

**Buffy St Marie** - vocals

**Pentangle**
Jacqui McShee - vocals
Bert Jansch - guitar
John Renbourn - guitar
Danny Thompson - bass
Terry Cox - drummer and percussion.

*Set list would probably have included*
A Maid That's Deep In Love
When I Was In My Prime
Omie Wise
When I Get Home
Rain And Snow
Helping Hand

So Clear
Three Part Thing etc

**Incredible String Band**
Robin Williamson - vocal, violin, guitar, flute
Mike Heron - lead vocal, guitar, bass, organ
Malcolm Le Maistre - bass, triangle, mandolin, xylophone, vocal
Licorice Mc Kechnie - vocal, bass, guitar

*Setlist*:
Log Cabin Home in the Sky
Dear Old Battlefied
Medley of reels:
Eyes like leaves
Sunday is my Wedding Day
Drops of Whiskey
Grumbling Old Men
You Get Brighter
Big Ted
Seasons they Change
Adam and Eve

**Steeleye Span**
Tim Hart - vocals, guitar
Maddy Prior - vocals
Ashley Hutchings - vocals, bass guitar
Martin Carthy - guitar
Peter Knight - violin, mandolin

*Setlist: probably included*
The blacksmith
Cold, haily, windy night
Jigs: Bryan O'Lynn/The hag with the money
Prince Charlie Stuart
Boys of Bedlam
The lark in the morning
Lovely on the water

**James Taylor Band**
James Taylor - vocals, guitar.

**Dave Swarbrick and Martin Carthy**
Martin Carthy - vocals, guitar.
Dave Swarbrick - violin.

# KNEBWORTH PARK
### NEAR STEVENAGE
### HERT-FORDSHIRE
## SATURDAY JULY 20th

FREDERICK BANNISTER'S
## BUCOLIC FROLIC
WITH

# THE ALLMAN BROS BAND
# THE VAN MORRISON SHOW
### FEATURING THE CALEDONIA SOUL EXPRESS
# THE DOOBIE BROTHERS
# THE MAHAVISHNU ORCH
### FEATURING JOHN McLAUGHLIN JEAN LUC PONTY
# ALEX HARVEY BAND
# TIM BUCKLEY

TICKETS IN ADVANCE £2.75 INC VAT     ON THE DAY £3.00 INC VAT     10 a.m. TO 11 p.m.

IF YOU HAVE ANY DIFFICULTY IN OBTAINING TICKETS FOR THE EVENT OR REQUIRE ADDITIONAL
INFORMATION PLEASE WRITE TO
THE KNEBWORTH PARK CONCERT c/o HARLEQUIN RECORDS 125 KINGS ROAD SW3

# Knebworth Festivals 1974 -79 Artists' Set Lists

NB. These lists are difficult to obtain and do not cover
every band that performed at these festivals.
No guarantee is made to their accuracy or to the personnel of the bands involved

20/7/74

## THE ALLMAN BROTHERS BAND

Wasted Words
Done Somebody Wrong
One Way out
Stormy Monday
Midnight Rider
Blue Sky
In Memory of Elizabeth Reed
**Set 2**
Statesboro Blues
Come and Go Blues
Ramblin' Man
Encore:
Trouble No More
Jessica
You Don't Love Me-
Les Brers In A Minor
**Encore 2**
Whipping Post

**Gregg Allman**
lead vocals, keyboards
**Dickie Betts**
lead and slide guitar
**Lamar Williams**
bass

**Chuck Leavell**
piano
**Butch Trucks**
drums and percussion

**Jai Johanny Johanson**
drums

## DOOBIE BROS

Listen to The Music
Black Water
South city Midnight
Lady
Rockin Down The
Highway
Don't Start Me To
Talking
Without You
Clear As The Driven
Snow
Eyes of Silver
Down In the Track
Road Angel
Jesus Is Just Alright

**Tom Johnston**
guitars, harmonica, vocals
**Pat Simmons**
guitars, arp, vocals
**John Hartman**
drums, percussion, vocals
**Tiran Porter**
bass guitar, vocals
**Michael Hossack**
drums, congas, timbales
**Jeff (Skunk) Baxter**
guitar

With Me
China Grove

## VAN MORRISON

Warm Love
Foggy Mountain Top
Street Choir
I Like It Like That
Its not the Twilight Zone
Listen to the Lion
Buffyflow
Bulbs
Into The Mystic
Since I Fell For You
Help Me
I Believe To My Soul
I've Been Working
Take Your Hands Out Of My Pocket
Naked In The Jungle
Brown Eyed Girl

**Van Morrison**
sax, harmonica, vocals
**Peter Van Hook**
drums
**Peter Wingfield**
piano
**Jerome Rimson**
bass

## THE MAHAVISHNU ORCHESTRA

Wings of Karma
Sanctuary
Vision is a Naked Sword
Band members introduced
Hymn to Him

**John McLaughlin** - electric guitar
**Jean-Luc Ponty** - electric violin
**Gayle Moran** - keyboards
**Ralphe Armstrong** - electric bass
**Michael Walden** - drums
**Carole Shive** - violin
**Marsha Westbrook** - viola
**Philip Hirschi** - cello
**Steve Frankewicz**
with the addition of Bob Knapp
- trumpet, fluegelhorn, flute
(featured in Hymn to Him)
**Steven Kindler** - violin

## ALEX HARVEY BAND

The Faith Healer
Midnight Moses
Can't Get Enough
Give My Regards To
Sergeant Fury
The Return of Vambo

**Alex Harvey**
**Zal Cleminson**
**Hugh Mckenna**
**Chris Glenn**
**Ted Mckenna**

The Man in the Jar
Money Honey
To Dream the Impossible Dream
Dance to the Music
Framed

## TIM BUCKLEY

| | |
|---|---|
| Nighthawkin' | **Tim Buckley** |
| Dolphins | vocal, guitar |
| Get on Top | **Art Johnson** |
| Devil Eyes | guitar |
| Buzzin fly | **Jim Fielder** |
| Sweet Surrender | bass |
| Honey Man | **Mark Tiernan** |
| Improvisation | keyboards |

NEAR STEVENAGE · HERTS

# KNEBWORTH PARK

SATURDAY JULY 5th · NOON TO 11.00 PM

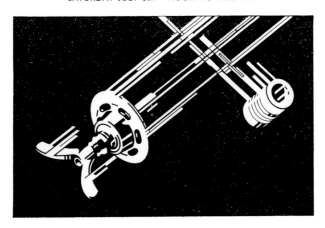

FREDERICK BANNISTER PRESENTS

# PINK FLOYD
# THE STEVE MILLER BAND
# CAPTAIN BEEFHEART
## AND HIS MAGIC BAND
# ROY HARPER
SPECIAL GUESTS · GRAHAM CHAPMAN (WITH FRIENDS) FROM
# MONTY PYTHON
# D. J. JOHN PEEL

TICKETS IN ADVANCE **£2.75** · ON THE DAY **£3.50**

PLEASE NOTE THE COST OF THE TICKET **INCLUDES VAT** AND TICKET SELLERS COMMISSION · **DO NOT PAY MORE**

**TRAINS** · THE NEAREST STATION TO KNEBWORTH PARK IS STEVENAGE AND A COACH SHUTTLE SERVICE HAS BEEN ARRANGED
BETWEEN THIS STATION AND THE PARK · DO NOT GET OUT AT KNEBWORTH STATION
**PEDESTRIANS** · MAKE FOR STEVENAGE THEN FOLLOW THE SIGNS TO KNEBWORTH PARK
**MOTORISTS** · KNEBWORTH PARK IS SITUATED DIRECTLY OFF THE A1(M) AT THE A602 INTERSECTION
AMPLE PARKING IS AVAILABLE IN THE PARK AND IS FREE OF CHARGE

*TICKETS AVAILABLE FROM ALL BRANCHES*
*OF HARLEQUIN RECORD SHOPS*

ABERDEEN Virgin Records, 411-413 George St.
BOURNEMOUTH Setchfields, 95 Old Christchurch Rd.,
 and 21-25 High St., Poole
BIRMINGHAM Cyclops Sounds, 8 Piccadilly Arcade, New
 St., Virgin Records, 177 Corporation St.
BRIGHTON Virgin Records, 126 North St.
BRISTOL Virgin Records, 1a, The Haymarket
COVENTRY Virgin Records, 11 City Arcade
CHELMSFORD Pop Inn, 11 Badow Rd.
CROYDON London Rd.
CARDIFF The Welsh Sports Shop, Quay St.
DURHAM The House of Andrews, 73-75 Sadler St.
EDINBURGH The Edinburgh Bookshop, 57 George St.
EGHAM Record Wise, 172 High St.

EAST GRINSTEAD L&H Cloake, 131 London Rd.
GLASGOW Virgin Records, 308-311 Argyle St.
HERTFORD Hosts, 5 Parliament Sq.
HARROGATE Joseph Nicholson, 8 Parliament St.
HOUNSLOW Music-craft
IPSWICH 16 Queen St., The Music Centre
KINGS LYNN Bayes Recordium, 26 Broad St.
LEICESTER Brees Records Ltd., 23 Churchgate
LETCHWORTH David's Bookshop, 14 East Cheap
LIVERPOOL Cosmopolitan Theatre B.O., 132 St. Georges
 Way, St. John Precinct
LEEDS Virgin Records, 20 Queen Victoria St.
LEAMINGTON SPA Deputy Amenities Officer, Warwick
 District Council, 35 Regent Grove
MIDDLESBROUGH Hamiltons, 26 Newport Rd.
MANCHESTER Hime & Addison, 8 St. James Sq., off John
 Dalton St.

NEWCASTLE Virgin Records, 29 Ridley Place
NORWICH George Wortley Ltd., 2/2a, Charing Cross
NOTTINGHAM Select-a-Disc, 16a Goldsmith St.
PLYMOUTH Virgin Records, 131 Cornwall St.
POTTERS BAR The Potters Bar Record Centre, 14 Barnet
 Rd.
RUGBY Berwicks, 12 Sheep St.
SWINDON Kempster & Son, 98 Commercial Rd.
SHEFFIELD Virgin Records, 137 The Moor
SOUTHAMPTON Virgin Records, 16 Bargate St.
SWANSEA Virgin Records, 34 Union St.
SALISBURY Ted Hardy, 24b Milford St.
STEVENAGE The Stevenage Record Centre, 26 Market
 Place
WORCESTER The Worcester Music Centre, Russell &
 Dorrel, High St.

A TEDOAR LIMITED PRESENTATION

IF YOU HAVE ANY DIFFICULTIES IN OBTAINING TICKETS OR REQUIRE ADDITIONAL INFORMATION PLEASE WRITE TO
THE KNEBWORTH PARK CONCERT · C/O HARLEQUIN RECORDS · 125 KINGS ROAD · LONDON SW3

## PINK FLOYD

| | |
|---|---|
| Raving and Drooling | **Dave Gilmour** |
| You've Got To Be Crazy | guitar, vocals |
| Shine On You Crazy Diamond | **Roger Waters** |
| Have A Cigar | bass |
| (with Roy Harper on vocals) | **Richard Wright** |
| Shine On You Crazy Diamond 6-9 | keyboard |
| Speak To Me | **Nick Mason** |
| Breathe | drums |
| On The Run | |
| Time | |
| The Great Gig In The Sky | |
| Money | |
| Us and Them | |
| Any Colour You Like | |
| Brain Damage | |
| Eclipse | |
| Encore: | |
| Echoes | |

## STEVE MILLER BAND

| | |
|---|---|
| Feel so Good | **Steve Miller** |
| Mercury Blues | guitar, vocal |
| Boogie Children | **Lonnie Turner** |
| Freight Train Blues | bass |
| Stagger Lee | **Les Dudek** |
| The Window | 2nd and slide guitar |
| Living in the USA | **Doug Clifford** |
| Space Cowboy | drums (ex Creedence |
| Shu Ba Da Da Ma Ma | Clearwater Revival) |
| Ma Ma | |
| Rock'n Me | |
| Come On In My Kitchen | |

## CAPTAIN BEEFHEART

| | |
|---|---|
| Moonlight on Vermont | **Captain Beefheart (Don Van Vliet)** |
| Abba Zabba | vocals, mouth harp |
| Band Introduction | **Winged Eel Fingerling** |
| Orange Claw Hammer | guitar |
| Dali's Car | **Ella Guru Davidson** |
| When it Blows Its Stack | guitars |

My Human Gets Me
When it Blows Its Stack
My Human Gets Me
Blues
Alice in Blunderland
Beatle Bones 'n' Smokin
Stones
Gimme Dat Harp Boy
Electricity
I'm Gonna Booglarize
You Baby
Scalp Flat Top
Improvisations
Big Eyed Beans From Venus

**Drumbo**
guitar, drums
**Jimmy Carl Black**
(introduced as Indian Ink)
drums
**Bruce 'fossil' Fowler**
trombone

## ROY HARPER

Commune
Twelve Hours of Sunset
Another Day
(Electric with Trigger)
Hallucinating Light
Referendum
Highway Blues
Too Many Movies
The Spirit Lives
Home
The Game
Grown Ups are Just Silly Children

**Roy Harper**
vocals, guitar
**Trigger**
**Chris Spedding**
guitar (ex Jack Bruce Band)
**Dave Cochrane**
bass
**Bill Bruford**
(ex Yes and King Crimson)

## LINDA LEWIS

(not comprehensive)

It's in His Kiss
Days of The Old Schoolyard
Rock a Doodle Doo

**Linda Lewis**
vocals
**Max Middleton**
keyboards (ex Jeff Beck)
**Jim Cregan**
guitar (ex Family)

Frederick Bannister
in association with Five~One Productions, presents
NEAR STEVENAGE HERTS
SATURDAY AUGUST 21st 1976 · 11.00am TO 11.00pm

The Rolling Stones
10cc
Lynyrd Skynyrd and
Todd Rundgren's Utopia
Knebworth Fair
August 21st.

All the Fun of The Fair!

TICKETS IN ADVANCE £4.25 · ON THE DAY £4.50

PLEASE NOTE THE COST OF THE TICKET **INCLUDES VAT** AND TICKET SELLERS COMMISSION · **DO NOT PAY MORE**

TICKETS AVAILABLE FROM

AYLESBURY Harlequin Record Shop, 31 Friars Square.
BARNET Harlequin Record Shop, 98 High St.
BASINGSTOKE Harlequin Record Shop, 1 Newmarket Square.
BEDFORD Harlequin Record Shop, 97 High St.
BELFAST Harrison Records, 50 Castle St.
BIRMINGHAM Cyclops Sounds, 8 Piccadilly Arcade, New St.
　　Virgin Records, 74 Bull St.
　　Virgin Records, 177 Corporation St.
BOURNEMOUTH Setchfields, 95 Old Christ Church Rd., and
　　at 21/25 High St., Poole.
BRADFORD Virgin Records, 37 Arndale Mall, Lirkgate Centre.
BRIGHTON Virgin Records, 126 North St.
BRISTOL Virgin Records, 1a The Haymarket.
BROMLEY Harlequin Record Shop, 157 High St.
CAMBERLEY Harlequin Record Shop, 14 Princess Way.
CAMBRIDGE Harlequin Record Shop, 4 Bridge St.
CARDIFF The Welsh Sports Shop, Quay St.
CHELMSFORD Pop Inn, 11 Badow Rd.
COVENTRY Virgin Records, 11 City Arcade.
CROYDON Diamond Records, London Rd.
DUBLIN EMI Records, 4 Cathal Brugha St.
DURHAM The House of Andrews, 73/75 Sadler St.

EAST GRINSTEAD L & H Cloake, 131 London Rd.
EDINBURGH Virgin Records, 18a Frederick St.
EGHAM Record Wise, 172 High St.
EPSOM Harlequin Record Shop, 16 High St.
GLASGOW Virgin Records, 308 Argyle St.
GUILDFORD Harlequin Record Shop, 14 Tunsgate Square.
HARROGATE Joseph Nicholson, 8 Parliament St.
HARROW Harlequin Record Shop, 280 Station Rd.
HERTFORD Hosts, 5 Parliament Square.
HOUNSLOW Music Craft, 63 High St.
HULL Virgin Records, 5/6 Mill St.
ILFORD Harlequin Record Shop, 84 High Rd.
IPSWICH The Music Centre, 16 Queens St.
KINGS LYNN Bayes Recordium, 26 Broad St.
LEEDS Virgin Records, 20 Queen Victoria St.
LEICESTER Brees Records Ltd., 23 Churchgate.
LETCHWORTH Davids Bookshop, 14 East Cheap.
LIVERPOOL Virgin Records, 169 Market Way, St. Johns Centre.
LONDON All branches of Harlequin Records.
LUTON Harlequin Record Shop, 12 Arndale Centre.
MAIDENHEAD Harlequin Record Shop, 2 Nicholsons Walk.
MANCHESTER Hyme and Addison, 8 St. James' Square,
　　off John Dalton St.
　　Virgin Records, 9 Lever St.

NEWCASTLE Virgin Records, 10/12 High Friars.
NORTHAMPTON Harlequin Record Shop, 13 Peacock Way.
NORWICH George Motley Ltd., 2/2a Charing Cross.
NOTTINGHAM Virgin Records, 7 King St.
　　Select-a-disc, 16a Goldsmith St.
OXFORD Harlequin Record Shop, 362 Cornmarket Square.
PLYMOUTH Virgin Records, 131 Cornwall St.
POTTERS BAR The Potters Bar Record Centre, 14 Barnet Road.
READING Harlequin Record Shop, 57 The Butts Centre.
RICHMOND Harlequin Record Shop, 2 The Square.
ROMFORD Harlequin Record Shop, 77 South St.
SALISBURY Ted Hardy, 24b Milford St.
SHEFFIELD Virgin Records, 137 The Moor.
SOUTHAMPTON Virgin Records, 16 Bargate St.
STEVENAGE Stevenage Record Centre, 26 Market Place.
SWANSEA Virgin Records, 34 Union St.
SWINDON Kempster & Sons, 98 Commercial Rd.
WATFORD Harlequin Record Shop, 77 The Parade.
WELWYN GARDEN CITY Harlequin Record Shop, 46 Fretherne Rd.
WEMBLEY Harlequin Record Shop, 421 High Rd.
WINCHESTER Harlequin Record Shop, 10 Kings Walk.
WORCESTER Worcester Record Centre, Russel & Dorrel, High St.

**TRAINS** · THE NEAREST STATION TO KNEBWORTH PARK IS STEVENAGE AND A COACH SHUTTLE SERVICE HAS BEEN
ARRANGED BETWEEN THIS STATION AND THE PARK. DO NOT GET OUT AT KNEBWORTH STATION
**PEDESTRIANS** · MAKE FOR STEVENAGE AND THEN FOLLOW THE SIGNS TO KNEBWORTH PARK
**MOTORISTS** · KNEBWORTH PARK IS SITUATED DIRECTLY OFF THE A1 (M) AT THE A602 INTERSECTION
AMPLE PARKING IS AVAILABLE IN THE PARK AND IS FREE OF CHARGE

MAIL APPLICATIONS FOR TICKETS SHOULD BE SENT TO KNEBWORTH FAIR, C/O HARLEQUIN RECORDS, 28 STRUTTON GROUND, LONDON SW1

PLEASE MAKE CHEQUES PAYABLE TO KNEBWORTH FAIR ALSO INCLUDE A S.A.E.

A Tedoar Limited presentation

## ROLLING STONES

Satisfaction
Ain't Too Proud to Beg
If you Can't Rock Me
Get Off My Cloud
Hand of Fate
Around and Around
Little Red Rooster
Stray Cat Blues
Hey Negrita
Hot Stuff
Fool To Cry
Star Star
Let's Spend The Night Together
You Gotta Move
You Can't Always Get
What You Want
Dead Flowers
Route 66
Wild Horses
Honkey Tonk Woman
A Line of Country Honk
Tumbling Dice
Happy
Nothin From Nothin
Outta Space
Midnight Rambler
It's Only Rock and Roll
Brown Sugar
Jumping Jack Flash
Street Fight Man

**Mick Jagger**
vocals
**Keith Richards**
guitar
**Ronnie Woods**
guitar
**Bill Wyman**
bass
**Charlie Watts**
drums
**Ollie E. Brown**
percussion and vocals
**Billy Preston**
keyboards, organ, clavinet,
synthesizer and vocals
**Ian Stewart**
piano

## 10cc

Une Nuit a Paris
Old Wild Men
Silly Love
The Wall Street Shuffle
The Worst Band in the World
The Second Sitting for
The Last Supper
I'm Not In Love
Ships Don't Disappear
In the Night (Do They)?
Neanderthal Man
Don't Hang Up
I'm Mandy Fly Me
2 New Tracks
Rubber Bullets

**Eric Stewart**
vocals, guitar, keyboard
**Kevin Godley**
vocal, drums, percussion
**Graham Gouldman**
bass, vocal, guitar
**Paul Burgess**
drums, percussion

## LYNYRD SKYNYRD

Working for MCA
I ain't the One
Saturday Night Special
Whiskey Rock-a-Roller
Travellin' Man
Searchin'
What's Your Name
That Smell
Gimme Three Steps
Call Me the Breeze
T for Texas
Sweet Home Alabama
Freebird

## HOT TUNA

*Set list would probably include*
Hot Jelly Roll Blues
Hot Single #1
Invitation
Serpent of Dreams
Walkin Blues etc

**Jorma Kaukonen**
guitar,vocals
**Jack Cassidy**
bass
possibly **Bob Steeler**
drums

# KNEBWORTH

**KNEBWORTH PARK Nr STEVENAGE HERTS**

**SATURDAY 24TH JUNE 11.00 A.M.–11.00 P.M.**

FREDERICK BANNISTER PRESENTS

A MIDSUMMER NIGHT'S DREAM

# GENESIS JEFFERSON STARSHIP

## TOM PETTY And The HEARTBREAKERS DEVO
## BRAND X
## ATLANTA RHYTHM SECTION

With D.J. Nicky Horne

PRICE OF TICKETS **£5.50** In Advance. **£6** On Day.

**PLEASE NOTE** The cost of this ticket includes VAT and Ticket sellers commission **DO NOT PAY MORE**
IF YOU HAVE ANY DIFFICULTIES IN OBTAINING TICKETS OR REQUIRE ADDITIONAL INFORMATION PLEASE WRITE TO
**KNEBWORTH CONCERT, 28 STRUTTON GROUND, LONDON S.W.I** (S.A.E. Please)

## GENESIS

Squonk
Burning Rope
Ripples
Fountain of Salmacis
One For the Vine
Deep in the Motherlode
The Lady Lies
Afterglow
Follow You Follow Me
Dance on a Volcano
Los Endos
I Know What I Like

**Phil Collins**
vocals and drums
**Mike Rutherford**
guitar
**Tony Banks**
keyboard
**Darryl Sturmer**
guitar
**Chester Thompson**
drums

## JEFFERSON STARSHIP

Ride the Tiger
Caroline
Pride of Man
Skateboard
Love too Good
Big City
Count on Me
Runaway
Sweeter than Honey
Wooden Ships
Dance with the Dragon
Fire
Volunteers

**Paul Kantner**
guitar and vocals
**Marty Balin**
vocals
**David Frieberg**
**John Barbata**
drums
**Pete Sears**
drums
**Craig Chaquito**
guitar

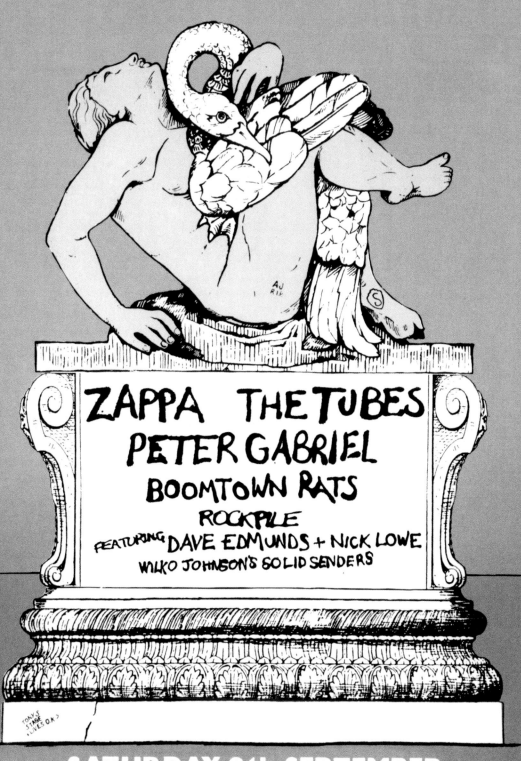

ZAPPA   THE TUBES
PETER GABRIEL
BOOMTOWN RATS
ROCKPILE
FEATURING DAVE EDMUNDS + NICK LOWE
WILKO JOHNSON'S SOLID SENDERS

**SATURDAY 9th SEPTEMBER**
OFFICIAL CONCERT PROGRAMME
50p

## FRANK ZAPPA

Deathless Horsie
Dancin Fool
Easy Meat
Honey Don't You Want
A Man Like Me
A Pound For a Brown
Bobby Brown
Conehead
Flakes
Magic Fingers
Don't Eat the Yellow Snow
Nanook Rubs It
St Alfonso's Pancake Breakfast
Father O'Blivion
Bamboozled By Love

**Frank Zappa**
**Dennis Walley**
**Ike Willis**
**Arthur Barrow**
**Tommy Mars**
**Peter Wolf**
**Ed Mann**
**Vince Colaiuta**

FREDERICK BANNISTER IN ASSOCIATION WITH PETER GRANT
PRESENTS

# LED-ZEPPELIN
## AT
## KNEBWORTH 1979

# OFFICIAL PROGRAMME 90p

## LED ZEPPELIN

The Song Remains The Same
Celebration Day
Black Dog
Nobody's Fault but Mine
Over the Hills and Far Away
Misty Mountain Hop
Since I've Been Loving You
No Quarter
Ten Years Gone
Hot Dog
The Rain Song
White Summer
Black Mountain Side
Kashmir
Trampled Underfoot
Achilles Last Stand
Guitar Solo
In the Evening
Stairway to Heaven
Rock & Roll
Whole Lotta Love
Heartbreaker

**Robert Plant**
vocals
**Jimmy Page**
guitar
**John Paul Jones**
bass
**John Bonham**
drums

## THE NEW COMMANDER CODY BAND
(also performed August 11th

George William Frayne - vocals
William Kirchen - guitar
Stephen Fishell - steel guitar
Anthony Carl Johnson - drums
Kim Ischliman - bass
Stephen Macay - saxophone

## CHASE AND DAVE
(also performed August 11th

Chase Hodges - vocals,piano
Dave Peacock - vocals,bass
Mick Burt - drums

The sideboard Song
Gertcha etc

# KNEBWORTH PARK

NEAR STEVENAGE · HERTS

## SATURDAY AUGUST 11TH

FREDERICK BANNISTER IN ASSOCIATION WITH PETER GRANT
PRESENTS

# LED-ZEPPELIN

## THE NEW BARBARIANS

RON WOOD, KEITH RICHARD, STANLEY CLARKE, BOBBY KEYES, IAN McLAGAN, ZIGABOO

## TODD RUNDGREN & UTOPIA

## SOUTHSIDE JOHNNY & THE ASBURY JUKES

### THE MARSHALL TUCKER BAND

### FAIRPORT CONVENTION · CHAS & DAVE

TICKETS £7.50 IN ADVANCE (THE PRICE OF THE TICKET INCLUDES VAT & AGENTS COMMISSION **DO NOT PAY MORE**)

11 AM TO 11 PM

IF YOU HAVE ANY DIFFICULTY IN OBTAINING TICKETS
OR REQUIRE ADDITIONAL INFORMATION PLEASE WRITE TO:
**KNEBWORTH CONCERT**, 201 OXFORD ST., LONDON W1 (S.A.E. PLEASE)

A TEDOAR LTD. PRESENTATION

## LED ZEPPELIN

The Song Remains the same
Celebration Day
Black Dog
Nobody's Fault but Mine
Over the Hills and Far Away
Misty Mountain Hop
Since I've Been Loving You
No Quarter
Hot dog
The Rain Song
White Summer
Black Mountain side
Kashmir
Trampled Under Foot
Sick Again
Achilles Last Stand
In The Evening
Stairway to Heaven
Rock and Roll
Whole Lotta Love
Communication Breakdown

## NEW BARBARIANS

| | |
|---|---|
| Sweet Little Rock'n Roller | **Ronnie Woods** |
| F.U.C. Her | guitar and vocals |
| Breathe on Me | **Keith Richards** |
| I Can Feel the Fire | guitar and vocals |
| Let's Go Steady Again | **Philip Chen** |
| Band introduction | drums |
| Worried Life Blues | **Bobby Keyes** |
| Honky Tonk Woman | saxaphone |
| Come To Realise | **Ian MacLagan** |
| Seven Days | keyboards |
| Before They Make Me Run | **Joseph Modeliste** |
| Jumpin Jack Flash | percussion |

Much of this information was obtained from GW Shark's Rock Festival Archives
htpp://tinpan.fortunecity.com/ebony/546

# BATH AND KNEBWORTH FESTIVAL MEMORABILIA 1969 - 1979.

**Posters from £4.95**
**T-shirts £10.95**
**Plus P & P**

1979Programme

# BATH AND KNEBWORTH FESTIVAL COMMEMORATIVE SETS

### BATH FESTIVALS OF BLUES AND PROGRESSIVE MUSIC 1969 - 70.

### 'JUST BROKEN EVEN'

This unique deluxe boxed set strictly limited to 1,000 worldwide includes the three reprinted programmes, handbills and tickets plus an album of 28 rarely seen photographs from both Bath Festivals and the 1971 Lincoln Folk Festival also the hard backed book 'Just Broken Even'

Only a limited number of these sets are left please phone for availability

### KNEBWORTH FESTIVALS 1974 - 79.

### 'THERE MUST BE A BETTER WAY'

A beautifully presented limited edition boxed Knebworth commemorative set containing 67 separate items. limited to 1,500 worldwide it is bound to appreciate. Each set is numbered and signed by Knebworth promoter, Freddy Bannister and can be personally dedicated if you wish. The set includes all the reprinted programmes, handbills and tickets from the first six festivals.plus a hardbacked book also a box of 43 7" x 9" photographs, including some never seen before of the Stones and Led Zeppelin,with a 55 minute video featuring clips from these Festivals.

**For further information or to order phone 01223 526073**
**Or write to Rockmusicmemorabilia.com Ltd. Suite 72 48 Regent Street**
**Cambridge CB2 1FD. email info@rockmusicmemorabilia.com**